D0308380

Valuing Quality in Early Childhood Services

NEW APPROACHES TO DEFINING QUALITY

Editors

PETER MOSS AND ALAN PENCE

TEACHERS
COLLEGE
PRESS

Teachers College, Columbia University
New York and London

Selection, editorial material and Chapter 12 Copyright © 1994, Peter Moss and Alan Pence.
All other material © as credited.

All rights reserved

Paul Chapman Publishing Ltd
144 Liverpool Road
London
N1 1LA

Apart from any fair dealing for the purposes of research or private study, or criticism or review, as permitted under the Copyright, Designs and Patents Act 1988, this publication may be reproduced, stored or transmitted, in any form or by any means, only with the prior permission in writing of the publishers, or in the case of reprographic reproduction in accordance with the terms of licences issued by the Copyright Licensing Agency. Inquiries concerning reproduction outside those terms should be sent to the publishers at the abovementioned address.

British Library Cataloguing in Publication Data

Valuing Quality in Early Childhood
Services: New Approaches to Defining
Quality
 I. Moss, Peter II. Pence, Alan R.
 372.12

 ISBN 1-85396-254-6

Typeset by Hewer Text Composition Services, Edinburgh
Printed and bound by Athenæum Press Ltd, Gateshead, Tyne & Wear

B C D E F G H 9 8 7 6

Contents

Contributors

GUNNAR ÅSÉN has worked as a researcher in different fields of education since 1973. In the 1980s, together with Gunilla Dahlberg, he conducted several studies in a programme on Educational Change in Early Childhood Education and Care. He is now a researcher at Stockholm Institute of Education and is leading a programme on Art and Creative Work in early childhood services.

JULIA BROPHY is a member of the Thomas Coram Research Unit at London University Institute of Education and is currently directing a study on the role of expert evidence in child care proceedings following the Children Act 1989. Her previous work has covered a range of areas including women's employment issues, the role of anti-sexism and anti-racism policies and practices and pre-school playgroups.

GUNILLA DAHLBERG has been a researcher in the field of early childhood education and care since 1971, and a member of two national committees developing pedagogical programmes for early childhood services. She is currently Associate Professor of Education at Stockholm Institute of Education and Director of the Research Unit at the Department of Early Childhood Education in Solna.

SARAH-EVE FARQUHAR originally trained as a kindergarten teacher but is now lecturer in the Department of Human Development, Massey University, Palmerston North. She currently teaches and researches on Human Development and Early Childhood Education and has recently completed a doctorate on constructions of quality in early childhood centres.

CLAUS JENSEN trained and worked as a pedagog (Danish child care worker), mostly with children aged three to seven in kindergartens. He currently works in BUPL, the trade union for pedagogs, where his responsibilities include the organization of further training of pedagogs in Arhus. He also teaches on in-service training courses.

CAROL JOSEPH has played an active role in developing anti-racist practices in early childhood services throughout her working life. She is a founder member of, and continuing contributor to, the Black Childcare Network, which helps to develop anti-racist policies and procedures, and continues this work in her current employment as a Human Resource Consultant. She was born in Grenada.

OLE LANGSTED is Professor at the Department of Communication at Aalborg University. A psychologist by discipline, his main research interest is the broad area of the everyday life of young children both at home and in early childhood services.

JANE LANE works in the Education Section of the British Commission for Racial Equality (CRE), where she has taken a special interest in early childhood services and especially the identification of policies and practices that are potentially discriminatory. She was responsible for preparing *From Cradle to School*, the CRE's guide to racial equality and early childhood services, and has lectured and written widely on this issue.

MARY LARNER began her career as a child care teacher. She is now director of early childhood care and education at the National Centre for Children in Poverty in New York. Her previous work has included projects on community-based family support programmes, training programmes for early childhood professionals and child care consumer education for low income families.

MARIE MCCALLUM is Assistant Director of Health and Social Development for the Meadow Lake Tribal Council (MLTC). She was formerly Director of the MLTC Indian Child Care Programme and has other experience in First Nation community development as an administrator and band councillor. She is a member of the Flying Dust First Nation, which is one of the nine communities served by the MLTC.

PETER MOSS is a member of the Thomas Coram Research Unit, London University Institute of Education, where he has researched and written about early childhood services and work/family issues. Since 1986, he has been Co-ordinator of the European Commission's Network on Childcare and Other Measures to Reconcile Employment and Family Responsibilities, which has involved reviewing policies and services in the European Union.

ALAN PENCE is Professor of Child Care at the School of Child and Youth Care, University of Victoria, British Columbia. Before moving into academic work in 1981, he was a child care worker, trainer and programme director. Since 1981 he has played a leading role in the development of Canadian early childhood care and education research; he was Co-director for the Canadian National Child Care Study.

HELEN PENN is a Visiting Fellow at the Department of Child Development and Primary Education at London University Institute of Education. Previously, she was Assistant Director of Education in Strathclyde Regional Council in Scotland where she had responsibility for the first integrated system of early childhood care and education services in Britain.

PAT PETRIE is a member of the Thomas Coram Research Unit, London University Institute of Education, where she researches play and care services for school-age children. She is one of the founders and co-ordinators of the European Network on School-age Childcare. Previous work has involved family day care and the training needs of nursery workers, and she has written extensively about child development.

DEBORAH PHILLIPS is Associate Professor of Psychology at the University of Virginia, but is currently on leave and serving as Director of the Board on Children and Families at the National Research Council's Commission on Social and Behavioural Sciences. She has been on numerous task forces and advisory groups concerned with child and family policy issues. A major and continuing research interest is issues of child care quality.

SUDESH SHARMA is Headteacher of a nursery school, having previously taught in both primary and secondary schools, as well as being a teacher adviser for multicultural education and involved in anti-racist training. Born in India, she came to live in Britain when her parents immigrated when she was three years old.

ANNE SMITH is an Associate Professor in the Department of Education, University of Otago, Dunedin. She teaches, writes and researches on Human Development, Early Childhood Education and Gender Issues in Education. For the last twenty years she has been involved in the process of reforming early childhood policies in New Zealand.

JUNE STATHAM is a member of the Thomas Coram Research Unit at London University Institute of Education. She lives in Wales where she currently directs a study of the implementation in Wales of the Children Act with respect to early childhood services. Her previous work has included non-sexist childraising, pre-school playgroups, open access family centres and integration of children with disabilities.

CHAPTER 1

Defining Quality:
Values, Stakeholders and Processes

PETER MOSS

The starting point for this book is that 'quality' in early childhood services is a relative concept, not an objective reality. Definitions of quality reflect the values and beliefs, needs and agendas, influence and empowerment of various 'stakeholder' groups having an interest in these services. 'Quality' is also a dynamic concept; definitions evolve over time. The process of defining quality involves stakeholder groups, and is not only a means to an end but is important in its own right. The central concern of this book is the process of definition, and how the many and varied perspectives of different stakeholder groups can be heard, respected and incorporated.

'Quality' is an international buzz word, not only in early childhood services but in connection with every kind of product and service. Yet in its mantra-like repetition, the word is in danger of being rendered meaningless. It attracts widespread support – for who could not want 'good quality'? – unless and until we have to say what we actually mean, at which point it becomes far more elusive. Many may secretly share the doubts voiced by a Swedish researcher:

> 'Quality' is not a very useful analytical concept . . . I have been struck from time to time with the thought that it would be a relief to have an agreement not to use (the term) 'quality' in scientific studies of early childhood services, at least for a couple of years.
>
> (Johansson, 1993, p. 22)

THE TWO MEANINGS OF 'QUALITY'

Given its elusiveness, some attention needs to be paid first to the meaning of the word 'quality' before considering the process of defining quality. The first step is to recognize two different meanings of the word, the one analytic and descriptive, the other evaluative. In the former meaning, 'quality' is used to analyze, describe and understand the essence or nature of something – what makes it what it is. It is in this sense that, most famously, the word is used when Portia in *The Merchant of Venice* considers the 'quality of mercy'.

Applied to early childhood services, this meaning of 'quality' requires the adoption of an essentially holistic approach: 'the distinctiveness and unique combination of characteristics are what defines a centre's quality' (Farquhar, 1990, p. 74); or, as Claus Jensen puts it in Chapter 10 in this volume:

> 'quality' was generally used . . . in describing an experience and as a way of expressing in shorthand complexity which was hard to define otherwise without using thousands of words – and even if thousands of words were used, the feeling remaining would often be that the description had only scratched the surface of what had actually been experienced.

Defining 'quality' in this sense means understanding the underlying dynamics of a particular service. It is a question of consciousness: 'Quality is what is under the surface, the persistent daily work done by the staff which can be hard to fully recognize without being together with a group of children in the service for a long time' (Andersson, 1990, p. 92).

In the evaluative meaning of 'quality', we are trying to assess how well a service performs or, more specifically, to what extent it meets its goals or objectives. For example, a common approach in child care research is to define quality indirectly in terms of certain processes in services (for example, child-adult interactions) or certain structural features of services (for example, staff ratios and training). These processes or features are usually selected by researchers because of their presumed or proven relationship with certain child outcomes. These outcomes may be short-term or long-term, possibly educational attainment or some other indicator of later achievement or failure but most often they cover some aspects of child development. The researchers assume these outcomes to be the service goals; the processes or features studied serve therefore as proxy measures of performance in relation to these service goals.

Or to take another example, 'customer' satisfaction may be considered a service goal and therefore the basis for evaluating quality. A 'good' service is one that attracts and satisfies 'customers': 'quality is defined as fully satisfying agreed customer requirements' (Bank, 1992, p. xiv). This objective of customer satisfaction will be considered particularly appropriate where market-oriented approaches are applied to early childhood services, with these services viewed as items of consumption and parents as the 'consumers' or 'customers'.

While distinct, these two meanings of 'quality' – the analytic and the evaluative – can complement each other. The understanding derived from the former analytic or descriptive approach can be used to explain results attained from the latter evaluative approach. To understand why an early childhood service is 'good quality' or 'bad quality', it is necessary to understand 'the quality' of that service.

GOAL SETTING AND STAKEHOLDERS

This book is primarily about the evaluative meaning of 'quality', or the performance of early childhood services in achieving their goals. But we are concerned not so much with *what* these goals might be, as *how* the goals are set and *how* they evolve over time – although the two aspects cannot be wholly disconnected since the process of goal setting or definition will determine what the goals will be. The process of goal setting, which is the process of defining quality, is therefore essential. What does it involve?

Goals for early chilhood services can be specified for any or all of a number of groups. *Education to be More* was the report of the Early Childhood Care and Education Working Group (Meade, 1988) established by the New Zealand Government 'to assist in establishing a more equitable system of early childhood care and education' (discussed in more detail by Anne Smith and Sarah-Eve Farquhar in Chapter 9 of this volume). The report proposes that the following groups will benefit from early childhood services: society, children, parents, the family, providers and employers. Other groups not specified in this report but which might be considered when defining service goals include staff working in services, local communities and particular ethnic, linguistic or cultural minorities.

Education to be More goes on to identify potential benefits, and therefore by implication possible service goals, for each of the groups that it specifies, for example (and the list below is only a selection from the full range of benefits proposed in Appendix 2 of the report):

CHILDREN: time out from intensive one-to-one relationships with parents; making friends with peers and other adults; learning a repertoire of social skills; given the chance to be children and to play, have fun and learn; construct more ideas through working at play; get opportunities to add a spiritual dimension to their lives; have mothers who are not overburdened.

PARENTS: women get the choice to join the labour force or control their lives in other ways; formation of a support network; opportunity for developing/maintaining Maori and Pacific Island languages and cultures.

FAMILY: a liveable income; more confident, relaxed and/or fulfilled parents who then have fewer angry interactions; siblings 'catch' some of the developmental benefits of care and education.

EMPLOYERS: continuity of work from employees; regular work attendance habits by parents who have their children in reliable early childhood services.

PROVIDERS: satisfaction from contributing to a publicly valued service; learning management skills.

SOCIETY: improvement to the social fabric (children start schooling on a sound foundation, parents get to play a fuller role, families are supported); the creation of networks within the social structure which help bind communities together in times of crisis.

Definitions of quality may be narrower or broader, depending on the groups identified as well as the goals specified for these groups. Especially in narrower definitions, some groups may not be specifically recognized in service goals, yet they may still be affected by services, for example because they contribute to them financially or because the service affects their neighbourhood. We refer to all groups who are affected by services, and therefore can be said to have an interest in them, as 'stakeholders'.

The process of defining quality involves stakeholders setting goals for particular groups. The goals set by stakeholders will reflect their needs, interests, concerns and priorities. These in turn will be influenced by values and beliefs. Karmel's conclusion about education applies equally to early childhood services: 'The notion of quality . . . is complex and value-laden . . . (prioritizing goals) are value judgements and depend on the educational philosophy and the ideological commitment of those involved' (Karmel, 1985, pp. 287, 286).

THE TWO RULERS

I am interested in not only the small 'r' *ruler* we use in attempting to measure quality, but also the capital 'R' *Ruler* who defines what it is that will be measured . . . '*Who* is the Ruler?' appears to be *the* question one must address before the questions of '*What* is the ruler and what is to be measured?' can be considered.

(Pence, 1992, pp. 2, 4)

Defining goals may suggest an open, democratic and orderly process in which values, beliefs, interests and needs are recognized, explicitly articulated then systematically discussed and considered; all stakeholders receive due consideration and exercise influence appropriate to the size of their stake; and decisions are reached by mutual agreement and consensus. In reality, things are usually much less perfect. In practice, the power of different stakeholders often determines the influence they have in the process: power can come from various sources, including economic resources, political or administrative position and professional status and expertise. Some stakeholders may be totally excluded or, if included, they may have little influence; other stakeholders, with more power, may dominate the process. A group or groups may exclude or marginalize others either consciously or unconsciously and for a variety of reasons: failure to recognize the legitimacy of the others' interest in services; belief in their superiority based on prejudice or other reasons; difficulties faced by excluded groups in asserting and implementing their right to participate.

A particular problem is how young children, who are obvious 'stakeholders' in early childhood services and almost invariably a group for whom goals are set, can be represented in the process of defining quality. At what age and in what ways can their views be articulated and comprehended? How can their views carry adequate weight given their lack of individual resources (material and information) and power?

Moreover, all of the key elements – power and influence, interests and needs, values and beliefs – may vary not only *among* stakeholder groups but also *within* the same group of stakeholders. For example, the same views may not be shared by all members of a particular ethnic group or by all parents or by all staff. Even within the same family mother and father may disagree on what they want for their child or from an early childhood service.

Defining quality is, therefore, a political process. It involves interplay, negotiation and possible conflict between, and sometimes among, those stakeholder groups who are included and who may have different perspectives about objectives and priorities arising from different values and beliefs, interests and needs. The final result of the process will be determined as much by the exercise of power and influence as by other considerations.

Yet *how* a definition of quality has been arrived at, *by whom* (and who was excluded from the process) and *why* is often not clear: just as defining quality may be a more or less inclusive process, so too the process may be more or less transparent. The values and interests underlying the choice of objectives and priorities may remain implicit and unacknowledged; agendas may be hidden or disguised; differences of opinion may go unrecognized or be disregarded or suppressed; and issues of power and influence may be ignored. That defining quality is a political process may not be acknowledged as such at all; instead, defining quality may be treated purely as the application of scientific, managerial or professional expertise or 'consumer' preference.

Any definition of 'quality' must be considered in this light. We need to recognize that there is a process of definition, and seek to understand the nature of that process. How has that definition been arrived at? Who has defined 'quality'? We need to ask *whose* views of 'quality' are included as well as whose views are not taken into account, *whose* measurement is being applied as well as what is being measured and how. The question of who is the Ruler should precede the question of which ruler should be used for measurement.

Defining quality is not only a complex process: it is also an on-going process. 'Quality' is never an objective reality, to be finally discovered and pinned down by experts. It is inherently subjective and relative, based on values and beliefs, that may not only vary among and within societies, but will undoubtedly vary over time. Views about 'quality' today are likely to be different from those held a generation ago and will in turn have changed in another generation's time. Any definition of quality, therefore, is 'to an extent transitory (since) understanding quality and arriving at quality indicators is a dynamic and continuous process of reconciling the emphases of different interest groups' (EC Childcare Network, 1991, p. 6).

The approach to quality adopted in this book contrasts in many ways with the approach that still dominates the current discourse on child care quality. The former focuses on values, relativism and the process of definition, the latter on the application and assessment of an objective reality. The former prioritizes the inclusion and empowerment of as wide a range of stakeholders as possible in defining and evaluating quality; the latter gives prominence to a narrower range of experts who control the process of definition and evaluation on the basis of technical expertise. Not that this book's approach precludes an important role for expert knowledge, both theoretical and applied. But this role primarily belongs to the stages of operationalizing goals and determining how best to achieve them, rather than to the preceding stage of defining what these goals should be. When it comes to defining goals, researchers and other professionals are themselves 'stakeholders', influenced by their own interests and priorities which reflect professional or disciplinary values and ideologies, and whose influence depends on their power.

THE ORIGINS OF A RELATIVE APPROACH
TO QUALITY

This approach to quality in early childhood services, with its emphasis on different values and perspectives and specific contexts, has begun to emerge in recent years from a variety of origins. One of these has been Bronfenbrenner's ecological model of human development. This is conceptualized to include an encompassing 'macro-system': 'the macro system is the overriding value system or cultural blueprint within which child care quality is provided. It is made up of societal and cultural attitudes and values and the political, economic and legal systems which enshrine those values' (Smith, 1992, p. 4).

The concept of the macro-system has been applied to an increasing number of cross-national studies of early childhood services, to illuminate and explain differences between services in different societies (e.g. Tobin, Wu and Davidson, 1989; Melhuish and Moss, 1991; Lamb *et al.*, 1992; Cochran, 1993). However, this concept allows not only for differences *among* societies, but also for differences of ideology and structure *within* particular cultures or subcultures.

> The close connection between criteria (of quality) and subcultural norms and value systems leads to difficulties in comparisons and a generalization of the content of the quality concept . . . methods (to measure) quality must be validated in the context where they will be used in order to strengthen their ecological validity.
>
> (Johansson, 1993; pp. 13, 21)

While this appreciation of the relative and values-based nature of quality comes in part from a growing ecological awareness, it also draws on post-modernist and feminist critiques of scientific 'knowledge', 'value-free' research and the positivistic paradigm.

> Child care research is not just an empirical issue but a value issue. The view that psychology can generate objective, neutral knowledge, independent of political and normative context is naive . . . Researchers are influenced by values and political context at every step of the research process.
>
> (Smith, 1992, p. 5)

There is therefore an increasing understanding that definitions of quality are values-based and relative. However, to date less attention has been paid to the practical implications of this emerging understanding or to the process of definition with its interplay of values and stakeholder groups. We know little about the process as it actually operates. Indeed, people involved in the process – for example, researchers, professional workers, other experts – may not perceive themselves as part of such a process but assume they are developing an objective, values-free concept as part of a strictly technical exercise.

We also know little about how the process might be better conducted. Which stakeholders are involved in practice? Which stakeholders should be involved? Which stakeholders currently exercise power and influence? How can all stakeholders have a significant voice, including children and other groups who may be less powerful? How can the process of defining and reviewing definitions of quality be made explicit and transparent? How can conflicts of interest and disagreements be dealt with? It has been argued that 'given such an inherent lack of agreement on "quality" perhaps the *process* of involvement should take precedence over the *product* of definition' (Pence, 1992, p. 5).

The issues go beyond the process of definition. Can groups with different views of quality, due to different values and beliefs, needs and interests, work together in partnership to mutual benefit? How can researchers studying quality take account of the relative nature of quality and introduce a reflective awareness of self into the research process? What are the implications of the relative nature of quality for the evaluation, regulation and public funding of services? Can a completely relative approach be accepted or must some common core of values and objectives be imposed across all services? If so, how should these core values and objectives be determined?

THE STRUCTURE OF THE BOOK

Valuing Quality contains contributions from eighteen experts on early childhood services, drawn from six countries, all of whom are operating within the paradigm of quality proposed in the book. The chapters fall into three main sets, although there is a lot of overlap between chapters in these different sets. The first set of chapters (2 to 4) introduces and examines the idea that defining quality is a process involving various key 'stakeholders', whose values, interests and perspectives may not always be shared and may sometimes even be in conflict. Issues of influence and empowerment are also raised, especially by Chapter 3 which considers whether and how children might have a significant voice in the process of defining quality in early childhood services.

The first two chapters in the second set (5 to 7) examine more closely issues in researching quality raised by recognition of the values-based nature of quality and of the fact that researchers themselves are one group of stakeholders in the quality defining process. For example, can researchers work with, rather than ignore, diversity in values and definitions of quality? Chapter 6 also introduces the issue of whether boundaries need to be imposed on the extent to which, in practice, a relativistic approach is permitted in early childhood services. Can anything go, as long as it reflects genuinely held values and beliefs, or should some limits be prescribed and some values deemed non-negotiable within a society? Chapter 7 takes this further by proposing that equality is one non-negotiable value in determining quality.

The third and final set of chapters (8 to 11) introduces examples of processes and structures which might support the development of what in the final chapter (Chapter 12) we refer to as a new, inclusionary paradigm in defining quality – a democratic and open approach based on cognition of diverse stakeholder groups and of the values, beliefs and interests that they bring to the process of definition. Chapter 12 draws together from the preceding chapters a range of indicators which provide some ideas about how to take forward this approach to quality – and invites readers to participate in the continuing process of exploring this inclusionary approach.

As we have already said, the chapters do not fall comfortably into three sets. There is far too much overlap. Most noticeably, perhaps, research and evaluation figure prominently in many chapters, not only Chapters 5 and 6, while issues raised in defining quality by the cultural and ethnic diversity of many contemporary societies recur throughout the book.

TERMINOLOGIES

Most of the contributions in this book come from what are often referred to as 'child care' and 'day care' services, rather than 'nursery education' or 'kindergarten'. In most countries, 'child care' or 'day care' and 'nursery education' or 'kindergartens' are operated as separate systems. This division reflects a continuing tendency to view 'care' and 'education' as separate functions.

In our perspective, however, the issues covered in this book are applicable to all care and education services for children under compulsory school age as well as to 'school-age child care' services for older children (which are the subject of one chapter). Our underlying assumption is that 'care' and 'education' for young children are inseparable and that, although it frequently occurs, it is artificial and inappropriate to divide services, conceptually or structurally, between 'day care' and 'education' or indeed between 'under threes' and 'over threes'. Services need to be appropriate for children's age and recognize various functions including the provision of safe and secure care and of a pedagogical approach: but such diversity can and should be developed within a common framework, providing a coherent and integrated approach to key issues such as funding, staffing, administrative responsibility and the concept of quality. This coherent approach has been adopted in some countries, such as Denmark, Sweden and New Zealand (all represented in this book) and Spain, where all services for children below compulsory school age are integrated into a common system of early childhood care and education services.

While Alan Pence and I share this perspective on services and on the scope of the book, as editors we have each become accustomed to use different terms for the broad range of care and education services for children below compulsory school age – 'child care services' and 'early childhood services'. As editors we considered selecting one term and applying it throughout the book, but decided it was neither necessary nor in the spirit of this book to be so exclusionary. Both terms have therefore been used interchangeably in the following chapters.

REFERENCES

ANDERSSON, B-E (1990) *Hur bra är egentligen dagis?* Utbildningsförlaget, Stockholm.
BANK, J. (1992) *The Essence of Total Quality Management*, Prentice Hall, Hemel Hempstead.

COCHRAN, M. (ed.) (1993) *International Handbook of Child Care Policies and Programs*, Greenwood Press, Westport: CT.

EUROPEAN COMMISSION CHILDCARE NETWORK (1991) *Quality in Services for Young Children: A Discussion Paper*, European Commission Equal Opportunities Unit, Brussels.

FARQUHAR, S-E. (1990) Quality in early education and care: what do we mean? *Early Child Development and Care*, Vol. 64, pp. 71–83.

JOHANSSON, I. (1993) Quality in early childhood services – what is that? Paper given at the Third European Conference on the Quality of Early Childhood Education, Thessaloniki, 1–3 September.

KARMEL, P. (1985) Quality and equality in education, *Australian Journal of Education*, Vol. 29, no. 3, pp. 279–93.

LAMB, M., STERNBERG, K., HWANG, C-P. and BROBERG, A. (eds.) (1992) *Child Care in Context: Cross-Cultural Perspectives*, Lawrence Erlbaum Associates, Hillsadale: NJ.

MEADE, A. (1988) *Education to be More: Report of the Early Childhood and Education Care Working Group*, Government Printer, Wellington.

MELHUISH, E. and MOSS, P. (1991) *Day Care for Young Children: International Perspectives*, Routledge, London.

PENCE, A. (1992) Quality care: thoughts on R/rulers, Paper given at Workshop on Defining and Assessing Quality, Seville, 9–12 September.

SMITH, A. (1992) Quality and its measurement: socio-political issues, Paper given at Workshop on Defining and Assessing Quality, Seville, 9–12 September.

TOBIN, J., WU, D. and DAVIDSON, D. (1989) *Preschool in Three Cultures: Japan, China and the United States*, Yale University Press, New Haven: CT.

CHAPTER 2

Working in Conflict:
Developing a Dynamic Model of Quality

HELEN PENN

Strathclyde Region in Scotland was a pioneer in the United Kingdom, seeking a more coherent approach to early childhood services, bringing together a wide range of services within an educational framework and making one department responsible for these services. Helen Penn draws on her personal experience of implementing this reform to illustrate how defining and developing quality is a process which needs to take place at many levels and involves a variety of stakeholders, often in conflict arising from different values, traditions and perceived interests.

INTRODUCTION

What is quality in early childhood services? This chapter is about the process of definition, about finding a route between competing and vociferous views about quality. It is about conflicts over principles, goals, strategies, practices and resources in early childhood services and attempts to resolve them.

It is commonly acknowledged that services to young children in the UK are characterized by fragmentation and lack of consensus. This situation is exacerbated by underfunding. Different kinds of services are competing for monies and the protagonists for each kind of service defend their position tightly. They are afraid to concede any argument about the relative value of the service they are offering since ideological speculation may lead to financial loss.

The arguments are rarely resolved by research since the research paradigm does not usually allow for the political, historical or economical context. Research is often highly specific and decontextualized, and located within a particular theoretical framework; daily practice is inevitably more complex.

Since I was myself a stakeholder in the processes I describe, it would be misleading to adopt a neutral tone, and write a measured discussion of the issues in the third person. I offer a description of what happened in a particular place over a particular period of time, but it is heavily based on personal experiences. Self-reflexive accounts are familiar and respected practice in social anthropology, but some in psychology have yet to come to terms with the tensions between subjectivity and objectivity.

QUALITY: THE DIFFERING PERSPECTIVES

Feminist perspectives

In 1986 I was appointed as Assistant Director of Education in Strathclyde Region in the West of Scotland. Following publication the previous year of a report which proposed bringing together and developing all of the Region's early childhood services within an educational framework (Strathclyde Regional Council, 1985), responsibility for all services was relocated in the education department having previously been split between the education and social work departments. This reform attracted widespread national attention because for the first time in the United Kingdom an attempt was made to introduce administrative and financial coherence to the diverse range of early childhood services (subsequently this course has been followed by a number of other local authorities in England). My job was to implement this reform; the task facing me was to manage, co-ordinate, develop and improve the whole range of early childhood services in the Region.

I came from a feminist background. I had worked for an organization which considered financial emancipation for women as a precondition of equality, and which considered both men and women should be able to balance work and domestic life by the provision of adequate services and appropriate employment legislation. As a teacher (but trained in England) I also had views about what constituted a high quality learning environment for children. I was delighted to come to Strathclyde, to have an opportunity to develop services in a coherent way, but I had badly misunderstood the context. I assumed that this feminist perspective would be widely understood and shared. In fact, as I detail below, equality issues were not then on the agenda. Providing services for working parents had not been seriously considered. Holding on to this feminist perspective, let alone promoting it, became, for me, a major issue.

The diversity of early childhood services

Strathclyde, like the rest of the United Kingdom, had a great diversity of early childhood services in the mid-1980s. The objectives of services, the training, working conditions and pay of the staff, their catchments and access by parents; in every way, the services differed. Within this diversity, there were four main types of provision: nursery education; public day nurseries; childminders; and playgroups. It was implicitly understood that all services, apart from childminders, would be part-time, except perhaps for some of the day nurseries and family centres where the distraught children who were referred were in need of more constant monitoring. Not only were most services part-time; in addition some required mothers to be present during the hours of operation.

Nursery education was provided in nursery classes attached to schools and free standing nursery schools which took three- and four-year-old children during the school year, almost all with a morning/afternoon shift system. About 24 per cent of children in the age group had access to these education facilities; the access was controlled by headteachers. The service attracted a middle-class catchment. Nursery education had in the past been managed by the education department.

Public day nurseries and family centres took two- to four-year-olds, from families under stress, and were open from 8 a.m. to 6 p.m. all year round. There were places for about 1 per cent of children, who were rarely from a middle-class background. Access was controlled by social workers and was confined to children defined as in need according to social work criteria with priority given to surveillance in cases of child protection. These services had been managed by the social work department.

Other services were in the main provided by the private and voluntary sector and regulated by the social work department of the local authority. The bulk of this provision was childminders, or family day carers, who offered the only provision for working parents, and playgroups which offered a very basic, very part-time play experience to children aged three and four, on a self-help basis with mothers acting as volunteers and organizers of the service. In addition, there were many miscellaneous services, including mother and toddler groups, where mothers were offered a chance to meet once or twice a week with their toddlers; toy libraries; home visitors; community development projects. Although the situation has now changed significantly, at that time there was a negligible number of private day nurseries.

The social context

The services of course did not operate in isolation. They were a small part of a much wider picture of social, political, historical and administrative traditions. This wider canvas determined the parameters of what was possible. I include a sketch of this wider picture, since some of the decisions and actions that were taken are inexplicable without it.

Strathclyde Region in Scotland has a population of two and a half million, and encompasses extremes of inner city deprivation and rural isolation. In Glasgow, the principal city of the Region, there were vandalized public housing estates where male unemployment was over 70 per cent, alcohol and drug abuse were endemic and there was up to 80 per cent absenteeism in schools. At the other extreme, the Region included small islands located up to a hundred miles into the Atlantic with small closely knit populations. Most people, however, expressed a view about the importance of affirming Scottish, as opposed to English or British identity. This assertion of nationalism was regarded as a more immediate concern than equal opportunities. There were then no policies or strategies within the Regional Council on race, gender or disability.

The political context

The political complexion of the authority was socialist, defiantly so in the face of a right-wing national government. A majority of the elected members were male ex-manual labourers, including the leader of the council who was an ex-miner, subsequently succeeded by an ex-railwayman. The chairman of the committee responsible for early childhood services (called the pre-five committee), which made my appointment, was a maverick intellectual who was extremely critical of the education department. He was succeeded by an amiable ex-factory worker whose main aim was to keep the peace, whatever the cost in policy terms. All these men were deeply concerned about the poverty and violence in the region, but all held deeply traditional views about the role of wives and mothers.

The report referred to above, which recommended bringing together and developing all early childhood services within an educational framework, had been commissioned by the leader of the council. The report had two main underlying assumptions. The first was that the main focus of any initiative was to combat poverty. The region had developed the concept of 'Areas for Priority Treatment' (APTs). The APTs were demographically designated, using a range of indicators such as housing, single parenthood and unemployment. The concept of the APT, which was essentially an administrative boundary, was rigidly applied, for instance cutting streets in half; those within the APT area had first call on new resources. There were some claims that this was a very divisive policy, since there was a great deal of poverty, including rural poverty, and the APTs were a crude administrative measure which did not necessarily reflect individual need, especially for services for pre-fives (Scott, 1989).

Secondly, there was an assumption that poverty could be challenged through parental involvement in early years. This had two aspects. Mothers' parenting skills could be improved to help break 'the cycle of deprivation'; by 'learning to play' with their children, mothers could improve their children's competencies. Secondly, by becoming involved, that is voluntarily participating in the service her child used, a mother would gain in confidence and become empowered to make changes in her deprived local community.

This rhetoric did not address several questions. What had led to the lack of confidence? What kind of experiences or tuition should be available to mothers to transform themselves from depressed and isolated women into concerned parents and community activists? What facilities should be available for children whilst their mothers were metamorphosing? The one small evaluative study which asked participant mothers what they thought of this approach suggested that they were uncomfortable with their status as volunteers and wanted more rights and powers in the project in which they were participating and/or paid employment. The organization which commissioned the study, an offshoot of the playgroup movement, dismissed the findings which were never referred to in the debate about parental involvement (Barr and Phillips, 1984).

Parental involvement was the buzz word in the report. The pre-school playgroup movement, which offered part-time care run mainly by volunteers and espoused the importance of full-time mothering, was seen to provide a glowing example of parental involvement. Administratively, so the argument went, the considerable resources of the education department could be used to promote and develop the philosophy of community development and parental involvement, even if this meant challenging the traditional view of educationalists. Resources were not seen to be a major issue. The fact that provision was unevenly spread, that so many premises were in appalling condition, and that there was a dearth of staff training, were reluctantly noted. But the mission was to change attitudes, to move away from traditional views of teaching and learning and to 'involve' and 'empower' parents.

The education context

Schooling in Strathclyde was denominational, either Catholic or Calvinist/ Protestant. Neighbouring and half-empty Catholic and Protestant schools would not amalgamate or share resources. There was a small minority ethnic community, mainly Pakistani, comprising about 4 per cent of the population in Glasgow, whose influence and whose cultural and religious traditions were barely acknowledged at that time within the school system.

Educational traditions were formal, rigid and hierarchical. The *tawse* (the cat of nine tails) had only just been abolished as an instrument of discipline in schools, largely because of European pressure, and many teachers lamented its passing. Not surprisingly, there were strongly held and ambivalent views about the education system. Some people regarded it as an excellent opportunity for children to progress and make something of themselves; in Calvinist terms, success equalled virtue. Others literally hated the education system, and saw it as an instrument of humiliation and rejection. Both views were frequently expressed to me by parents, teachers, social workers and elected members of the regional council.

There was a great deal of deference to authority, in the education department in particular, but also more generally. There were several colloquial expressions to describe status consciousness; for instance being *placey* was a praiseworthy attribute, that is knowing one's place in relation to someone else. People in positions of authority, or aspiring to them, were known as *high heid yins*. Every senior manager in the education department was male, and all had been recruited from the formal secondary education system and from within Scotland. None had any knowledge of early years, and none had any particular interest in it. All children, whether aged two or sixteen, were referred to as 'youngsters', a word more commonly used to describe teenagers. Put crudely, the notion of quality within the education department was implicitly tied to the observance and continuance of existing educational traditions – although it is only fair to note that this has subsequently changed.

Not only was tradition highly valued, but to adapt, extend or change traditional practices was procedurally laborious. The region was divided into six semi-autonomous districts, each run by its own mini-education office. There were a series of highly formalized meetings at district, regional and political levels, and at a union level with three different unions who did not speak to one another, where papers proposing change were discussed – and frequently rejected. Quite apart from any views that the workers or the users in the service had about change, any proposal – even a minor one like altering the procedures for staff appointments to nurseries – could take more than a year to gain agreement and involved months of lobbying and meetings. One of my yardsticks of quality became ability to play the system, the wit which people showed to deal with and circumvent these absurd procedures.

PURSUING QUALITY: THE PROCESS

The irregularity of the process

In order to give an account of how we pursued the elusive goal of quality, the narrative that follows is coherent; in practice we seized whatever advantage we could when we could. Our long-term strategy was to develop policy; to confront traditional views about mothering and to introduce ideas about women's rights; to reinvigorate the debates about children's learning and staff training; to acknowledge and build upon the council's community and anti poverty strategies; and to incorporate all of them into a workable policy framework for early years. We hoped to create a programme of change and development based on this policy, and to argue for the resources to implement it.

Our short-term strategies, however, were opportunistic. If there was a chance of gaining some money through an unexpected budget adjustment or of steering a paper unexpectedly through a committee or of finding a loophole in the regulations, then we took it. This expediency was a risk. It undermined our attempts to create a climate of democratic debate and it made enemies in the education department. On the other hand the level of services was so low, the resourcing of them so meagre and the wider political climate so bleak that I felt that we had to grasp whatever small advantages we could. In writing about the process I am largely ignoring these small and frequent compromises, and categorizing and grouping our initiatives, somewhat arbitrarily, after the event.

The management of change

I managed a central policy unit, the Pre-Five Unit, within the education department. I worked with a small team of colleagues who were also newly recruited to develop the service. We came from widely differing backgrounds, in education, social work, community development and educational psychology. We met regularly to compare notes, thrash out principles and devise strategies. We did not necessarily hold the same perspectives amongst ourselves, given our very different experiences, but attempted to resolve our differences and arrive at a coherent view and a coherent strategy in dealing with the issues which confronted us. We offered each other support; the sounding board we offered each other was important for our sanity.

We realized that the ideological differences, and the intensity and conviction with which they were held, meant that we had to engage all the participants in early childhood services – 2,000 or more staff with very different experiences and views, parents, politicians, trade unions, educationalists – in discussion about these services. If we wanted to put forward an idea we had to try to convince most if not all of these stakeholders of its validity and relevance. But we also believed that as a method of introducing change, discussion was inherently right, a view fortunately shared by politicians. How sophisticated and democratic discussion about complex issues might be achieved in a region as large and diverse as Strathclyde was a test of our ingenuity. We also had to accept that there would always be dissenters, and that no decision would ever be final. We had, in short, painfully discovered that arriving at a definition of quality, and putting it into practice, was a process.

Debate and counter debate

In the five years gestation of the report which led to the reorganization of responsibility for early childhood services, there had already been considerable debate. Much of this debate was polarized. Apart from parental involvement, much of the argument concerned how much educational services could be expected to change so as to offer more flexible hours and more opportunities to parents and other interested local people to become 'involved'. Teachers had expressed considerable opposition to the community development model. They considered they had already adapted by embracing the concept of parental involvement and were afraid any further change would mean a 'dilution of the service', that is a poorer service in part administered by non-teachers. At worst they feared their conditions of service would change or that their nursery class or school would be closed.

We attempted to introduce ideas which were outside the usual frame of reference of this embittered debate. We engaged constantly in meetings at every level, from grass roots community meetings, political caucuses and practitioners' conferences to academic seminars. We addressed community and tenants associations about the council's policy of bringing services together; we presented papers about what the service might look like to the ruling group of Labour Party councillors and at other political and trade union meetings; we organized meetings for cross-sections of workers and for cross-sections of those who trained the workers, who had rarely if ever met together.

We launched a newsletter to publish ideas and new initiatives. We solicited correspondence. We engaged in the formal requirements of the council consultation processes, issuing closely worded documents on A4 paper. But we also published thousands of simply written leaflets asking for comments. We issued press releases, and cultivated journalists.

This approach of radical self-examination and publicity was not well-received in the education department, where obedience was a virtue and being unnoticed was a sign of doing your job well. Permission to do these things was reluctantly given and bureaucratically impeded. Many teachers regarded it as flamboyant, eccentric or dishonest behaviour. A continual complaint was that to try to introduce change showed a lack of understanding and lack of sympathy with the Scottish education system.

Research initiatives

One of the ways in which we hoped to broaden the debate was by using and generating research. We were fortunate in having on our doorstep three universities, and in each of them there were individuals with a major interest in early years, from the perspective of child development, education, and sociology respectively. In a paper to the education committee, we defined research broadly as systematic investigation of problematic areas which could be carried out at many levels by practitioners as well as by trained researchers. We set up a research policy group, with a cross-section of practitioners – teachers, nursery nurses, voluntary organization representatives, childminders as well as academics – which discussed research strategies and evaluated research proposals.

A number of research projects were launched by this group, some obtaining funding from academic sources, others funded by the regional council. We undertook a survey of 1,000 mothers of children under five in the region, investigating their take-up of services, their opinions on the services they used and their preferences for services, and related this to socio-economic circumstances (Penn and Scott, 1989). This research was critical in challenging traditional views of mothering. A second project investigated the extent of early literacy and numeracy in day nurseries (Munn and Schaffer, 1991). A third project looked at methods of self-evaluation in nurseries and on the monitoring of new nurseries set up by the council (Wilkinson, forthcoming), while a fourth studied how teachers and nursery nurses in nursery schools dealt with non-English speaking children (Ogilvy et al., 1992).

We sponsored places for an M.Ed degree at Glasgow University, which had newly devised early years modules including one on research. We negotiated places on the course for non-teachers as well as for teachers, and encouraged them to research into aspects of the history of their practice as part of the degree. One of the most interesting pieces of research was from a Chinese student, who carried out a comparative study of the policies of nurseries in Guandong Province and in Strathclyde Region; she illustrated that, while in China the national curriculum for nurseries ran to 18 volumes, as a way of standardizing provision, in Scotland the activities and curriculum depended on the autonomy of the headteacher.

Part of the strategy was to familiarize ourselves with current research and to disseminate it. We ran a series of research seminars at Glasgow University. These were open to anyone, free and organized with a minimum of bureaucracy for two-hour sessions in the early evening. We invited a range of researchers working in the fields of child development, education, health, social work and community development to talk about research they had either just completed or which was in progress. Several hundred people turned up for the first few seminars, although interest gradually tailed off. We also organized one-off day conferences and residential conferences on particular subjects, for example for the council's link-up groups, which were an attempt to organize community-based forums for discussion of early years.

Reviewing practice

Since the mission of the Pre-Five Unit was to develop a more coherent service, with a common set of principles and shared resources, we had to look at what services were currently doing, and to see to what extent the aims, objectives and practices of existing services were unregenerate. A change in philosophy or administration does not guarantee a change in practice, and many of the service providers found it difficult to envisage in what way they could develop or extend their work or link with those coming from another sector; indeed, many questioned whether it was necessary to do so. There was clearly a conflict for some staff, particularly within the education department, about the extent of their loyalty as paid employees of the regional council, since they regarded themselves as having a particular professional standard to uphold which they saw as being above the whims of politicians.

The intention of the politicians in integrating the service was not only that resources between the different sectors should be pooled, but that in doing so the service was to become more relevant in meeting the needs of parents. Each sector, however, as well as the politicians, claimed to know best what parents needed and wanted. As one group of nursery teachers firmly told us, in reply to one of our attempts at consultation: 'We feel as a staff we are providing the best service suited to the needs of the community'. The difficulty was that those arguing for a very different kind of service made equally assertive claims.

There was an additional simmering argument about what the children should be doing which hinged on who should be allowed to work with them – the level of skill and training needed to care for and educate children. Teachers argued, through their union, that only they had sufficient and requisite training. Anything less than a teaching qualification would 'dilute' the service. The other unions argued that although less rigorous, the level of qualification of their members was more appropriate. However, all unions opposed the employment of any unskilled workers drawn from the voluntary sector.

Despite our initiatives, it proved very difficult to either pool resources or bring about changes in practice because of the entrenched nature of the views amongst professionals. It is useful to explore why this was so, by looking at each of the sectors in more detail.

Nursery education

Nursery education, although reaching less than a quarter of three- and four-year-olds, was one of the most widespread forms of provision. Almost all nursery teachers in Strathclyde had trained at one of three teacher training colleges, and had always worked within the authority. This meant that there was a uniformity of view amongst teaching staff, and surprisingly little variation in practice between them, either in terms of the type of service or in the curriculum they offered. Most nursery education offered a part-time two and a half hour session, with a fairly fixed routine, and a curriculum built around the idea of 'themes', each theme lasting for a term or more.

The classroom was organized according to the requirement of the theme – transport, nature etc. It was questionable to what extent this classroom organization enriched learning, and whether children could grasp an abstract theme or be interested by its application for months at a time. The classrooms often seemed, to a casual visitor, rather barren places. There was hardly any consideration of race and gender issues, even in the few nurseries where black children formed more than half the catchment. In addition, partly because of the weather, partly because of vandalism, but mainly for cultural reasons, there was very little outside play and the children, in our view, were restricted physically.

From our perspective we felt the nursery schools and classes were some-what impoverished environments compared with some of the richly equipped English services we had seen. Again, compared with the more liberal traditions of English nurseries, the children were over-disciplined. It was possible to go into a nursery for 120 children at 11 a.m. in the morning and not hear a sound, because it was story time and the children were all, without exception, listening to the teacher or nursery nurse.

The nurseries mirrored the hierarchical tradition of the education depart-ment. Headteachers were firmly in charge and dressed for the part in suits and career clothes rather than in the casual clothes more suitable for working on the floor with children, while the nursery nurses (who worked with the teachers) often wore uniforms. The staff were often introduced by their designation rather than their name – the senior teacher, the first assistant nursery nurse and so on. The demarcations between these categories were usually made clear to visitors.

The most positive aspect of practice was that many nursery schools had parents' rooms which had been developed in response to the politicians' calls for more parental involvement and community participation. There were some excellent participative schemes, where the community education service offered taster courses to mothers while their children were attending school.

As well as perceiving it as sabotage of their professional standing, one of the reasons the nursery teachers were so defensive about any new development was that the politicians had threatened to close the nurseries in the more well-to-do areas and transfer their resources to deprived areas. The continual attacks on their integrity had demoralized the teachers and they felt the nurseries must be defended against change, since change was a prelude to closure. Teachers organized several well-publicized demonstrations, also attended by parents, against changes which they perceived, mistakenly or not, as being inimical to their interests.

Day nurseries

The public day nurseries were not so hostile towards change. Neglected for years, many of them in terrible premises and poorly equipped, they were mostly offering a dismal service and wanted improvements. The worst had bare rooms, equipment locked up in safes and the children were hygienically cared for but little else. There was almost no understanding of curriculum issues or of the potential to provide a learning environment.

There were a couple of new family centres, lavishly equipped and more generously run, which were the social work department's last attempt to develop the service before handing over to education. There were other family centres, created on the community development principle, with local participation. Often they were based in cramped and dingy converted flats in APTs, the argument being that local people would be alienated from any service that did not immediately reflect the experience of living in a poor, run-down area.

Playgroups

The playgroups were the most widespread service of all. They offered a part-time service of very variable quality, run mainly by volunteers. The representatives of the playgroup organization at regional level put forward a strongly articulated ideological claim to best represent the interests of mothers through their 'self-help' approach. Their notion of mothering, as discussed above, was a conventional one. They saw mothers essentially as tied to and responsible for their children, rather than as potential members of the workforce. The playgroup representatives had been led to expect that they would get a £500,000 grant from the Pre–Five Unit but it was simply not in the budget. As they had already appointed development staff in expectation of receiving the grant, they decided they had been subject to 'cuts'. They led deputations to the council and wrote furious letters to the papers denouncing all our initiatives and arguing that the politicians' intentions to involve parents was being subverted. It was a long time before we reached an equilibrium with them.

Childminders

Childminders were in some ways the easiest and most amenable group to deal with because their representatives had a non-confrontational, non-ideological approach and were entirely pragmatic. Moreover they were the only group likely to gain substantially from our initiatives. They had been so little acknowledged that everything was a bonus. We set up a working party with representatives of the childminders organization to produce guidelines on regulation and training and support of childminders, and were able to grant their association a small amount of money to develop and articulate the concerns of their members.

Developing practice

Following discussion within the Pre-Five Unit team, and with the agreement of politicians, a series of position statements were issued on curriculum, training, assessment and evaluation of practice and the type and hours of the service which could be developed according to parents' needs. These position statements were produced as leaflets in a widely accessible style, with a tear off slip for comments, and distributed both to professionals and parents. This gave us a basis on which to begin to discuss changes in practice.

We then considered what support and advisory staff were available to develop and extend the notions of good practice within the range of early childhood services. In each of the six divisions of the education department there was an Early Years Inspector, a person fairly senior in the hierarchy, skilled in curriculum matters and respected by teachers. They had substantial experience of the nursery education sector, but little or none of other early childhood services. They were unsure how to relate to these services, formerly the remit of the social work department, and were, with one sterling exception, fairly uncomfortable about doing so.

In addition, we had been able to appoint five new Development Officers to work at a divisional level to support new developments. They were drawn from both teaching and non-teaching backgrounds but were appointed at a less senior grade than the inspectors. Given the hierarchical nature of the education department, this immediately led to conflict about who should lead on new initiatives.

Finally there were over thirty Pre-school Organizers already in post. Their job had been to register playgroups and childminders from within the social work department and to encourage the development of mother and toddler groups and other small scale community initiatives. They were initially extremely hostile at being transferred to the education department and, as they saw it, losing the support structures they had had from working within social work teams. They were uncomfortable with the formality and hierarchy of the education department, and uneasy about the changes proposed by the politicians.

In addition, we drew on the contributions and expertise of lecturers and other staff at the teacher training colleges and colleges of further education in providing some of the training initiatives we wished to stimulate.

We worked with the various support staff to try to develop a programme of in-service training and to discuss and think about service development. The situation was both exciting and fraught. There were regrading claims, resignations, long-term sickness and threatened strikes and other indications of staff 'burn-out'. There were the inevitable setbacks. For instance, staff who had formerly worked for the social work department were represented by two separate unions. The union officials were both men who had a somewhat macho view of the women they represented. They had a narrow view of jobs and services, based on manual working. So for instance when we proposed to organize a two-day residential training course for day nursery workers at the luxurious teachers' centre to which they had never before been allowed access, the union insisted their members boycott it because we were not offering overtime pay for the evening and overnight time.

On the other hand, for the first time through the work of the support staff there were cross-sector meetings, joint training programmes and other new training initiatives and opportunities to compare practice and exchange ideas. We used the newsletter to focus on practice with information about what different groups of staff or parents were doing or thought about the services.

We tried to highlight 'good practice' by asking those service providers who were providing a slightly different service to talk about what they were doing and why. For instance one of the family centres offered a moving example of integration of profoundly disabled children; another service had an anti-racist under-fives project which had truly involved the local Pakistani community; and so on.

We arranged visits for a cross-sector of staff to services outside Strathclyde, elsewhere in the United Kingdom and abroad. The visits were carefully prepared and staff were asked to report back and give their impressions of what they had seen and understood. One group of staff visited Italy and were very impressed by the art work they had seen. As a result, a nursery school head and a day nursery head were seconded part-time to develop a similar art project with a group of nursery schools and day nurseries in an area of Glasgow.

The European perspective proved fruitful since assumptions about the provision of services were very different from current practice in the United Kingdom. We therefore became involved in a number of European projects besides arranging further exchanges and visits. We organized a seminar/conference on 'Men as Carers' where we worked with a small group of men to articulate their perceptions of themselves either as fathers at home with small children or men working with young children, and created an exhibition around this theme. We arranged a Scottish-wide residential conference to look at European initiatives.

Creating new services

The existing services in Strathclyde were not only diverse; they were unevenly spread and underfunded. Many of the premises were terrible, leaking, rotten and vandalized. One of the assumptions of the original report had been that if educational resources were more evenly shared and redistributed, there would be considerable improvements. But there was little to redistribute and those who were in possession of resources were determined to keep them.

For instance one of the family centres was housed in a suite of rooms in a large semi-derelict building, an abandoned school, which finally became uninhabitable. Children were having to come in waterproof boots because of the puddles inside the building. The kitchen had been condemned. We proposed that they be moved to the local primary school, a spacious building in reasonable condition where there were a number of spare rooms. The school objected violently; parents occupied the school in protest and teachers went on strike and formed a human barricade around the building. They argued that the school did not really have enough room, and they did not want 'social service children' in the school. The divisional education officer supported the teachers. The children and staff of the family centre were split up and bussed to empty places in other family centres. Many left and the family centre eventually had to be closed. There were other examples of schools showing this extreme reaction to sharing and amalgamation with early childhood services which had previously been the responsibility of the social work department. There was no question of redistribution. Unless we were also able to upgrade services and provide new services, things were unlikely to change.

Unfortunately there was little money for expansion. A school closure programme, due to a fall in the child population, had created some extra money. But there was only two weeks in which to submit bids for this money – partly a result of the cumbersome council procedures, but also because it had not occurred to anyone that we might wish to bid. There was also some money through the urban aid programme.

My own preference would have been to ask community groups to bid for money and experiment with developing services, rather than commit ourselves to a particular kind of provision. But the paternalism of the authority was such that this had never been done. Local groups had suggested schemes, but then the authority representatives had moved in, applied local authority staff designations, insisted on local authority grades and local authority management and in effect stamped out anything independent. One group, for instance, wanted to act as a collective, and to employ the cook as one of the collective. This was not merely unacceptable – it was inconceivable.

We did not want to fund more nursery schools or day nurseries along the existing divisive lines. We therefore proposed to set up a number of pilot 'community nurseries' which were intended to be flexible, multi-purpose centres taking children from early months to school starting age and open to cover working hours and the working year, with all staff working the same hours and conditions. These proposals degenerated to near farce; it was impossible to match the capital bids and the revenue bids because they were treated separately within the department. We could have revenue money, but there was a five-year capital programme on which we were not yet registered. There were endless negotiations about staff gradings for those who might work in these centres; we ended up with eighteen grades of staff for one small centre. The education officers in the divisions did not share our priorities about getting the work started once we had compromised horribly over everything else, and the teachers were determined to boycott anything that was not a nursery school. Last, but not least, the admissions policy, heavily influenced by social work lobbying, decreed that social need was still the most important criteria for admission and should take precedence over any other criteria, including the need for parents to work.

Our attempt to provide these pilot services proved fraught. The new community nurseries were set up, but they limped along. The three-year monitoring programme we initiated to evaluate them had to have an extension since the nurseries were so slow in starting. Nevertheless despite the drawbacks, the evaluation did suggest that children progressed as well in the community nurseries as in conventional nursery schools, and that the community nursery met parents' needs more effectively than conventional types of provision. The teachers' union dismissed the research as 'flawed', but more recently the council has been sufficiently convinced by the evidence to commit itself to a further programme of development of community nurseries. This has encountered resistance, mainly inspired by the teaching union, but implementation is now easier. There are precedents; the capital and revenue programmes are better reconciled; and both senior officers and members are now more solidly behind the ideas.

Formulating the policy

After three years we were able to submit to the council a new policy statement about services. This proposed ten principles and objectives:

1. The ultimate objective is to provide appropriate provision for all pre-school children and their parents.
2. All provision should recognize children's need for learning and education as well as care.
3. All services should reflect an equal opportunities approach which is anti-racist, anti-sexist, and recognizes the right of either men or women to work or care for children.
4. Parents and staff together should be actively involved in planning and running pre-school services for the long-term benefit of their children.
5. Pre-school services should be community based and sensitive to local needs, including employment and training needs.
6. There should be active co-ordination of services in each community (or group of communities) involving parents, council staff, voluntary organizations, health services and other appropriate agencies.
7. Voluntary organizations and community groups should be treated as partners in the provision of services capable of enhancing and complementing council provision.
8. Pre-school provision should be developed according to regional priorities in those areas having poorest services at present (i.e. APT areas).
9. Places should be allocated according to agreed admissions criteria. Referrals from social work and health should be given priority and accommodated within the complete range of services.
10. Services should be organized so that any provision can accommodate and meet the needs of children with a handicap or chronic illness, however severe the condition. The emphasis should be on directing resources to the community where the child is. No child should be denied access to a service on the grounds of health or disability.

This policy statement was flawed and ambiguous. But it did reflect the concerns of most of the interest groups with whom we had worked. It would have been possible to use it as a basis for planning the development of the service.

However, at this point, the circumstances changed. The politicians, finally exasperated with the education department, commissioned a consultant to examine it. His report was extremely critical of the departmental centralization, hierarchies, traditions and lack of educational objectives, as well as the absence of an equal opportunities perspective. It recommended that the department be fundamentally reorganized and that strategic and executive powers be devolved to local level. There was a major restructuring, and the new director, deeply ambivalent about the autonomous Pre-Five Unit, argued that it should also be devolved to local level. This eventually happened, and the unit was disbanded, although none of the policies were reversed; to that extent the debate had been too thorough. More seriously, from having had a slightly expansionist budget, the council was forced, by changes in national government legislation and funding, to start cutting its services. I felt I was in an untenable position, to have to advise on cutting back services which were so underfunded and so much in need of development. So, in 1990 I resigned.

CONCLUSIONS

Strathclyde as a representative example

Was Strathclyde typical? It is an unusual authority within the United Kingdom because of its size and diversity (it is also, at the time of writing, due to be abolished in a new round of local government reorganization). By English, and perhaps by Scottish standards, and for historical and religious reasons, it had a peculiar and enduring tradition of hierarchy. Because this sense of hierarchy was so engrained, there was also a lively sense of opposition to it, and radical and collectivist ideas were also vigorously held. Criticism escalated rapidly into inflamed confrontation and this aggressive confrontation permeated many areas of public life.

In this cultural context, introducing change was almost inevitably problematic. However, the fact that early childhood services were unified, with a common management structure and a common budget across the different service sectors, made it possible to plan for and develop services across the region. It would have been an impossible undertaking to review and develop services on the basis of goodwill, with the management responsibility for the different sectors vested as previously in different departments, because of the ideological differences between them. In order for change and development to happen, there had to be some kind of spearhead and some kind of coherent responsibility for services. The Pre-Five Unit crucially provided these.

A further difficulty was the vacuum at national government level. At this level there was no policy, no appropriate legislation or strategies, conflicting guidance from different government departments and worst of all, diminishing funding for local authority services. As Strathclyde was also the first local authority to attempt to provide a coherent service in the United Kingdom, there were no precedents – only a constant and premature stream of visitors wanting to come and see how we were managing.

Quality as a process not as a finite attribute

Strathclyde was unusual in the scale of its conflicts and in its diversity. In these respects, it is an atypical example. Nevertheless, it can be used to illustrate that quality is a process; that it is impossible to uphold a values-free and context-less definition of quality in early years services. If values and contexts differ, then the differences can only be resolved by informed debate and careful experimentation. The outcome of such debate is inevitably a compromise. People do not readily relinquish long-held views or abandon well-established practices, and adopt new ones. So the process is necessarily continuous, to take account of new ideas and changing circumstances and to allow for people's accommodation to them.

The process takes place at many levels

How young children learn and develop depends on the beliefs and practices of the adults they are with and where they are. These are not merely abstract considerations for child development experts and educationalists; they are also political questions. Quality cannot be achieved at the level of daily practice alone. Without a policy framework and the resources to implement it at local and national level, attempts to develop daily practice flounder. Otherwise there is no rationale or incentive for change.

The inadequacy of other models of quality

This conclusion, that arriving at a definition of quality is a complex process which needs to be worked out at many levels, is not generally agreed. The more familiar notion of quality is a finite, static and mechanical one, of a product which meets certain agreed and measurable criteria. This is the simplistic model implicit in 'validated' rating scales on various aspects of provision. Such scales may serve as a comparative research tool, but it is difficult to see how they can be used as a method for initiating and evaluating development and change. Similarly any regulatory model based solely on minimum standards rather than on principles and process has the effect that many providers, particularly in the private sector, equate meeting such standards with quality provision. Providers can claim that because they have met the regulatory requirements, they are offering 'a quality service'.

Where the level of services is poor and there are many different providers, regulating services by specifying a minimum standard below which certain services may not fall may be a useful preventative measure. But it runs the risk of lowering expectations; what is achieved is all that is expected. It is a very unambitious definition of quality.

We do a disservice to children, parents and workers unless we involve them all, in as many ways as possible, in exploring their understanding of what can be achieved in providing services. Arriving at that vision is a process, but given the fragmented nature of services to young children and the disregard in which they are often held, not an easy one to articulate or follow through.

REFERENCES

BARR, J. and PHILLIPS, K. (1984) *Evaluation of the Stepping Stones Project in Glasgow*, unpublished report.

MUNN, P. and SCHAFFER, R. (1991) Literacy and numeracy events in social interactive contexts, *International Journal of Early Years Education*, Vol. 1, no. 3.

OGILVY, C., BOATH, E., CHEYNE, W., JAHODA, G. and SCHAFFER, R. (1992) Staff-child interaction styles in multiethnic nursery schools, *British Journal of Developmental Psychology*, Vol. 10, pp. 85–97.

PENN, H. (1992) *Under Fives: The View from Strathclyde*, Scottish Academic Press, Edinburgh.

PENN, H. and SCOTT, G. (1989) *1000 Mothers of Children under Five*, Strathclyde Regional Council, Glasgow.

SCOTT, G. (1990). The concept of Areas of Priority Treatment in relation to services to children under five, *International Journal of Sociology and Social Policy*, Vol. 10, no. 1, pp. 1–13.

STRATHCLYDE REGIONAL COUNCIL (1985) *Pre-Five Report*, Strathclyde Regional Council, Glasgow.

WILKINSON, E. (Forthcoming) Evaluation of community nurseries in Strathclyde, *Monograph of the Journal of Early Education and Care*.

CHAPTER 3

Looking at Quality from the Child's Perspective[1]

OLE LANGSTED

Denmark has one of the most highly developed and coherent systems of early childhood services in the world. Using results from research and innovative projects undertaken in this system, Ole Langsted introduces an important but rarely heard stakeholder group in early childhood services – the children who attend them – and argues that they have a right to be heard in discussions about quality. He provides examples of how this might be done and of children's perspectives on quality, and emphasizes that while structures and procedures are needed for ensuring children's involvement they depend on a cultural climate which values children's opinions.

INTRODUCTION

Denmark has a large number of centres providing early childhood services for children before compulsory schooling, which starts at seven. These centres include day nurseries (*vuggestuer*) for children under three, kindergartens (*børnehaver*) for three- to six-year-olds and age-integrated centres (*aldersintegrerede institutioner*) taking children from a few months old to school age at seven and in some cases even older. There is a long tradition of experts being allowed to define quality in these centres. Experts in psychological and physical development, nutrition, safety, etc. have been asked for their opinion about the design of these centres and the standards which should be met to ensure good, healthy development for children. The politicians have listened to these experts (but not always followed their advice) during the decision-making process. The trained staff who work in the centres have also been regarded as experts in this connection. Thanks to their training and daily contact with children, their views about the best way to treat children have been listened to – although not sufficiently, they would say themselves.

In recent years there has been a tendency for public services to take the wishes of their users into account to a greater extent. With regard to early childhood services, this has led to the idea that parents should have greater influence on the daily life of centres. But what about the influence of the primary users – the children themselves? Is anyone interested in the kind of daily life the *children* want? Does anyone regard children as experts when it comes to their own lives? This chapter will describe various Danish experiences and research results concerned with taking seriously children's views about their daily lives and what makes for quality child care.

THE DANISH CONTEXT

In Chapter 10, Claus Jensen describes the development of Danish early childhood services during the past twenty years as a change from a situation in which the adults controlled and made the decisions in centres (the adults were supposed to teach the children something) to a situation in which provision is on the children's terms to a greater extent (children and adults learn from each other). This increasing willingness to listen to the wishes and needs of children reflects a trend running throughout the twentieth century, which has been described as 'the century of the child'. However, there is still a tendency to listen too little to children.

Claus Jensen's chapter presents the Danish context in detail. Consequently, I shall only summarize some of the most important features of Danish early childhood services here. Danish mothers of young children have been increasingly active in the labour market during the past thirty years. At first they were slow to find work, and often preferred part-time jobs. But today 95 per cent are active participants in the labour market and half of this number are employed full-time. During the same period, Danish society has introduced and organized a system of publicly-funded early childhood services, including both centres and family day care. Today there are places for 55 per cent of children aged six months to two years (22 per cent at centres, 33 per cent in organized family day care) and 72 per cent of the three- to six-year-olds (65 per cent in centres, 7 per cent in family day care); in addition, out-of-school care places are available for 40 per cent of seven- to ten-year-olds. There are still waiting lists, but the aim of the present government is to provide publicly funded places by 1996 for all children over the age of twelve months whose parents want a service.

Staff-child ratios in Danish centres are high compared with most other countries. On average the ratio for children aged six months to two years is 1:3, for three- to six-year-olds it is 1:6 and for seven- to ten-year-olds it is 1:8. There are very few deviations from this norm in the homogeneous Danish system (Langsted and Sommer, 1992; 1993). Although the number of places in centres has increased greatly during the past thirty years, influenced by the growing numbers of women joining the labour force, staff-child ratios have hardly altered at all. But educational theories and practice have.

STATE REGULATION: LISTEN TO THE CHILDREN

The educational content of, and theories behind, Danish early childhood centres are not subject to a great deal of state regulation. Responsibility is decentralized, with these areas controlled primarily by the staff and parents at each centre. However, a few years ago new general principles were laid down by the Ministry of Social Affairs (responsible at national level for all early childhood services) which all centres now have to observe:

1. Children's development, well-being and independence must be encouraged.
2. Children must be listened to.
3. Parents must have influence.
4. Centres must be regarded as a resource in connection with preventive work, i.e. the staff must, in co-operation with other professionals, ensure the special support that is needed for some families with children.
5. Centres must be regarded as one of each neighbourhood's facilities for children, i.e. the staff must co-operate with other facilities in the neighbourhood, both public and private.

Item two is particularly relevant to the subject of this chapter. It shows that the cultural battle for the amount of influence children should have has now reached a stage at which such influence can be required by law. The principle of listening to children is elaborated in the following way:

> It must be emphasized that children should be included in the planning and execution of activities in daytime child care facilities, according to their age and maturity, and that children in this way are able to gain experience of the connection between influence and responsibility on a personal and social level.
>
> (Danish Ministry of Social Affairs, 1990, Chapter 2)

There are also other ways in which the state has attempted to increase children's influence. In connection with the United Nations Convention on the Rights of the Child, the Danish Ministry of Social Affairs published a number of leaflets and books for children. The Convention has been described in three leaflets for three different age groups, and distributed to all Danish schoolchildren to inform them of their rights under the convention. For instance, a class of twelve-year-olds was asked to express the Convention in words that children can understand. The children expressed the lengthy Article 12 of the Convention in the following way: 'Children have a right to their own opinion, which must be respected' (Danish Ministry of Social Affairs and Danish UNICEF Committee, 1991, p. 39).

In another book for three- to six-year-olds in centres, written by adults and published by the trade union for untrained staff and two private organizations running centres (about 40 per cent of publicly funded early childhood services in Denmark are provided by non-profit private organizations, the rest by local authorities), the following words are used about the same topic: 'Grown-ups have lots of set ideas about how things should be organized. But children have their own ideas, and grown-ups must listen to children's ideas. Grown-ups must listen to what children have to say. Children must also have a say in things' (Pædagogisk Medhjælper Forbund *et al.*, 1991).

In this way the state and other organizations have tried to live up to Article 42 of the Convention, which in the children's own words sounds like this: 'The state must ensure that everyone knows about these articles' (Danish Ministry of Social Affairs and Danish UNICEF Committee, 1991, p. 41).

The extensive 'Children as Citizens' Project is another more direct way of listening to and including children. The Project was set up by an inter-ministerial working party concerned with children, and the general aim was to increase children's influence on issues relevant to themselves. The more specific aims were: to focus on children's everyday life and their possibilities for participation in decision-making; to strengthen children's right and opportunities to say things that will be heard and to which importance will be attached; to give children information that makes real participation in decision-making possible; to develop working methods where children can exert their influence; and to make adult practices and attitudes to children the subject of debate (Larsen and Larsen, 1992).

The Project was carried out in five selected local authorities and included many different ways of giving children greater influence. Most involved teenagers but some focused on younger children. The example quoted here is written by a trained worker from an early childhood centre. She describes one part of the Project, where children from the seventh form in a school (aged about thirteen to fourteen years) wanted to study how much say children in kindergarten (aged three to six years) had in their daily lives. The school-children made observations in the kindergarten for two days, and afterwards they met with staff and parents to tell what they had observed and what they thought was good and what was bad.

> After two children (Tina and Morten from the seventh form) had pointed out several areas where they felt we trampled on children's rights, we made certain structural changes in the daily running of our daycare centre. Tina and Morten pointed out that:
> - it was unlikely that the children were all hungry at the same time, and it was therefore unreasonable that they were all expected to eat at the same time (the time the adults considered suitable):
> - it might be healthy for children to go out to play, but only if they wanted to – and nothing indicated that they all wanted to go out at the same time, just because the adults thought they should:
> - it was not reasonable that the children could only have drinks from the water tap between meals, while the adults could have a cup of tea or coffee whenever they wished.
>
> The parents and staff listened to Tina and Morten's views, and decided to take the following steps:
> - we dropped the joint lunch, staffed the playground with one adult all day, and placed a jug of squash on the table for any child who was thirsty.
> - In addition, we decided to give the children the right and power to make important decisions about their life in the kindergarten, remov-ing this right and power from the hands of the adults. We had no idea what we had opened up, especially from the adults' point of view, but over the years the children have made an increasing number of decisions, and the result is a life that children and adults really

share. It is still the responsibility of the adults to introduce the children to the social world, but countless decisions are now taken by the children, and our mutual relationships are what really matter.

(Hare, 1993, p. 19)

The youngest children have also been involved in the 'Children as Citizens' Project. Very young children have not been asked themselves about their daily lives but staff and parents have tried to find out how to be attentive to the children's needs and wishes in their everyday life. One project described by Larsen and Larsen (1992) concerns a nursery for children from six months to three years. Here the staff have been preoccupied with rules, frequently regulating the behaviour of the children by prohibitions. On the assumption that even very young children have the right to control themselves in their everyday life, and that they are able to do so, the staff have reviewed the rules and try to listen more to the children. This means, among other things, that children have got the right to say 'no'. If a child does not want to eat, she should not be pressed; and if a child leaves the dinner table to do something else it is all right – but it is not all right to run back and forth all the time. Thus, some rules are preserved, including those rules that concern the safety of the children, but a lot of the former rules have been abandoned.

One of the consequences is that there are fewer conflicts between adults and children. On the other hand there are more conflicts between the children. But this is seen as another right that children have – the right to try to solve their own conflicts. And on many occasions they are able to do so.

From the start not all parents were happy about the project. When the children were allowed to jump on the furniture in the centre, how could you explain to them that it was not allowed at home? But practice has proved that the children are fully able to distinguish between the rules at home and the rules in the centre if the reasons for the differences are explained to them. Through meetings between staff and parents and through daily practice the parents have gradually realized that children are able to decide more for themselves.

The 'Children as Citizens' Project continues for the next two years. Through children's everyday life in centres, schools, libraries, clubs, etc. an attempt is made to encourage their active participation in society. This Project and other examples show how Denmark, even on an official level, has become increasingly interested in making sure that children are listened to and that they are included in decisions that are important in their own daily lives.

THE CULTURE OF CHILDREN

In Denmark, importance is also attached to the wishes and needs of children at less official levels. Pressure from these less official channels may well have helped to influence official policy. The Centre for Children and Young People's Culture at Odense University has been studying children's own cultural patterns for several years. The myth that children's activities are often chaotic and without direction has been exposed. The Centre prefers to listen to children and try to understand things which adults find incomprehensible *in children's terms*. This technique has also enabled the Centre to expose another myth: that children learn all the important things in life through learning situations organized by adults. The following example, taken from Jessen (1993), reveals some of the central features of this approach to children's culture.

The culture of play is used by children to learn in their own special way. The adult method is to allow children to practise things for a long time and then perform the activity concerned once they have learned to do it right. Children do not divide the learning process up in this way. They play, practise and learn at the same time. The game itself and social relationships are the most important things. Skills and competence are by-products.

Peter is just over six years old, and attends a daycare centre. He has still not started school, and will start nursery class in a few months. But he can already do arithmetic. He can add up in play, and arithmetic is still a game for him. He spends a good deal of time each day adding up figures in his own head. Not just 'two plus two makes four' and other multiplication tables learned by rote, but figures ranging from 2 to about 30 or 40.

It is not unusual for a child of six to do sums, of course. Arithmetic is one of the most important skills in our society and parents often start giving their children adding up lessons at an early age. But this is not the case with Peter. His parents are adamant that they have *never* tried to teach him arithmetic. They are proud of the fact that he simply seems to have picked it up naturally, and confident that he is bound to succeed in life as a result.

This story would probably have been forgotten – but Peter suddenly started doing arithmetic with figures of more than 100, counting in intervals of 5 and 10 (which seemed strange). Peter had just returned from a holiday with his grandmother, so everyone assumed he had been taught the new technique by her. He was asked what he had done at grandma's house. Had he done any arithmetic? 'No,' he answered – but he had played a card game with grandma. Each player had seven cards, which were placed on the table in order and added up. Some cards counted five, others ten. The winner was the first to have a total of five hundred. When asked whether he did the counting himself, he answered that he had. Otherwise grandma might have been cheating!

It is worth mentioning that there were several reasons why Peter was ready to learn arithmetic. He had done a good deal of arithmetic already during games of 'school' with his sister, involving his first unofficial teaching in how to add up.

This story shows that children can learn skills without needing a formal learning system, and that such skills are a by-product of their central activity (play). Peter learned arithmetic after a few hours of teaching by his nine-year-old sister and by playing cards for hour after hour with his grandmother. But the point of the story is not merely that card games teach children to add up painlessly. The point is that the story has been noticed and regarded as interesting because it deals with *arithmetic*, which is regarded as a complex and important skill in our society. If the story had been about learning to walk, dance, talk or sing, no-one would have remembered it. Children learn all these skills without anyone noticing much – despite the fact that talking (for instance) is far more complicated than adding up figures.

INTERVIEWING CHILDREN

Most of the information we have about the psychological development of children is derived from adults. Very few research projects interview the children themselves, preferring to obtain their information from the adults who have close daily contact with the children concerned. In many cases, this is because information provided by adults is regarded as being more reliable and valid than information obtained from children.

With regard to this point, Tiller (1988) argues that in many cases it is both relevant and necessary to obtain information about the situation of children (and their understanding of this situation) from children themselves. He asks how such information can be regarded as objective (i.e. reliable) and how the reliability of children's statements can be confirmed. The commonest way of determining reliability is by making comparisons with other test results. But first the reliability of these other tests must be determined: it is possible that the independent observations of children we use as a criterion of reliability may be less reliable than the children's own statements. If information provided by children corresponds poorly with other observations, this may also be because the information given by the children is unique. In such cases an apparent lack of reliability can actually provide an argument in favour of using the information provided by children, since such information cannot be obtained by any other means.

The problem of validity is another matter:

> If we are interested in the child's experience and interpretations, the criterion for validity is hard to derive from any other source than the child itself. In such cases validity depends partly on consistency, on the relationship of the parts to the whole; and individual statements can be understood in the light of the overall picture obtained. But because the subject matter is children, the problem is that our adult logic has rules about what represents reasonable consistency; and to put it simply the logic and consistency of children is different from that of adults.
>
> (Tiller, 1988, p. 42)

In other words, the problems of reliability and validity differ when it comes to interviewing children. But this fact does not mean that children should not be asked about their own lives in all relevant circumstances.

A number of research projects have used interviews with children as their method, particularly when focusing on older children. However, we still have little experience of interviews with young children. A good deal of imagination and creativity is required to design interviews for this age group. Here is an example of how it can be done.

The *BASUN Project* is a comparative study of the daily lives of ordinary young children in the five Nordic countries: Denmark, Finland, Iceland, Norway and Sweden.[2] *BASUN* is the abbreviation (in Nordic languages) for Childhood, Society and Development in the Nordic Countries. We have studied 123 children living an ordinary modern childhood. Ordinary in this context means that the children have not had treatment for any serious physical illnesses or psychological problems. In the Nordic countries, modern childhood involves living in an urban area with parents who are in the labour force and the child taken care of outside the home on a regular basis. We have studied four groups of boys and girls aged five years: two groups living with both biological parents, one middle-class and the other working-class; and two groups living with a single mother, one with little or no contact with the father and one with frequent contact.

In the *BASUN Project*, the five-year-old children were interviewed about their daily lives. Based on the theory that children acquire skills and understanding of their surroundings and themselves from the regular social interactions that take place each day, the interviews were focused on the child as an actor in the social interactions of daily life. Before interviewing the children, they were observed in their centres and interviews were conducted with parents and centre staff. These adult interviews were scrutinized closely, so that we had detailed insight into the structure and content of the children's daily lives before interviewing them.

We had already met the children concerned before the interviews, often several times, so the children knew the interviewer. In the introduction to the interviews we made a great point of telling the children about the objective of our conversation. We pointed out that we had already spoken to their fathers, mothers and centre staff and that we already knew a lot about their families and centres. But we also said that *they* were the only ones who were five years old in their families, so *they* were the only ones who knew what it was like to be five years old. We tried to make the children *experts in their own lives*, and to inform them that this was the case. Many of the children were clearly unused to being regarded as the most important sources of information about their own lives in this way – certainly by an adult whom they hardly knew. It was obvious that the realization made them highly motivated to take an active part in the interviews.

We used *time and space* as structural factors of the interviews. We asked what the children did on a specific day from morning to evening, so the cyclical progress of a day provided the structure of the interviews. Five-year-olds find it difficult to sit still and be interviewed and it is often a help and support for the child (and the interviewer) to conduct the interview in the environment which is being discussed. So the conversation about the flow of events from morning to evening took place in the child's home. The daily routine takes a child from the bedroom where he/she wakes up; to the bathroom and getting dressed; to the kitchen and breakfast. The interview took the same route, with the child taking the interviewer on a sightseeing trip of his/her daily life. For example, the interview started in the morning with a discussion of what it was like to wake up. We asked each child to show us where he/she woke up. Inside the bedroom we asked the child to show us how he/she lay in bed and asked what waking up was like – did someone wake them up, or did they wake up on their own? Andenæs (1991) gives more details of these aspects of the interview, and (taking a girl as an example) goes on to explain that:

Once details of waking up had been given, we asked what she did when she was awake. When she said she went to the bathroom, I asked if she could show me the bathroom, and we both went there. If the next step was getting dressed, I asked the girl to show me where she kept her clothes and how she got dressed. I took the opportunity of asking why the clothes were arranged as they were. The answers to this type of question can reveal whether the child is aware of her role in the events of the household, or whether she feels that events simply happen at random without any motives and without pondering on the reasons for events. The demonstration of dressing also gives an opportunity to ask how much help the child is given in various situations, and how much she can manage without help. In addition, the description of what happens at home can be compared with what happens at the daycare centre or the house of the family day carer.

(Andenæs, 1991, p. 280)

In other words, interviewing children provides information about their own views of their daily lives which could not be acquired by any other method.

CHILDREN'S VIEWS ON QUALITY

The lives of children these days are said to be split into compartments, something which is regarded in a negative light as being a potential constraint on their development. It is claimed that because children switch between various social situations each day of their lives, confusion and at worst permanent problems of identity can result. In the *BASUN Project* we studied the ordinary daily lives of children in at least two different worlds – the family home and the centre where they go while their parents are out at work. These days, the characteristic feature of the lives of children in the Nordic countries is that they live in both worlds from a very early age. In attempting to understand this daily life, we therefore believe that the conventional distinction between primary and secondary socialization is insufficient. We prefer to speak of *dual socialization*, in order to understand the dual nature of the way children acquire experience from their two worlds (Dencik, 1989).

The analysis outlined below is based on the experience of twenty-four Danish children, all of whom attend a standard kindergarten or an age-integrated centre. In order to understand the children's own experiences when living in two different worlds, and to appreciate what children regard as quality in each of these two worlds, we subjected our interview material to the following analytical questions (naturally, these are not the same questions as those asked in the interviews):

• Which of the two worlds was preferred, and what did the children like about their families and centres?
• Who makes decisions, and what was the child allowed to decide, in each of the two worlds?
• What rules apply in each of the two worlds?

It is difficult to get five-year-olds to say what they like about their families. The family is taken for granted by children. In other words, the family *is* quality and all other contexts are judged in relation to the family. We know that this causes problems in other areas of life. The social system is familiar with the loyalty of children to their parents, even parents who neglect them, beat them or sexually abuse them. But great loyalty to the family also applies to what we here define as 'ordinary' children.

The children had far more to say about quality in the centres they attended. When we asked what the children liked best about their centre we were given different answers, but there was one distinguishing feature about all the answers. The primary factor determining children's views about the quality of their centre was the presence of other children. Here is a typical answer:

> INTERVIEWER: Let's talk a bit about your daycare centre. Do you like going there?
> CHILD: Yes, I do.
> I: What do you like about it?
> C: There's lots of children there to play with.

The presence of children is also important in the home environment and this is expressed in many ways. For instance:

> I: Where do you like being best?
> C: At home.
> I: Why is that then?
> C: Because at home I can play with the children I like.

However, contact with other children is not necessarily pleasurable for all children at all times:

> I: (We had just discussed being picked up at 2.00 or 3.00 p.m.) What time do you like being picked up best?
> C: I like two o'clock best.
> I: Why is that then?
> C: Because there's so many children that tease me at the centre.

In other words, the presence of other children was the greatest attraction at the daycare centre. But depending on the situation, other children could make it difficult or even impossible to attend the centre.

Several factors were mentioned as being of secondary importance (all three were given equal weight): activities; toys; nice staff.

> I: Do you like Mum going out to work?
> C: Yes. At the centre it's always fun, because there's so many toys – far more than I've got at home. Sometimes we get new toys – we've got some new toys at the centre today. Pearls, felt tips, and plasticine. There's lots more I can't remember.
> I: Is it more fun sometimes being at the centre than being at home?
> C: Yes (nodding vigorously).
> I: Why is that then?

C: Because I don't like being at home at weekends. I'd much rather be at
 the centre.
I: Why's that?
C: Because I don't like being at home.
I: What makes the centre so much fun? What do you like best about the
 centre?
C: When we go out for a walk, and when they take photos of us. And I
 like playing with my friends.

The daycare centre staff clearly play an important role for the children,
although they are far from being the most important factor (which is what
adults often believe).

One of the most important differences between home and centre for the
children is the degree to which they are allowed to decide for themselves in the
two environments. In general they feel that they can decide a lot themselves at
home, even though they are perfectly aware that their parents decide in the
last resort, a fact generally regarded as natural. At the centre things are a little
different:

I: Who makes the decisions at your daycare centre?
C: The grown-ups.
I: Are the children allowed to decide anything?
C: Yes – who we want to play with.

Another child said:

I: At meal times do you decide for yourself more at home or at the
 centre?
C: At home with Mum and Dad
I: What are you allowed to decide at home that you can't decide at the
 centre?
C: What I eat. At the centre we just get what Grete makes. She decides. I
 don't mind that. But I don't like the grown-ups always standing up
 there getting the food, because they leave the children all alone.

To a large extent children accept the fact that adults decide more at the centre
than at home. They seem to accept that life at the centre is simply like that,
and have no difficulty functioning both in a social system where they have
great influence on small daily routine tasks and in a system in which the adults
decide to a larger degree. But when the adults decide more, the child is often
forced to develop strategies to handle the situation, such as the following
child:

I: Do they tell you to do things in the daycare centre sometimes that you
 don't want to do?
C: Yes.
I: What, for example?
C: To make garlands or something out of leaves. I don't like doing that,
 but we have to.

I: What do you say when they tell you you have to?
C: I say no, then they say I've got to, then I say alright I will.
I: Why do you say alright in the end?
C: Because I don't want to argue with them.

However, deciding for yourself is only fun to a certain extent, as the following story shows:

I: What's it like at the daycare centre? For instance, are there things you're not allowed to do?
C: Yes . . . I can't really remember what . . . Once we were allowed to do anything we wanted. We threw liver pâté sandwiches at each other and at the windows.
I: Is that what you always do?
C: No, we were only allowed once. All the children asked to decide themselves what to do. Some children went to the toilet in the middle of the playroom, and we threw the toys around, but it wasn't much fun tidying up afterwards.
I: So you had to tidy up afterwards?
C: Yes, and the grown-ups just lay on the mattresses all day.
I: Was it a good idea to let the children decide what to do?
C: It was fun alright, but it wasn't much fun tidying up afterwards.

The fact that children are allowed different degrees of self-determination in their two worlds is due to the fact that the two worlds have different rules. These different rules and standards are often believed to confuse children. But the truth is that children not only have a clear picture of the differences, but also an understanding of the reasons for the differences:

I: Are there rules at the daycare centre that you don't have at home?
C: Yes. If you want to go down into the common room you always have to ask a grown-up from your own room first, and usually only two children from each room are allowed down there each time.
I: Why do you have to ask the grown-ups when you want to go down into the common room? Why can't you just go down there yourselves?
C: Because sometimes we have pillow fights down there, and it gets a bit out of control.
I: What happens then?
C: Someone might start crying if they get a pillow straight in the eye.

Or another child:

I: Is there a big difference between home and your daycare centre?
C: Yes! Very, very big.
I: What are the differences? Can you decide more at home?
C: Yes. Eating rules – at home I can decide where to sit when I eat lunch. And . . and when we go out I'm allowed to decide at home. And when we eat . . . when I want something to eat like a carrot or

apple, I can help myself at home from the fridge, but when I'm at
the centre I can only have fruit and other stuff . . . and . . .

I: At regular times?

C: Yes.

I: Do you like it best at home, then?

C: Yes.

I: Do you think it's funny sometimes that there's such a big difference?

C: Yes. I don't know why. I think there ought to be the same difference,
that there shouldn't be any differences.

I: Why is that? Is it easier to work things out then?

C: No, it's easier to work out for me . . . there's only, there's only three
children. At the centre . . . I know why we're not allowed to up at
the centre. It's because there's so many children, isn't it, so just
because someone asks if we . . . if he can have some milk, and if
he's allowed to have some, then *all* the children will want some too,
isn't it?

I: Is that why?

C: Yes, that's why we eat at regular times.

However, some children associate the difference in rules between home and
daycare centre not with the control and decisions of adults, but with quite
different rules:

I: Are there a lot of rules to obey at your centre?

C: I don't know.

I: Is there anything you're not allowed to do there?

C: Yes, sometimes.

I: What aren't you allowed to do?

C: You're not allowed to stand in the middle of the goal, because you'll
get the football right on your knee.

It is very difficult to draw any firm conclusions from the rich and varied
material provided by these interviews with children. Any attempt to do so will
undoubtedly blur the variation and differences in the answers given. None-
theless, I intend to try.

It is not difficult to define quality in the life of five-year-old children today.
The family is regarded as the quality standard. But children also regard their
centre as representing quality. Children regard the other children as by far the
most important factor in determining the quality of their centre. This
conclusion underlines the importance of a factor which experts, parents
and centre staff are all aware of but may tend to forget from time to time,
i.e. that children are important for children's development. The conclusion
also underlines the fact that it is important for children to have a world in
which there is room for contact with other children.

If the presence of other children is the most important quality criterion,
activities, toys and nice staff are also important criteria for children. The fact
that staff are no more important than toys might make them seem superfluous.
This is not at all the case. The children clearly understand that the staff
control the daily routine, helping and comforting them when conflicts arise

which they cannot manage themselves. But the staff certainly do not have the same importance as the other children.

Any discussion of the quality of centres must also include the other side of the coin: concern that the life of children these days is split into different compartments and that this compartmentalization between home and centre will harm children and their development. When we ask five-year-olds themselves about the differences between home and centre (differences in terms of the degree of self-determination and the rules applying in each social environment), it appears that children are perfectly capable of coping with such differences. They might think that the differences are strange and that certain rules should be changed. But they accept virtually all the differences and many children show that they understand the reasons for the differences that apply.

So is there no reason to be concerned about modern childhood? Yes, there is. The ability of children to bring coherence to a world of differences depends on the presence of professional staff with the ability to guide and support children's relationships with each other and the integration of each child's different worlds into a single entity. The theories applied in many Danish centres, based to a large extent on the wishes and needs of the children themselves, and the high level of professional training for workers in these centres (described in Chapter 10) mean that these centres are able to help children build up an increasingly complex network of social relationships with both adults and children and create coherence in their own lives.

CONCLUSION

This chapter presents several Danish examples of how to take even young children's views and opinions about their own lives seriously. They also reflect (to a varying extent) the views of children on the quality of their daily lives. These examples show that even young children have strong opinions about their everyday life, and there is evidence that you can improve the life conditions of children by listening to and going along with their opinions. When we speak of quality in early childhood services, it is therefore important not only to listen to the views of adults, as is traditionally done, but also to ask the children themselves since they have important things to tell us.

How to find out about children's opinions is exemplified in this chapter. There is no 'correct' way to do this. It is important to experiment with different ways to bring forth children's views. The appropriateness of different methods depends to a large degree on the age of the children: the younger the child the more you must use methods that are more indirect than just asking the child directly. However, in developing methods it is most important to adopt an open and listening attitude to what children have to say.

If you are not only going to experiment with giving more influence to children but also want to keep the influence already obtained you have to build structures and procedures for this. If this chapter says little about structures and procedures it is not because they are unimportant. But more important is the cultural climate which shapes the ideas that the adults in a particular society hold about children. The wish to listen to and involve children originates in this cultural climate. This wish will then lead to structures and procedures that can guarantee the involvement of the children.

It is important to emphasize that the examples in this chapter all relate to a Danish context. In other circumstances and other cultures, children may have completely different wishes and needs. The results are not even necessarily representative of Danish society as a whole; here, too, much greater efforts are needed before sufficient attention is paid to the views of children. However, the examples do at least indicate one conclusion which is applicable internationally: it is an advantage to regard children as experts when it comes to their own lives to a far greater extent than has been the case until now.

REFERENCES

ANDENAES, A. (1991) Fra undersøgelsesobjekt til medforsker? Livsformsintervju med 4–5-gåringer (From investigated object to co-researcher? Way-of-life interview with 4- to 5-year-old children), *Nordisk Psykologi*, Vol. 43, no. 4, pp. 274–92.

DANISH MINISTRY OF SOCIAL AFFAIRS (1990) *Cirkulære nr. 203 om dagtilbud for børn og unge efter bistandsloven* (Government Circular no. 203 concerning child care for children and young people according to the Danish Public Assistance Act).

DANISH MINISTRY OF SOCIAL AFFAIRS and THE DANISH UNICEF COMMITTEE (1991) *Konventionen om Barnets Rettigheder* (Convention on the Rights of Children), Danish Ministry of Social Affairs, Copenhagen.

DENCIK, L. (1989) Growing-up in the post-modern age: on the child's situation in the modern family, *Acta Sociologica*, Vol. 32, no. 2, pp. 155–80.

HARE, J. (1993) Voksne har svært ved at høre efter (Adults find it hard to listen), *Børn & Unge*, Vol. 24, no. 48, p. 19.

JESSEN, C. (1993) Børns legekultur – en introduktion (Children's culture of play – an introduction), *Nul til fjorten*, Vol. 3, no. 4, pp. 35–41.

LANGSTED, O. and SOMMER, D. (1992) *Småbørns livsvilkår i Danmark* (Conditions of life for young children in Denmark), Hans Reitzels Forlag; Copenhagen.

LANGSTED, O. and SOMMER, D. (1993) Denmark, in M. Cochran (ed.) *International Handbook of Child Care Policies and Programs*, Greenwood Press, Westport.

LARSEN, H. R. and LARSEN, M. (eds.) (1992) *Lyt til børn – en bog om børn som medborgere* (Listen to children – a book on children as citizens), Det tværministerielle Børneudvalg og Kulturministeriets Arbejdsgruppe om Børn og Kultur, Copenhagen.

PAEDAGOGISK MEDHJAELPER FORBUND, MENIGHEDERNES DAGINSTITUTIONER and LANDSFORENINGEN FRIE BORNEHAVER OG FRITIDSHJEM (1991) *Børns rettigheder – en fagbog for børn i daginstitution* (The rights of children – a non-fiction book for children in child care centres).

TILLER, P. O. (1988) Barn som sakkyndige informanter (Children as reliable sources of information), in M. K. Jensen (ed.) *Interview Med Børn* (Interviews With Children), National Institute of Social Research, Copenhagen.

NOTE

1. The research reported in this chapter has been supported by the Danish Social Science Research Council and the Danish Ministry of Social Affairs.
2. The participants in the *BASUN project* are research leader Lars Dencik; Anja Riitta Lahikainen and Harriet Strandell (Finland); Baldur Kristjánsson (Iceland); Agnes Andenæs and Hanne Haavind (Norway); Gunilla Dahlberg (Sweden); and Dion Sommer and Ole Langsted (Denmark).

CHAPTER 4

Defining and Valuing Quality As a Parent

MARY LARNER AND DEBORAH PHILLIPS

Few would disagree that parents are a key child care stakeholder group, but what is known regarding parental perspectives on quality care? Mary Larner and Deborah Phillips address this question from studies based in the United States, contrasting parental perspectives with those of child care professionals. Acknowledging the diversity of parents and their socio-economic resources, the impact of a free market economy on the provision and utilization of child care services emerges in this chapter.

I read some articles previous to going out and actually looking. But in the back of my mind, I was looking to find someone who was going to hold my baby as much as I hold him.

(EDK Associates, 1992, p. 6)

For my son, I would like someone to pay attention to him . . . someone that will take him out for fresh air, to play with him. To teach him about books.

(Porter, 1991, p. 22)

I said, 'You don't even know these people . . . and I'm going to leave you . . . and you're not going to cry?' I felt kinda funny. I was like, 'You're supposed to want to come with me?'

(Holloway *et al.*, 1993, p. 9).

INTRODUCTION

Quality counts in child care – on that, parents and professionals agree. They share an interest in ensuring that young children are safe, nurtured, and given opportunities to learn and grow. Parents and professionals differ sharply, however, in their relationships to children. Parents have only their own children in whom all their hopes and affections are invested; professionals usually see sets of children not related to them who change from one year to the next. Some professionals work as child care providers, others train child care providers, study them, and supervise their work; parents rely on the child care services they offer. Divergent experiences give rise to different values, and parents think about child care quality in a different way from professionals. Further, parents are not a homogeneous group: they include both mothers and fathers; parents of infants, pre-schoolers and older children; men and women of different racial and ethnic groups; and those with ample resources as well as those living under conditions of scarcity. This chapter will examine the ways parents differ from professionals and from one another in their ways of defining and evaluating child care quality.

Based on research in the United States, the chapter focuses on full-day child care that enables parents to work outside the home; the distinct role played by part-day early childhood programmes is not addressed. The chapter first examines the differences between professional perspectives on child care and those of parents. Next, it reviews in some depth what is known about how parents select child care and how different parents judge the quality of care. The chapter concludes with a call for a concerted effort by professionals – researchers and practitioners – to expand their view of child care quality to encompass the priorities and values parents have for the care of their children. A brief description of pertinent aspects of child care in the United States sets the stage.

CHILD CARE IN THE UNITED STATES

Child care is a fact of life for most families in the United States, including those with infants under one year of age. Yet ideologies about free enterprise capitalism, the privacy of the family, and the supremacy of exclusive maternal care have worked against the development of a stable, adequately funded system of non-parental child care that meets the needs of most families. Instead, a patchwork of child care has evolved in incremental steps, supported predominantly with parent fees, leaving many holes and uneven coverage (Phillips, 1991). There is no public consensus that either the government or employers have a responsibility to invest in efforts to make child care available, affordable and of decent quality. As a consequence, the vast majority of families in the USA face the search for child care on their own, without substantial assistance in paying the cost of care (which averages about $3,300 per year for full-time care).

Today, values that stress family privacy are seen in child care policies that promote the rights of all parents (including those who receive publicly-funded child care) to choose freely among child care arrangements, and to reject any measures that limit the availability of care. The goal of promoting parent choice is invoked by policy-makers who seek to restrain the use of regulations aimed at improving standards. Many states have eliminated requirements that public subsidies go only to child care arrangements that meet an agreed standard of safety, again because of the effects those requirements might have on parent choice. The rationale is that such restrictions diminish the overall supply of care and, thus, limit the number of child care arrangements available for parents to consider. Others argue, however, that what parents want most is a range of good, affordable child care options to choose among as they decide how best to meet the family's child care needs.

To the extent that the safety and quality of care are regulated by government agencies in the USA, it is entirely a state-level responsibility, applied primarily to child care centres that are not run by churches or the public schools. Regulations concerning home-based child care vary widely and, in many states, are ineffectively enforced (Adams, 1990). Moreover, the quality provisions of child care regulations are very minimal. One example is the area of staff training: most states require only that child care providers have graduated from high school. As a result, parents are left on their own to judge the safety and quality of whatever child care options they locate, without the benefit of a publicly-supported system that assures or guides them to quality arrangements. Even parents' choice about when to first place their child in child care is limited by the fact that the United States has only a weak parental leave law, enacted in 1992. The law provides twelve weeks of job-protected but unpaid leave; it thereby forces families who cannot afford the loss of twelve weeks of a parent's wages to return early to work, and to find child care.

In theory, parents' child care options compose a dizzying array of possible arrangements including, for some, the grandmother or another relative, and for many, the next door neighbour, a near-by adult who cares for several children, or a child care centre. Most of these arrangements, with the exception of centres, operate beyond the purview of public regulatory scrutiny, and the vast majority offer care by untrained adults. Although many of the nation's centre-based child care programmes are run by non-profit organizations, a growing number are business enterprises. Family day care providers who care for children in their homes also work as individual entrepreneurs.

Child care in the USA is also, to a great extent, economically stratified. Child care is usually a neighbourhood-based service because many parents want child care that is close to home and similar to the culture of the family. As a result, the income segregation of United States neighbourhoods is reflected in a segregated child care market – the quality and variety of alternatives available to well-to-do families outstrip the range of options open to families who live in poor communities. In reality, then, most parents' choice of care is severely restricted by their need for a convenient and affordable arrangement.

DIVERGENT PERSPECTIVES OF PROFESSIONALS AND PARENTS

The views of early childhood professionals have long dominated discussions of what constitutes quality in early childhood programmes: professionals determine the content of training for those who establish and staff child care programmes; they set criteria for recognizing excellence within the profession; and their expert judgements about quality may inform the policy-makers who set regulatory policies. By contrast, the voices of parents have long gone unheard. Yet no one who has been or known a parent who used child care would suggest that parents do not care about child care quality. In large measure, parents are silent because they have not been asked their views. Fathers, in particular, are invisible players in the process, despite recent evidence that husbands and wives both juggle their work schedules to keep child care within the immediate family (O'Connell, 1993). For the most part, parents make their child care arrangements quietly and privately. Their thoughts and priorities are evident only when they make actual child care choices, or when they act to change unsatisfactory arrangements. By examining those actions and asking parents to explain them, researchers in recent years have given us a glimpse of how parents think about and judge the quality of child care. That evidence reveals how different the perspectives of parents and professionals truly are.

When professionals assess child care quality, their goal is typically to identify the features of child care settings that are associated with positive experiences and outcomes for children. Their concepts of quality are designed to be concrete, objective and quantifiable, so they can be applied fairly across a wide range of programmes. That interest leads professionals to focus on structural features of child care programmes such as adult-child ratio, group size and caregiver qualifications that are often associated with safe, positive experiences for children.

Research studies which include observations of children in centres and (less frequently) in family day care homes (Kontos, 1992; Phillips, 1987; Whitebook, Howes and Phillips, 1989; Zaslow, 1991) have confirmed professionals' conceptions of quality. Children attending programmes in which adult-child ratios, group size and caregiver training meet professional standards are more likely to be secure, comfortable and interested. For instance, one reviewer explained the impact of adult-child ratios as follows: 'The number of children with whom each caregiver can engage in a stimulating and sensitive fashion is obviously limited. With too many children to care for, the caregiver's interactions with each child are likely to become brief and cursory' (Phillips, 1987, p. 5). However, while structural features like ratios and staff training are conditions that a number of studies have indicated will make it more likely that children will fare well in a given setting, they do not measure quality directly, or guarantee it.

In contrast to professionals, parents want assurances that their individual child's experiences will be safe, pleasant and developmentally sound. The critical difference between parent and professional perspectives on child care is that parents are seeking a child care arrangement that will meet the needs of their own child and family; they bear no broader responsibility for the child care field. They need only find one arrangement, but their stake in the quality of that arrangement is immense. Averages and probabilities that structural child care features will somehow translate into positive experiences for children are not reassuring to most parents, who must find a single caregiver or programme to which they are willing to entrust their child's safety, happiness and development.

The words parents use to describe their search for child care reveal how important they consider that decision to be. One father in California arranged to work a different shift from his wife's so they could manage the care of their toddler between them. He explained why: 'I'm absolutely astounded at how important [our child's daily child care arrangement] is, and how insignificant childless people think it is. My colleagues and relatives think I am crazy to be as involved as I am. They just don't understand' (Leventhal-Belfer, Cowan and Cowan, 1992, p. 170). A parent in Alabama echoed that view: 'I was really scared. When they are babies they can't tell you what happens to them' (Bernard van Leer newsletter, 1993, p. 1). And a mother who recently left welfare in Illinois commented, 'It's hard to find someone. I will not leave my child with just anyone' (Siegel and Loman, 1991, p. 76). Finally, a middle-income mother from Hartford summed up her feelings about the child care she found for her three-year-old this way: 'I just prayed everything would work out' (EDK Associates, 1992, p. 4).

Parents care about child care quality, but they define quality in relation to the needs of their own children. They have little control over the child care that is available to them, and they often feel vulnerable as child care consumers – more worried about preventing harm than about maximizing benefits. This position sharply contrasts with the role of professionals, who strive to improve the quality of child care generally and who focus on the best, rather than the worst, aspects of the programmes with which they come into contact.

Child care is a multidimensional service, so parents must juggle a range of concerns as they choose care arrangements – from schedules and cost to the physical appearance of the setting and the caregiver's behaviour with children. The parents' own rapport with the caregiver is often a major consideration, as well. In the remainder of this chapter, we examine what is known about how parents make child care choices, and consider how such factors as the age of the child, the family's language and cultural heritage, and values about parenting roles influence those choices. We also look closely at the barriers that make it especially difficult for families with limited incomes to find the child care they would prefer. Finally, we propose a broadened conception of child care quality that takes the interests and concerns of parents into account.

PARENTS AS CHILD CARE CONSUMERS

Parents' values and perceptions regarding child care have attracted attention in recent years. The traditional image of parents as relatively passive partners in programmes that care for children has been joined by a new image of parents as consumers seeking to maximize their purchasing power in the child care marketplace. The interest of professionals who need funds to improve quality have come into direct conflict with the economic interests of parent-consumers who seek affordable forms of care, and who may construe quality in a different way from professionals. The new emphasis on parent choice in public child care subsidy programmes for low-income families has also demonstrated the extent to which parents' choices diverge from professional recommendations (Kagan and Neville, 1993; Mitchell, Cooperstein and Larner, 1992; Stoney and Genser, 1992). Vouchers can now be used to pay not only for child care centres but also relatives, friends and neighbours. In many states, more than half the parents who receive vouchers are turning to these unlicensed arrangements.

This fresh evidence of parents' actions as child care consumers comes at the same time as new research has illuminated how parents think about and choose child care. Studies conducted during the 1980s probed the decision-making of selected groups of parents who sought child care through resource and referral agencies or who used either centre-based or family day care (Bogat and Gensheimer, 1986; Fuqua and Labensohn, 1986; Fuqua and Schieck, 1989; Pence and Goelman, 1987; Powell and Eisenstat, 1982; Rapp and Lloyd, 1989; Shinn, Galinsky and Gulkur, 1989). More comprehensive studies followed in the 1990s. The National Child Care Survey of 1990 interviewed a random, nationally representative sample of 4,392 parents with children under thirteen years of age to determine what child care arrangements they made, what factors influenced their choices, and how satisfied they were with those arrangements (Hofferth *et al.*, 1991). A number of studies have posed similar questions concerning child care to current and former welfare recipients (Siegel and Loman, 1991; Kisker *et al.*, 1989; Meyers, 1993; Sonenstein and Wolf, 1991). Other researchers have used ethnographic approaches, interviews and focus group discussions to let parents describe how they think about child care (EDK Associates, 1992; Porter, 1991; Zinsser, 1991). These recent studies provide information on the full range of child care arrangements that parents actually use – including efforts by parents to work different shifts to keep child care within the family, and private arrangements made with relatives or friends, as well as care in centres or family day care homes.

Before summarizing the findings of this research, it is essential to note again that 'parents' and 'consumers' in these studies are mothers, not fathers. No research specifically examines fathers' perceptions about child care. Perhaps of greater concern, no US researcher has attempted to decipher the process of negotiation that occurs between mothers and fathers as they select and manage child care. One would think child care is exclusively a maternal role from the literature, despite solid and growing evidence that mothers and fathers go to extreme measures to co-ordinate and adjust their work schedules to accommodate their child care preferences. A recent study by the US Census Bureau, for example, found that the proportion of children under age five cared for by fathers increased from 17 per cent to 23 per cent between 1977 and 1991 (O'Connell, 1993). Children whose fathers worked night shifts were almost twice as likely as those with fathers on day shifts to be cared for by their father (30 per cent versus 17 per cent). Discovering how families balance the work commitments and schedules of both parents, family finances and child care arrangements ought to be a high priority for researchers interested in family, labour force and child care issues.

SEARCHING FOR CHILD CARE

The process of searching for child care begins with the family's decision that the demands of work or education make non-parental child care necessary. That decision is unquestioned for some parents, but it is a stressful one for many others, since it often involves trade-offs between the family's child-rearing values and its financial security. Families who can survive on one parent's wages tend to weigh the personal and economic costs of using child care against the income the mother can earn by working outside the home. One often hears the lament: 'More than half my earnings go to buy child care –

I don't know if it's worth it!' However, when parents believe the child care experience promotes the child's development in critical ways, by reducing shyness or teaching skills that will be useful in school, the calculus often changes. In such cases, the full household income may be scrutinized to see whether the requisite fees or tuition can be afforded.

By the same token, when the child care experience is damaging or troublesome for the child or the parents, the family may decide to sacrifice income to keep the child in family care. Low-income parents, who earn relatively little and find it almost impossible to secure decent child care, are especially likely to give up their employment and training plans in the face of child care problems. A study of participants in California's welfare reform programme found that women who were unhappy with their child care were twice as likely to drop out of job training as were women whose child care was satisfactory (Meyers, 1993). Similarly, an Illinois study found that child care problems led women who had left welfare for employment to quit working and return to public assistance (Siegel and Loman, 1991). Even parents who do not decide to stay at home feel torn at times. A middle-income mother interviewed for a television programme on child care commented, 'I'm comfortable with the care that my son receives, but I just have a hard time because I wish it was me.'

Once they decide to use non-parental child care, most families seek advice close at hand, asking friends, relatives and neighbours for suggestions. The 1990 national household survey mentioned earlier indicated that 66 per cent of parents who arranged child care outside the family relied on informal sources of information about child care, while only 9 per cent turned to resource and referral agencies (Hofferth *et al.*, 1991). The help offered by resource and referral agencies reaches a limited number of families because many communities are not yet served by these agencies, although there are now over 500 across the country. However, even when corporations offer access to resource and referral services as an employee benefit, relatively few parents use the services. Parents are often frightened by reports of abuse and poor conditions in child care, and are reluctant to rely on an impersonal source of information. Taking the advice of kin and confidants is a different matter. People who are close to the family usually know the child well, they probably share the family's basic values, and their primary interest is in the well-being of the child and the family. By contrast, child care experts may be seen as having a vested interest in promoting a particular form of child care. Moreover, kin and friends are usually willing to recommend or criticize child care options that they know from experience or by reputation. That is something that community service organizations like resource and referral agencies are unable to do, lest they be accused by child care providers of steering business towards or away from particular programmes.

Whatever sources of information they seek, most parents actively consider several child care alternatives. The 1990 National Child Care Survey revealed that nearly half the families who used non-parental care had seriously considered more than one type of care (care in a centre, a family day care home, or by someone in the child's own home). The parents who arranged child care within the family were the least likely to look at several alternatives – family ties, trust and economics commonly make relatives the first choice as caregivers for very young children. Deciding between a neighbourhood centre and a family day care home down the street is a different type of choice, however. Just under half the families who found child care outside the kin network investigated more than one provider, visiting more than one centre or interviewing several family day care providers. Overall, the child care search process took parents an average of five weeks.

For many parents, those are uncomfortable weeks, during which they attempt to find options that are feasible, given the family's budget and work hours, and they try to screen out any that may be untrustworthy. Then they visit and ask questions of the remaining providers to try to envision how well the child would fare in each setting. All the while, most parents are painfully aware that they are unlikely to know which arrangements may actually pose problems. A New Jersey mother who interviewed a family day care provider liked the provider but had other worries: 'I didn't want to put my child in a home because I don't know who enters that house during the day' (Porter, 1991). An Illinois mother found a good centre, but then discovered that the building triggered environmental allergies in her asthmatic child. Another mother in Illinois found a centre with a teacher she liked, but that teacher left and was replaced by a less patient young teacher whom the mother did not trust. A mother in California began to feel desperate when all her leads for infant care led nowhere, until a friend of a friend agreed to help out. 'It seemed like it was working out okay. Then, two days before I had to go back to work, she called me and said she couldn't do it' (EDK Associates, 1992, p. 4). No visit or friendly interview would have warned these parents of the problems that loomed. It is not surprising that few parents feel they are informed consumers who can make child care choices that will meet their requirements, expectations and hopes.

CHILD CARE CHOICES

Whether or not they feel well-informed, parents are the ones who decide which child care arrangement they will trust and invest in. Although no family's choices are unconstrained, the arrangements parents make to place a child in a particular type of care reveal a great deal about their preferences and values. The most comprehensive data on this topic are from the 1990 National Child Care Survey. That study showed that, although the popularity of centre-based care has grown, in families with an employed mother, nearly half the children under five were cared for within the family network – 30 per cent by the parents themselves, and 18 per cent by relatives. Just over a quarter of the children were in centre-based care, and almost a fifth were in family day care homes.

That basic pattern varies only slightly by family income and ethnicity. Low-income families earning less than $15,000 per year relied on care within the family more often than did families earning over $50,000 per year (55 per cent of low-income families used parent or relative care compared to 35 per cent of the wealthier families). Hispanic families depended more extensively on family care (55 per cent) than did African-American or non-Hispanic Caucasian families (44 per cent and 48 per cent respectively). By contrast,

African-American families were most likely to use centre-based care (45 per cent used centres, compared to 26 per cent of Caucasian and 23 per cent of Hispanic families). The pattern of care use differed most sharply for children of different ages. Sixty per cent of infants were cared for in the family and 14 per cent were in centres – in part because very few centres offer infant care, and in part because of a widespread preference for keeping infants within the family. In contrast, 37 per cent of pre-schoolers were with parents or relatives, compared with 43 per cent who attended centres.

What factors do parents weigh as they make these choices? Is 'quality' an important value for parents, and if so, how do they describe it? In one study, 167 Michigan parents who found care through a resource and referral agency rated ten child care characteristics as important or very important to them: 99 per cent considered 'health and safety' important, 95 per cent checked 'how the children get along with each other and the adults', and 93 per cent regarded 'provider's childrearing philosophy' as important (Bogat and Gensheimer, 1986). However, space and equipment were checked less often, and convenience factors were important to still fewer parents.

The 1990 National Child Care Survey included families using all types of care arrangements, and interviewers grouped parents' reasons for choosing their care into six categories: quality, general preference for relative care, availability, cost, hours and location. The parents most often explained their choice in terms that referred to quality features including the number of adults and children; provider warmth, training or style; programme characteristics like curriculum or cultural content; and the setting's safety and equipment for children. The next most common explanation given was a general preference for having a relative as a caregiver. Again, answers stressing adult needs like reasonable cost, location or hours were much less common.

Low-income families interviewed in California, Illinois and New Jersey expressed similar views (Siegel and Loman, 1991; Meyers, 1993; Porter, 1991). Those parents gave top priority to safety and trust, closely followed by the quality of the care (described as including both nurturance and educational opportunities). Factors like location and cost had to be weighed by low-income parents, but they are valued very differently from factors that directly affect the child's well-being. The Illinois parents described their image of quality child care in phrases like the following: 'taking the time for each child' and 'really caring about them and their well-being', as well as 'teaching them' and being 'qualified to care for children'. Parents receiving public assistance stress the importance of safety and trust in part because they 'live in high crime inner-city areas, where violent behaviour and excessive drug use are common occurrence. Concern for the safety of children in these settings often takes precedence over everything else' (Siegel and Loman, 1991, p. 3).

Research suggests that parents pay relatively little attention to the indicators of quality that professionals suggest they use to screen child care options, such as licensing and caregiver training. Over 40 per cent of the low-income parents in the Illinois study did not consider it important that their child was cared for by a provider with a licence from the state, in part because many of the unlicensed providers were relatives of the parents. The parents had only a vague sense of what licensing involved, and fewer than one in four said anyone had ever talked to them about child care licensing. In general, few parents are aware of the regulatory requirements that apply to family day care homes, or know where the boundary between unregulated care and regulated family day care is drawn. (In some states, care of one child is considered family day care; in other states, regulations do not apply until the home includes six or more children.) Parents more often realize that centres should be licensed, but some assume that any open centre is licensed, or it would not be operating. However, parents often do not believe that licensing makes a difference in the quality of the care an individual child would receive. They may know of a top-notch child care building in which a college-trained caregiver was harsh or indifferent to a given child, or of an inspired, attentive caregiver working in a dilapidated environment that could not meet regulatory standards.

Some parents are also sceptical about the importance of specialized child care training, explaining that 'you can't teach someone to love children.' While professionals argue that training gives caregivers the skills that make it easier to keep loving children even in groups all day long, parents hope to find one special person who 'will care for my child the way I would.' Not surprisingly, they do not think that can be taught. However, as parents watch their children grow older and focus more on their mastery of academic and social skills, they tend to place more stock in the expertise of specially trained caregivers or teachers. One parent commented:

> If it's a little baby, I don't care if they have a degree in something. If they're going to hold that child and love it and nurture it, then that is good enough for me. But on the other hand, if I have a three- or four-year-old, then I want to know what kind of activities they're going to be doing.
>
> (EDK Associates, 1992, p. 10)

THE IMPACT OF VALUES ON CHILD CARE CHOICES

Parents are not all looking for the same thing when they set out to arrange child care. Their expectations reflect their understanding of what safe, good child care looks like, and depend on the role that child care is to play in the life of the child and the family. Parents' beliefs about the experiences that will be most important to their children and their attitudes towards work and family roles also affect what they value in child care. These attitudes vary with the age of the child, and they are profoundly affected by the family's cultural and ethnic values.

Children of different ages

Some parents, especially those with children under three, view child care as a substitute for parental care that is necessary only because of the demands imposed by the work or educational commitments of the parents. Given the opportunity, they would prefer to be at home with the child. Many other countries protect that parental right by providing parent leave and child allowance policies that enable very young children to remain at home in the care of a parent (Cochran, 1993). When parents view child care as a necessary evil, their objective is likely to be that of finding a form of child care that is as similar to parental care as possible – for instance, care in the child's own home or another home setting, care in a small sibling-style group, or care that exposes the child to the same language, values, foods and activities that are present in the family's home. An additional goal may be to minimize the amount of time the child spends in child care, by finding arrangements that do not require that the child be present or the caregiver be paid for full-time care that is not needed.

Parents who think of child care in this way often want to make decisions about how things are done with the child, by leaving schedules and instructions for naps and feeding at the infant centre, or arranging with the nanny that she will pick up the baby when he cries, or let the children use fingerpaints. Basic caregiving practices are more salient during the first years of life than educational activities. Many parents are confident in their views of how babies should be held, fed and played with; and they have opinions about how much toddlers should be restrained or encouraged to explore and do things on their own. Most do not expect to argue with their child's caregiver over such issues. A mother in Vermont who did not give her children sweets had to accept the fact that her family day care provider served chocolate milk: 'The thing I was expecting at first and realized I couldn't expect from anybody else was that the babysitter would do things the way I wanted them done' (Nelson, 1989, p. 23).

In contrast, parents with children over three often view child care as an important educational opportunity for the child, a setting in which children become independent and learn social, verbal and academic skills. For instance, one Illinois parent boasted of the advancements her son made after entering child care: 'He knows how to count, sing, cover his mouth, and he knows how to do everything by himself' (Siegel and Loman, 1991, p. 95). Thirty per cent of the families in which the mother is not employed enrol their three- and four-year-old children in centre-based programmes, to ensure that they benefit from those developmental experiences (Hofferth *et al.*, 1991). Parents whose children spend their earliest years in the care of relatives or family day care providers often want to shift child care arrangements as the child's third birthday nears, to have a more structured environment where the child will learn more. Some families whose primary language is not English see child care as a setting in which the child can begin to learn the language that he or she will need in school; although others prefer an arrangement in which the child can communicate in the language used at home (Chang, 1993; Kagan and Garcia, 1991).

Parents who believe that child care offers important educational opportunities to children are likely to value the extent to which the child care environment complements the family environment, often choosing centre-based programmes over family day care homes (Pence and Goelman, 1987). Such parents may also trust and defer to the expertise of a professionally-trained caregiver or teacher. A 1977 study of a co-operative nursery school in Berkeley, California, revealed that African-American parents were especially likely to view early childhood programmes in this way. One mother explained, 'I want the nursery school to be an extension of my own home – what I can't do for my kids, I want the school to do. Take reading – you have to learn the right way. You only learn it once and I want them to get it right' (Joffe, 1977, p. 91).

Families with different cultural backgrounds

The influence of a family's cultural and ethnic values on their choice of and comfort with using child care has not been prominently studied in the United States. This is particularly ironic given that the United States, always a multiethnic and multiracial society, is becoming more diverse every year. Ethnic minorities now account for almost one-third of the nation's population of children and youth, and the recent growth has come primarily among Hispanics and Asians – two groups that are themselves extremely diverse. Today, 2.3 million children in US schools are not proficient in English, and this number is increasing rapidly with the current influx of immigrant groups who also have relatively high rates of birth (Edmonston and Passel, 1992).

These trends pose serious challenges to our educational institutions, and early childhood programmes are dealing now with issues of cultural and linguistic diversity that will increasingly face primary and secondary schools. In California, a recent study of 450 child care centres revealed that in only 4 per cent were all the children from the same racial group, in 34 percent the children came primarily from two racial groups, and in another 24 per cent multiple races were represented (Chang, 1993). Nationwide, 20 per cent of the children enrolled in Head Start – the premier early intervention programme for children in poverty – speak a language other than English (Kagan and Garcia, 1991). Most, but far from all, of these children are Spanish-speakers. The capacity of child care programmes to provide culturally and linguistically appropriate care to the diverse children who now make up the child care population has thus become a very pressing issue. For many children, child care provides the first exposure to a 'school-like' setting. Whether the experience makes a child feel accepted or alienated can set the stage for subsequent attitudes about and performance in school.

However, little attention has been given to the implications of diversity for child care policy and programme design, although many acknowledge that the domain of childrearing is fraught with cultural meaning. What is known is that non-Caucasian children in child care centres are less likely to be cared for by a teacher from the same racial background than are their Caucasian peers. Many are cared for by adults who do not speak their home language. Given the lack of training caregivers receive that prepares them to care for ethnically diverse children, significant cultural and linguistic barriers can arise between child care providers and parents. Forty per cent of the centre teachers surveyed in the California study described above reported that they had difficulty communicating with parents because they do not share a common language.

Clashes between professionally-trained teachers and parents over programme practices regarding academic instruction, physical discipline, play that breaks gender stereotypes and messy play are all too familiar (Bredekamp and Willer, 1993; Feeney, 1987; Rodd and Clyde, 1990). Identifying the role that culture and values play in these struggles between professionals and parents can help to explain why the debates are so intense, and it can put the two groups on somewhat more equal footing. Janet Gonzales–Mena has explored the potential for cultural conflict between infant caregivers and parents over such issues as changing nappies, feeding, comforting, toilet training and 'educating' babies (1993). Her analysis points out how strongly held the views of both caregivers and parents are, and she suggests strategies caregivers can adopt to reduce children's exposure to what she calls 'cultural assault.' It is perhaps not surprising that many parents avoid doing battle with their caregivers over such emotionally charged issues by looking for caregivers who share the family's values from the outset.

Divergent values about parenting roles

Independent of their cultural heritage, families also differ in their views of the appropriate work and family roles for mothers and fathers. Values related to parenting roles can influence child care decisions both directly and indirectly (Hock, McBride and Gnezda, 1989; Leventhal-Belfer, Cowan and Cowan, 1992; Rapp and Lloyd, 1989). As Ellen Hock's research has shown, mothers may be dissatisfied because they want to work but are at home, or because they wish they could be at home but must work. Other researchers have found that parents with traditional views concerning maternal employment and those who feel guilty about working are more likely to choose family day care and other home-based care arrangements over centres (Molnar, 1982; Nelson, 1989). In contrast, parents who are more comfortable in full-time work roles often use centre-based care, and they report that they value the educational benefits that care offers the child.

Interactions between parents and caregivers are also affected by values about parenting roles. Several researchers have begun to probe the attitudes centre-based caregivers hold about the parents whose children are in their care (Galinsky, 1989, 1990; Kontos and Wells, 1986). The Galinsky study of Atlanta centres revealed that a quarter of the teachers disapproved of mothers who worked while their children were young and only 41 per cent thought it was a good idea. Although the mothers felt guilty about working and wished they could spend more time with their children, only 25 per cent believed their children would be better off at home all day.

It is ironic that, as noted above, the parents who are most conflicted about working tend to place their children in home-based settings, where they often come face to face with disapproving caregivers. Several studies have shown that family day care providers hold especially traditional values about family roles and many feel it is wrong for mothers to work. In one in-depth report exploring the relationships between parents and caregivers in Vermont, a provider explained her view: 'The bottom line is I feel every mother at every expense should stay home with their children . . . I always felt in the back of my mind, why don't they stay home with their children . . . I can't understand why it was more important for them to shuffle papers' (Nelson, 1989, p. 12).

The disapproval of caregivers in centres or homes often makes itself felt when job demands force parents to compromise or cut corners with their children – by arriving late to pick them up; by bringing them to child care even when they are ill; or by being preoccupied, rushed and impatient. As is so often the case, problems tend to pile up. The parents who are most stressed by their dual roles also face the most criticism and hostility from the caregivers on whom they rely as partners in childrearing.

CONSTRAINTS THAT LIMIT PARENTS' CHILD CARE CHOICES

For all their importance, preferences and values do not determine child care choices alone, or even primarily. Although parents do not focus on logistical factors like location, cost and hours when they are interviewed about child care, in practice they cannot ignore those considerations. Logistical factors often define the pool of options that the parent will even explore. After all, why bother visiting a centre that costs far more than you can afford to spend? Why hope that it will work out for your sister to keep your child when she lives two bus rides away from both your home and your job? Parents are not pleased that their decisions must be based not only on the well-being of the child, but on the fit between a given arrangement and their financial resources and work obligations. Nevertheless, those factors influence child care choices and they affect the ability of the parents to manage the demands they face as workers, students, or trainees. When non-negotiable adult requirements confront rigid child care policies, low-income parents are likely to drop out of employment or training programmes to stay at home (Meyers, 1993), and mothers with higher status jobs experience more stress and health problems (Galinsky, 1990).

The influence of adult needs on child care choices can best be seen by considering the situation of low-income parents, because poverty influences child care choices by intensifying the urgency of adult needs and turning them into constraints that limit the options that are feasible for the family to consider. For instance, low-income parents have less money to spend on child care than do wealthier parents, yet child care costs are not usually discounted in relation to family income. In a recent national poll, the Philip Morris Companies found that business executives reported paying an average of $244 per month for child care, while the single mothers polled paid $221 per month – a difference of only $23 per month (Harris, 1989). As a result, child care costs in low-income households consume an average of 23 per cent of total family income, more than twice the 10 per cent that is considered affordable (Hofferth *et al.*, 1991).

The jobs held by many low-income working mothers also pose problems for them when it comes to making child care arrangements. Low levels of education consign many to pink collar jobs in the service industries, where they are expected to work shifts that extend beyond the traditional work hours of between 8.00 a.m. and 6.00 p.m. In one study of 382 welfare mothers with pre-schoolers, close to 30 per cent of the child care users needed care before 6.00 a.m., after 7.00 p.m. or on weekends (Sonenstein and Wolf, 1991).

Low-income families also tend to live in neighbourhoods that are poorly maintained, underserved by public transport, and inhabited by other families that have too little money to meet basic family needs. Such a community context cannot support an array of high-quality child care services aside from Head Start or publicly-funded child care programmes. Adequate physical facilities for child care are hard to come by, and child care providers cannot survive on the fees nearby parents can afford to pay. Parents cannot turn to child care settings in better neighbourhoods unless they have reliable transport. Those who have no car must make their way during rush hours from home to child care setting to work and back again by bus or train, with tired children in tow.

Low-income parents recognize that their children are not getting the quality of care that they deserve, or need. Welfare mothers interviewed in New Jersey (Porter, 1991) complained of dirt-filled playgrounds and too little supervision, and they were concerned about staff turnover and the adults' indifference to children's development and educational progress. Similarly, some of the parents Zinsser (1991) interviewed described settings with broken toys, too much television and passive adults. While surveys of the general population of employed mothers show that over 90 per cent are very or mostly satisfied with their child care arrangements, only 70 per cent of the welfare mothers studied by Sonenstein and Wolf (1991) felt that way. The hopes and aspirations of low-income parents are not different from those of more advantaged parents, but they face many more obstacles when they attempt to find satisfactory care.

SUCCESSFUL CHILD CARE SITUATIONS

This focus on parents' views of child care quality serves as a reminder that child care is only one slice of a child's experience, and the 'quality' of that slice cannot be judged without reference to its fit with the family environment. Fit can mean several things. Child care may fit well with family because there is congruence and similarity between the child's experiences in both settings. There may be deliberate complementarity, as when the parents choose a child care setting that will afford new or contrasting experiences for the child's benefit (Powell, 1989). Interviews with mothers from several ethnic groups in a working class community led one researcher to conclude that 'parents search for arrangements they trust and are often reassured by continuities between home and caregivers. At the same time, parents want the advantages of professional care if it means early childhood education, reliability, a healthy and safe environment, nutritious meals, kindness, affection and fairness' (Zinsser, 1991, p. 167). Parents juggle a variety of different considerations as they evaluate child care alternatives. To get the quality they want on the dimension that matters most to them (for instance, cultural or language similarity), they must often accept alternatives that are disappointing in other ways.

The concept of fit should be considered not only from the child's perspective, but from the family perspective. High-quality child care is designed to enable adult family members to meet their goals both as workers or students, and as parents – without worrying about the safety, the well-being, and the development of their children. Too often, the current system forces parents to choose between opposing values – enrolling a child in part-day Head Start for its educational value, and assembling a patchwork of babysitting and transport schemes to cover the remaining hours of the parents' workdays; or relying on a sister's care because she will accept the child for whatever hours the parents need to work, even though her busy, rundown home is neither safe nor nurturing. Families all want care that is good for their children, that meets their needs as workers, and that they can trust to support their childrearing efforts without questioning their choices about work and family roles and without adding to the guilt that many parents already feel.

When parents speak about what child care means to them, they remind us how strongly they feel about sharing their childrearing role with others. It is time that we all – professionals, policy-makers, researchers and advocates – paid more attention to the parents' perspective on child care. Researchers must continue and expand their efforts to understand the parental perspective on child care. Greater reliance on qualitative approaches that elicit the words, phrases and topics that are salient to parents will help ensure that parents' voices are heard without distortion. Longitudinal studies are also needed that capture the dynamic quality of parents' relations with child care, because child care use is a process that plays out over time and is influenced by changing requirements, relationships and opportunities. Next, researchers can use what they learn to integrate the features of child care that parents value with professional standards, to come up with a more comprehensive conception of child care quality, including educational aspects of the care setting, safety and trustworthiness, and the level of communication and value consensus between the parent and provider.

Increasing the 'family friendliness' of child care in these ways will pose a long-term challenge to professionals. Although the idea of 'parent-professional partnerships' is widely touted, few professionals have been trained or feel prepared to manage relationships with parents. Training is needed to prepare professionals to relate to parents as equals, not only as experts, and to help them understand the implications of cultural diversity for programme practices and relationships with families. Even with training, however, it will be difficult for professionals to invite parents to join them as full and equal partners in discussions of child care and its quality, since that necesssarily involves sharing control and relinquishing status. The battle to ensure that policymakers and the general public understand that child care is not an unimportant domestic service but a legitimate profession is far from over, and the bitterness of that drawn-out battle contributes to an undercurrent of competition between early childhood professionals and the parents they serve. The challenge of placing families at the centre of child care will require a new commitment on the part of professionals to insist that good practice must be respectful and inclusive of parents.

Even with that commitment, it will not be easy to convince parents to actively express their views of the child care they want and need for their children. Parents use child care for only a few years in their lives, and those are typically the years when they are busiest, and most anxious, insecure and overwhelmed. However, child care programmes that offer parents genuine opportunities to share decision-making power and to influence the aspects of the care that they care most about – discover how much energy and creativity parents can bring to the child care programme and provider. Shared caregiving brings with it both tensions and richness, and it is critical that parents and professionals work together to ensure that the child benefits from the best of both worlds.

REFERENCES

ADAMS, G. (1990) *Who Knows How Safe? The Status of State Efforts to Ensure Quality Child Care*, Children's Defense Fund, Washington: DC.

BERNARD VAN LEER FOUNDATION (1993) USA: mothers talking, *Bernard van Leer Foundation Newsletter*, vol. 71, pp. 8–9.

BOGAT, G. A. and GENSHEIMER, L. (1986) Discrepancies between the attitudes and actions of parents choosing day care, *Child Care Quarterly*, vol. 15, no. 3, pp. 159–69.

BREDEKAMP, S. and WILLER, B. (1993) Professionalizing the field of early childhood education: pros and cons, *Young Children*, vol. 43, no. 3, pp. 82–4.

CHANG, H. (1993) *Affirming Children's Roots: Cultural and Linguistic Diversity in Early Care and Education*, California Tomorrow, San Francisco.

COCHRAN, M. (1993) Public child care, culture, and society: crosscutting themes, in M. Cochran (ed.) *International Handbook of Child Care Policies and Programs*, Greenwood Press, Westport: CT.

EDK ASSOCIATES (1992) *Choosing Quality Child Care: A Qualitative Study Conducted in Houston, Hartford, West Palm Beach, Charlotte, Alameda, Los Angeles, Salem and Minneapolis*, Child Care Action Campaign, New York: NY.

EDMONSTON, B. and PASSEL, J. S. (1992) *The Future Immigrant Population of the United States*, The Urban Institute, Washington: DC.

FEENEY, S. (1987) The working mother: summary of reader responses, *Young Children*, Vol. 43, no. 1, pp. 16–19.

FUQUA, R. A. and LABENSOHN, D. (1986) Parents as consumers of child care, *Family Relations*, Vol. 35, no. 2, pp. 295–303.

FUQUA, R. and SCHIECK, R. (1989) Child care resource and referral programs and parents' search for quality child care, *Early Childhood Research Quarterly*, Vol. 4, no. 3, pp. 357–65.

GALINSKY, E. (1989) A parent/teacher study: interesting results, *Young Children*, Vol. 45, no. 1, pp. 2–3.

GALINSKY, E. (1990) Why are some parent/teacher partnerships clouded with difficulties? *Young Children*, Vol. 45, no. 5, pp. 2–3, 38–9.

GONZALES-MENA, J. (1993) *Multicultural Issues in Child Care*, Mayfield Publishing Company, Mountain View: CA.

HARRIS, L. and ASSOCIATES (1989) *The Philip Morris Companies Inc. Family Survey II: Child Care*, Philip Morris Companies, New York.

HOCK, E., MCBRIDE, S. and GNEZDA, M. T. (1989) Maternal separation anxiety: mother-infant separation from the maternal perspective, *Child Development*, Vol. 60, pp. 793–802.

HOFFERTH, S., BRAYFIELD, A., DIETCH, S. and HOLCOMB, P. (1991) *The National Child Care Survey 1990*, University Press of America, Washington: DC, Lanham: MD.

HOLLOWAY, S., FULLER, B., RAMBAUD, M. and EGGERS, C. (1993) What is high-quality child care? Views of low-income women, Paper presented at the Second Annual Head Start Research Conference, Harvard University, Cambridge: MA.

INSTITUTE FOR APPLIED RESEARCH (1991) *Child Care and AFDC Recipients in Illinois: Patterns, Problems, and Needs*, Division of Family Support Services, Illinois Department of Public Aid, Chicago: IL.

JOFFE, C. (1977) *Friendly Intruders: Childcare Professionals and Family Life*, University of California Press, Berkeley: CA.

KAGAN, S. L. and GARCIA, E. (1991) Educating culturally and linguistically diverse preschoolers: moving the agenda, *Early Childhood Research Quarterly*, Vol. 6, pp. 427–43.

KAGAN, S. L. and NEVILLE, P. R. (1993) *Parent Choice in Early Care and Education: Myth or Reality?* A. L. Mailman Family Foundation, White Plains: NY.

KISKER, E., MAYNARD, R., GORDON, A. and STRAIN, M. (1989) *The Child Care Challenge: What Parents Need and What is Available in Three Metropolitan Areas*, Mathematica Policy Research, Inc., Princeton: NJ.

KONTOS, S. (1992) *Family Day Care: Out of the Shadows and Into the Limelight*, National Association for the Education of Young Children, Washington: DC.

KONTOS, S. and WELLS, W. (1986) Attitudes of caregivers and the day care experiences of families, *Early Childhood Research Quarterly*, Vol. 1, pp. 47–67.

LEVENTHAL-BELFER, L., COWAN, P. A. and COWAN, C. P. (1992) Satisfaction with child care arrangements: effects on adaptation to parenthood, *American Journal of Orthopsychiatry*, Vol., 62, no. 2, pp. 165–77.

MEYERS, M. K. (1993) Child care in JOBS employment and training program: what difference does quality make? *Journal of Marriage and the Family*, Vol. 55, pp. 767–83.

MITCHELL, A., COOPERSTEIN, E. and LARNER, M. (1992) *Child Care Choices: Consumer Education for Low-income Families*, National Center for Children in Poverty, New York: NY.

MOLNAR, J. (1982) *Choosing a Child Care Arrangement: Reasons 'Why'*, Cornell University Department of Human Development and Family Studies, Ithaca: NY.

NELSON, M. (1989) Negotiating care: relationships between family daycare providers and mothers, *Feminist Studies*, Vol. 15, no. 1, pp. 7–33.

O'CONNELL, M. (1993). *Where's Papa? Father's Role in Child Care*, Population Reference Bureau, Washington: D.C.

PENCE, A. R. and GOELMAN, H. (1987) Silent partners: parents of children in three types of day care, *Early Childhood Research Quarterly*, Vol. 2, pp. 103–18.

PHILLIPS, D. (ed.) (1987) *Quality in Child Care: What Does Research Tell Us?* National Association for the Education of Young Children, Washington: DC, pp. 81–8.

PHILLIPS, D. (1991) The social context of child care in the United States, in P. Moss and E. Melhuish (eds.) *Day Care for Young Children: International Perspectives*, Routledge, London.

PHILLIPS, D. A., HOWES, C. and WHITEBOOK, M. (1992) The social policy context of child care: effects on quality, *American Journal of Community Psychology*, Vol. 20, no. 1, pp. 25–51.

PORTER, T. (1991) *Just Like Any Parent: the Child Care Choices of Welfare Mothers in New Jersey*, Bank Street College of Education, New York: NY.

POWELL, D. (1989) *Families and Early Childhood Programs*, National Association for the Education of Young Children, Washington: D.C..

POWELL, D. R. and EISENSTADT, J. W. (1982) Parents' searches for child care and the design of information services, *Children and Youth Services Review*, Vol. 4, no. 3, pp. 239–53.

RAPP, G. S. and LLOYD, S. A. (1989) The role of 'home as haven' ideology in child care use, *Family Relations*, Vol. 38, pp. 426–30.

RODD, J. and CLYDE, M. (1990) Ethical dilemmas of the early childhood professional: a comparative study, *Early Childhood Research Quarterly*, Vol. 5, pp. 461–74.

SHINN, M., GALINSKY, E. and GULKUR, L. (1989) *The Role of Child Care Centers in the Lives of Parents*, New York University, Department of Community Psychology, New York.

SIEGEL, G. and LOMAN, A. (1991) *Child Care and AFDC recipients in Illinois: Patterns, problems and needs*, St. Louis: Institute for Applied Research.

SONENSTEIN, F. and WOLF, D. (1991) Satisfaction with child care: perspectives of welfare mothers, *Journal of Social Issues*, Vol. 47, no. 1, pp. 15–31.

STONEY, L. and GENSER, A. (1992) *Establishing Effective Certificate Programs: Issues for States*, National Association of Child Care Resource and Referral Agencies, Rochester: MN.

WHITEBOOK, M., HOWES, C. and PHILLIPS, D. (1989) *Who Cares? Child Care Teachers and the Quality of Care in America*, Child Care Employee Project, Oakland: CA.

ZASLOW, M. J. (1991) Variation in child care quality and its implications for children, *Journal of Social Issues*, Vol. 47, no. 2, pp. 125–38.

ZINSSER, C. (1991) *Raised in East Urban: Child Care Changes in a Working Class Community*, Teachers College Press, New York: NY.

CHAPTER 5

Measure for Measure: Values, Quality and Evaluation

JULIA BROPHY AND JUNE STATHAM

The United Kingdom has a diverse range of early childhood services. From their experience of using the Early Childhood Environment Rating Scale in researching one of these services, playgroups, Julia Brophy and June Statham illustrate the problem of applying a universal measure of quality, with an implicit values-base, to a specific service with a distinctive identity reflecting a particular set of values. They conclude that if scales are to be useful, they need credibility and acceptability with the service to which they are applied; that the values underlying scales must be explicit; and that there is a need for diversity of measures, some of which are developed for specific services.

INTRODUCTION

The United Kingdom has a diverse range of early childhood services. Children under statutory school age may attend a nursery school or class, an infant class, playgroup, childminder, day nursery or a family centre, depending on such factors as their age, where they happen to live and what their parents can afford. These services are provided by different agencies, including education and welfare departments, voluntary organizations, private businesses and individuals. Compared to the rest of Europe, the UK has little publicly funded provision for pre-school children (Moss, 1990). Most provision is in the private market and depends on parents' ability to pay. The expansion of early years services in the last decade has been primarily in the private sector; between 1980 and 1991 the number of places in private day nurseries more than trebled and places with childminders more than doubled. Despite this expansion, playgroups and early entry to primary school (by four-year-old children) remain the most common form of provision for children under five (Sylva and Moss, 1992).

There is no national policy in the UK that can provide a coherent framework for the development of early childhood services. The various types of provision differ in their priorities and objectives, as well as in the resources available to them and the conditions and training of their staff. Thus local authority day nurseries and family centres generally provide for children who are defined by social work agencies as 'in need', with an emphasis on family support and child protection. Nursery education and playgroups aim to foster the social and educational development of three- and four-year-olds and childminders and private day nurseries attempt to meet the child-care needs of working parents.

While the desire for an easy-to-use, 'objective' scale to measure quality in early childhood services is understandable, it also raises a number of issues. In particular, in such a fragmented and diverse system, is it possible or desirable to develop a measure of quality which can be used in all early childhood settings? In this chapter we describe our experience of using one measurement of quality in research in a particular child-care setting in order to illustrate the practical and theoretical problems inherent in seeking such a measure. We conclude by identifying a number of issues which it is crucial to address if the concept of quality in early childhood services is to be operationalized.

THE DEVELOPING DEBATE ON QUALITY

In recent years there has been an increased emphasis in the UK on the importance of quality and standards in early years services, by both child care practitioners and the government. In the private sector, a 'kitemark' system of quality assurance has been developed for use in private child care facilities (British Standards Institute, 1990). In the voluntary sector, a number of organizations have produced guidelines and codes of good practice (e.g. Kids Club Network, 1989; Pre-school Playgroups Association, 1990; National Childminding Association 1991; National Children's Bureau, 1991). At government level, a Committee of Inquiry was set up to report on the quality of the educational experience offered to three- and four-year-olds (Department of Education and Science, 1990), and new legislation affecting the provision of early childhood services, the Children Act 1989, was implemented in October 1991.

The Children Act has provided a particular spur to the debate on quality services for young children. The new legislation requires local authorities to review every three years all existing 'day care' services for children under eight in their area, and 'to inform themselves about the quantity and availability' of nursery and primary education facilities. Although local authorities regulated private and voluntary provision for children under five before the Children Act, the new legislation has led to a reform of regulation, extending it to child care services for children up to age eight (i.e. school-age child care services), requiring inspection of all services at least annually and leading local authorities to overhaul the standards they require of services. The Children Act was accompanied by detailed guidance from the Department of Health which expanded on the statutory duties the Act placed upon local authorities. The volume of guidance covering 'Day Care and Educational Provision for Young Children' (Department of Health, 1991) suggests that the registration process for new services should be 'an enabling process which helps intending providers and childminders offer *good quality* services' (our emphasis) (ibid., para. 7.3).

The guidance also includes a wide-ranging discussion of 'quality of care', relevant to the theme of this book. The discussion begins by listing a number of 'main factors which influence quality of care', most of which concern structural and inter-actional features of services which have been shown to be linked to child development outcomes (e.g. the nature of adult/child inter-action, size of group and numbers of staff, recognition of children's developmental needs etc.). The guidance then goes on to suggest three different ways in which quality and its definition can be approached.

The first is headed 'child development', which

involves focusing on the child's experience in terms of the potential advantages and disadvantages that the [child care] experience offers the child and the possible effects of the care upon child development. One aspect of good quality care is that it is developmentally beneficial to the child and poor quality care is that which inhibits, or at least does not facilitate, child development. Most research on quality has been explicitly or implicitly guided by this approach.

(ibid., para. 6.27)

The second concerns 'rights and expectations', starting with children:

Children have a right to an environment which facilitates their development. An approach based on children's rights would encompass all the factors necessary for their development. However, depending on the values held by society at large, the child may be regarded as having rights which go beyond the provision of an environment which can be empirically demonstrated to facilitate development. For example: children have the right to be cared for as part of a community which values the religious, racial, cultural and linguistic identity of the child. The justification for the awarding of such a right would be in terms of fostering the child's sense of identity. Children's sense of identity is a fundamental aspect of their development and so such a right could be included within a definition based upon the facilitation of children's development. Other examples of rights [include] freedom from discrimination such as racism or sexism and [rights to] cultural diversity . . . The extent to which a day care setting fulfils these rights may be used in defining the quality of care for that setting.

(ibid., para. 6.28)

The guidance extends this 'rights' approach to quality to parents and workers in services. For example, 'certain parental rights should be considered as part of a definition of quality of care because this enables parents to influence the nature of their children's care environments' (ibid., para. 6.29). And 'conditions for workers can be shown to influence the nature of children's experience in ways which have implications for their development' (ibid., para. 6.30).

This part of the discussion of the meaning of quality is based, as the guidance recognizes, on the view that quality should be defined in terms of 'a child's experience in a care environment'. But in conclusion the guidance

recognizes that the particular aspects of child experience that it proposes are
'not the only definition'.

> Deciding whether services run by day care providers or offered by
> individuals (childminders) are of an acceptable quality involves a value
> judgement. There should be a clear understanding about the value base
> and the criteria used for assessing the quality of care in these situations.
>
> (ibid., para. 6.38)

The guidance does not take this issue further. In particular, it does not explore
what adopting a values-based notion of quality might imply in practice. Nor
does it develop the related notion of a rights-based approach to defining
quality.

Faced by the need to modernize their regulatory systems, and encouraged
to see regulation as promoting quality, many local authority officers who have
a responsibility under the Act for registering new services and inspecting all
services annually have felt the need to find the new ways of defining and
assessing the quality of early years services. Not surprisingly, they have
sought help with this. The National Children's Bureau, a voluntary organization in London which offers advice and information on children's issues,
reported a large increase in 'urgent requests for an immediate and author-
itative statement of quality and standards' in the period leading up to
implementation of the Act in October 1991 (Elfer and Wedge, 1992). It is
in this context – of tentative recognition of the values-based nature of quality
in the official guidance, yet a demand for 'objective' measures of quality to
implement a duty to regulate services – that we turn now to consider our
experience of using one such measure in a particular child care setting.

PLAYGROUPS AND THE PLAYGROUP
RESEARCH PROJECT

Playgroups are a form of pre-school provision which has typically developed
in countries with relatively low levels of publicly funded nursery schooling,
such as the UK, Ireland and the Netherlands (Statham, Lloyd and Moss,
1990). In the UK, playgroups were originally set up in the early 1960s as a
self-help response by mothers to the lack of nursery education. By 1991, in
England alone, they were providing some 420,400 places for three- and four-
year-olds (and for increasing numbers of two-year-olds) and were attended by
around 700,000 children. They provided more places and for more children
than any other type of pre-school service.

However, places in playgroups are commonly part-time. A typical session
lasts between two and three hours and although playgroups are open on
average for four sessions a week, places are often shared so that each child may
attend only two or three times a week. Playgroups are funded largely from
parents' fees, and workers often receive only a token wage. They seldom enjoy
purpose-built accommodation and are generally held in church or village
halls, with problems of storage arising from sharing the premises with other
users. And, although they are required to be registered with the local Social

Services Department, there is substantial variation in the amount of oversight and support that these Departments are able to offer (Brophy, Statham and Moss, 1992).

While originally set up as a stopgap measure until adequate nursery education was provided, the playgroup movement has over the years developed its own distinctive identity. In the 1990s, the movement sees itself as offering a valid alternative form of pre-school provision, with a particular set of values, rather than as a cheap substitute for nursery education. The Pre-school Playgroups Association describes the distinctive features of the playgroup movement as its emphasis on self-help, on the value of parental involvement, and on the importance of play rather than formal instruction as a means of helping young children to learn. The association describes playgroups as 'a special form of provision . . . synonymous with parental involvement and parent-run education' (PPA, 1989, p. 2).

Despite their numerical importance in the UK, playgroups until recently had received little attention from researchers and policy-makers. However, between 1988 and 1991, a major research project on playgroups in England was commissioned by the government, the results of which have been reported elsewhere (Statham *et al.*, 1990; Brophy, Statham and Moss, 1992; Brophy, 1994).

As part of that study, we undertook to do some observational work in forty-five playgroups from three contrasting geographical areas. Limited time and resources precluded developing our own 'tailor-made' measures. However, it quickly became apparent that there were few 'off-the-peg' measures available and a completely appropriate existing measure of quality would be difficult to find. Indeed, the comparatively recent growth of interest in measuring quality in early childhood services had not been matched by a comparable growth in available research tools for this exercise (but see Prescott, Kritchersky and Jones, 1972; Day, Phyfe-Perkins and Weinhaler 1979; Fiene, Douglas and Kroh, 1979). The measurement we finally selected was the Early Childhood Environment Rating Scale or ECERS for short.

THE EARLY CHILDHOOD
ENVIRONMENT RATING SCALE

The ECERS was developed by Thelma Harms and Richard Clifford in the United States in the early 1980s and has been used on an international scale by both researchers and practitioners (e.g. Bjorkman, Poteot and Snow, 1986; Phillips McCartney and Scarr, 1987; Goelman and Pence, 1988; Whitebook, Howes and Phillips, 1989; Melnick and Fiene, 1990; Kontos, 1991; Bryant, Clifford and Peisner, 1991; Dunn, 1993). The ECERS has been described by its authors as offering 'a relatively short and efficient means of looking seriously at the quality of the [early years] environment' and as covering 'the basic aspects of all early childhood facilities' (Harms and Clifford, 1980, p. iv). It was designed for use in a variety of forms of group child care in the United States, including day nurseries, playgroups, kindergartens and private nursery schools. Following training, it can be used by various people (including evaluative teams outside the child care setting) as a basis for both evaluation and planning. It can also be used by child care workers themselves to provide a more objective picture of how well their group is doing.

The scale is intended to provide an overall picture of the surroundings that have been created for the children and adults who share the setting. Environment is given a broad definition and encompasses the layout and use of space, provision of materials and experiences to enhance children's development, organization of the daily schedule, levels of supervision provided, and provision for the needs of adults (both workers and children's parents).

The ECERS contains thirty-seven individual scales, each carrying a possible rating from 1 (inadequate) to 7 (excellent). Each scale offers a description of what it is necessary to observe in order to score a 1, 3, 5 or 7; and, where appropriate, alternative scales are provided for use with babies and toddlers. An example is given in Table 5.1. The individual scales are organized into seven main topic areas, as listed in Table 5.2. Scores are based on observation of the current situation, and it is intended that the schedule be completed after one 2–3 hour observation session, backed by information given by staff. The ratings applied in our research, however, were based on two visits to each of the 45 playgroups, rather than just one.

RATING SCALES AND SERVICE VALUE SYSTEMS

Our experience of using the ECERS to structure observations in the *Playgroup Research Project* raised a number of issues about the assumptions underlying the construction of the scale and its appropriateness for use in all kinds of group child care settings. For example, any attempt to provide an objective rating scale for measuring quality in such settings has to assume that there is an explicit and agreed model of what constitutes 'good' quality child care. In the case of the ECERS, the instrument was validated against the views of American experts in the early childhood field. Seven 'nationally recognized experts' were asked to rate each item on the scale in terms of its importance to early childhood programmes. Seventy-eight per cent of their ratings indicated high importance while only 1 per cent indicated low importance, confirming that in the view of this group, the ECERS was indeed measuring relevant aspects of early childhood settings (Harms and Clifford, 1980, p. 38).

Secondly, the scale was tested by comparing its ability to distinguish between classrooms of varying quality as determined by trainers who had been working with the staff in those classrooms. Ratings on the ECERS made by observers were compared with the ratings of the trainers familiar with the classrooms. Expert observers reached a closer agreement with the trainers than those with less experience. Harms and Clifford note that although the findings are 'clearly supportive of the validity of the scale', they also indicate the 'lack of universally acceptable norms for early childhood environments' (ibid.).

We would argue that there are, in fact, a number of different stakeholders in the process of defining quality in early years provision and that these stakeholders may hold different views: but rating scales such as ECERS are generally validated by reference to the values of one particular group in one country. In this case the experts were drawn from the field of child

TABLE 5.1
example of a scale from the ECERS

ITEM	INADEQUATE	MINIMAL		GOOD		EXCELLENT		
	1	2	3	4	5	6	7	
MEALS/SNACKS	Meals/snacks served on a haphazard, irregular schedule and of questionable nutritional value.		Well-balanced meals/snacks provided on a regular schedule but strict atmosphere, stress on conformity, meals not used as a pleasant social time or to build self-help skills (Ex. pouring milk, setting table, etc.).		Well-balanced meals/snacks provided on regular schedule. Staff member(s) sits with children and provides pleasant social environment during meals and when possible at snacks. Small group size permits conversation.		Everything in 5 plus time planned as a learning experience, including: self-help skills; talking about children's interests, events of the day, and aspects of foods (colour and where foods come from).	
OR	1	2	3	4	5	6	7	
MEALS/SNACKS (INFANTS)	Feeding is not timed to child's needs and is of questionable cleanliness and nutritional value (Ex. bottles not sterilized, nipple uncovered, too rigid a schedule, etc.).		Clean, nutritionally adequate feeding on schedule suited to child's needs; but lack of social interaction (Ex. bottle is propped up, child is not held or talked to, no talking when child is spoon fed, etc.).		Clean, nutritionally adequate feeding on a suitable schedule, plus child is held and talked to while bottle fed. Solid food is spoon fed with pleasant adult-child interaction and conversation. Individual attention given.		Everything in 5 plus self-help is promoted in feeding (Ex. infant/toddler encouraged to finger feed self, then use spoon as ready).	

TABLE 5.2
Individual scales in the ECERS organized by main topic areas

1. Personal care routines	2. Furnishings and display for children
Greeting/departing	Furnishings (routine)
Meals/snacks	Furnishings (learning)
Nap/rest	Furnishings (relaxation)
Diapering/toileting	Room arrangement
Personal grooming	Child related display

3. Language-reasoning experiences	4. Fine and gross motor activities
Understanding language	Fine motor
Using language	Supervision (fine motor)
Reasoning	Gross motor space
Informal language	Gross motor equipment
	Gross motor time
	Supervision (gross motor)

5. Creative activities	6. Social development
Art	Space (alone)
Music/movement	Free play
Blocks	Group time
Sand/water	Cultural awareness
Dramatic play	Tone
Schedule (creative)	Exceptional provisions
Supervision (creative)	

7. **Adult needs**
Adult personal area
Adult opportunities
Adult meeting area
Parent provisions

development in North America. However, an assumption that such scales are completely value-free and can be applied to a wide range of child care situations creates problems: we illustrate this below by focusing on our experience of using ECERS. We identify four issues where ECERS either has different values from our day care settings (playgroups), or gives low priority to values we wished to stress. These issues are play; parent involvement; ethnic, gender and other diversity; and interpersonal relationships.

Play

ECERS attaches a high value to directed learning, where teachers structure a child's environment to achieve planned curriculum goals. On many of the individual scales, it is necessary to observe evidence of planned programmes (for instance to promote social development or to develop learning concepts) in order to give a score of 7 or 'excellent'. To some extent, this emphasis on structure and curriculum is counter to the philosophy held by the pre-school playgroup movement, which stresses the importance of the child learning through free play, sometimes extended by adults, but initiated by the child. The Pre-school Playgroups Association considers the education provided by playgroups to be distinctive, and to differ from that provided by nursery classes: 'education . . . is seen as a "pervasive" process, involving all adult/child contacts, and not as a specialized activity' (PPA, 1989, p. 65).

Parental involvement

Parental involvement is another key tenet of the playgroup philosophy. In community playgroups, with which the PPA has become identified, parents are expected to be 'responsible for all aspects of running the group, from fund-raising to the employment of staff to the purchase of equipment' (ibid., p. 64). They are also encouraged to help in the group on a regular basis, since the association believes that 'parents learn and develop from working with their own children; children benefit from the involvement of their parents' (ibid, p. 65, but see also Brophy, 1994.) The ECERS includes a scale which rates 'provision for parents', but this proved insufficiently sensitive to the variety of ways in which parents could be involved in playgroups.

Ethnic and other diversity

The Children Act 1989 has created a particular need for sensitive ways of assessing services with regard to equal opportunities because, for the first time in United Kingdom legislation concerning child care services, it requires local authorities and voluntary organizations, in considering the care provided for any children looked after by them, to 'have regard to [their] religious persuasion, racial origin and cultural and linguistic background' (Section 22 (5) (c)). ECERS includes a scale measuring 'cultural awareness' which attempts to assess how far the pre-school environment is a multi-cultural and a non-sexist one. However, it gives few examples of how to judge anti-sexism or the kind of staff behaviour that would merit a high score. Moreover, issues such as equality of access to the provision and how far membership and management of the playgroup are representative of the local community are difficult to address in an observational scale of this nature, and the ECERS does not attempt to do so. Nevertheless representation in terms of race, ethnicity, gender and disability can provide important indicators for parents concerned both about the value which a child care setting places on diversity, and for the development of self-esteem and self-perceptions of those children who might attend.

Interpersonal relationships

Interpersonal relationships are also not addressed in any depth in the ECERS. Indeed the original intention of the authors of the scale was to produce a separate instrument to examine relationships between workers and children. However, they found it impossible to ignore completely interpersonal behaviour and still deal adequately with the environment, so relationships between adults and children and between children and their peers do appear in the scale (for instance in the item which rates the 'tone' of the group), but this aspect of quality is not covered in any detail. American researchers who have used the ECERS as a global measure of the pre-school environment have generally supplemented it with other data, such as records of the number of verbal interactions between staff and selected children (Phillips, 1987) or a measure of staff sensitivity (Whitebook, Howes and Phillips, 1989).

USING ECERS IN PLAYGROUPS

The particular features of different types of early years provision need to be taken into account when using the ECERS and to interpret the meaning and significance of the ratings that it produces. In the case of playgroups, sessions rarely exceed two to three hours or include a midday meal; some of ECERS scales covering such items as personal grooming, space for nap or rest and notions of a balanced diet were therefore obviously less relevant, and in fact the 'nap' item was excluded from our analysis of the scores. Criteria such as 'used weekly' or 'available every morning' were difficult to apply consistently when groups opened for differing numbers of sessions. Moreover, scales which stressed the need for regular periods of outdoor play in order to score highly were generally less relevant to the playgroups in the rural area of the study, where virtually all children had gardens at home and spent no more than a few hours a week at the playgroup.

It is also important to remember that ECERS is a measure of the pre-school environment. It makes no claim to describe the experience of individual children within that environment, which would require time-consuming observation of target children. It is therefore possible for a pre-school environment to score highly on particular scales, for instance in the provision of gross motor activities, and yet for individual children to engage in little or no such activity during the course of the day. This is particularly likely to be the case in playgroups where there is an emphasis on free play and on allowing children to choose how they spend their time. Environments therefore create an important potential for good quality individual experiences, but they do not necessarily ensure it.

Context and interpretation of scores

ECERS is designed to be completed in a single visit to an early childhood setting, and this gives it an advantage as a research tool, especially where lengthy observation would be impractical. However, what it offers is a 'snapshot' of the pre-school environment at one particular point in time. It is important, therefore, to be aware of some of the factors that may affect the scoring, such as when the visit takes place and which particular staff are observed.

All services are dynamic; they change from week to week, from term to term, and over the years. Playgroups are not unique in this respect but serve as a useful illustration. At the start of a new term, staff were often settling in new children so the routine and interactions observed may have been untypical. At the end of term, there were often seasonal activities such as preparations for Christmas or other cultural festivities, which again involve a departure from normal procedures. Some playgroups provided extra 'educational' activities for older children, generally in the half-term before they started school, which would not be observed at any other time of the year and could substantially affect the scoring on many scales.

The particular staff members observed also affect the score. Some scales in the ECERS (for example, those which rate the understanding and use of expressive language or the development of reasoning concepts) involve assessing staff-child interaction and this may vary substantially both between individual workers in the same session and between workers in different sessions or shifts. Again, playgroups provide a particular example because many groups rely on voluntary help, and sessions may vary depending on which workers are present or even which (volunteer) mothers are helping on the rota. For example, in one playgroup in the rural area of the study, a different group of women ran each of the four morning sessions and although the premises remained the same, the environment differed in terms of the activities they provided, the equipment they chose to bring out, the interactions with children and the general tone of the session. Making two observational visits to playgroups with such a staffing pattern could therefore result in a compromise score which attempted to take account of such variations. Visiting only once would have avoided this problem, but provided a less valid assessment of the environment.

The 'snapshot' nature of the ECERS therefore makes it difficult to assess both the dynamic nature of a pre-school environment and how far it offers variety and new challenges to children. A group may have a good supply of toys and games to encourage fine motor skills, for instance, and score highly on the relevant scale. But if the same toys are brought out every session for the two years that a child may attend before starting school, they will be less effective than a smaller number of toys that are regularly changed.

An invaluable back-up to the observational sessions was provided by the detailed interviews with playgroup leaders, which lasted on average for three to four hours and explored in depth the playgroup's organization, history, funding, admission policy, aims and values, structuring of sessions and attitude to parent involvement. This material provided a context within which to make sense of the scores obtained in a playgroup setting. Any assessment of quality has to go beyond the application of checklists and frameworks, and consider what the scores actually mean. When we came to interpret the numerical ratings provided by the scale, this additional information allowed us to take into account factors peculiar to playgroups. For example, some groups may *have* sand and water trays – but be unable to use them indoors because of village hall restrictions; or they may *possess* pieces of large equipment such as climbing frames – but rarely use them because of the problem of dismantling and putting away such equipment after every session. This additional information also helped us to understand the scores obtained by playgroups in the light of what this particular service is aiming to achieve.

CONCLUSION

Our experience of using ECERS should not be taken as a condemnation of this scale or rating scales in general. On the contrary, ECERS had a number of benefits. As a scale, it provided a helpful method of categorizing and highlighting many aspects of the pre-school environment which may have a bearing on 'quality'. It provides both researchers and practitioners with a systematic way of recording certain observable aspects of child care settings.

The ECERS also stimulated much discussion within the research team as to what constitutes 'quality', how to measure it and the way in which particular, established methods (e.g. sophisticated quantitative techniques) can limit perceptions and exclude certain issues, and the meaning and value of the information we produce. The practice of using the ECERS and the ensuing debate demonstrated that the 'problem' is not the ECERS as such, but rather the fundamental paradigm presented by the search for a universal measure of quality with which to assess a diversity of values, philosophy and service provision in the child care sector. Using the ECERS therefore was not an end in itself but rather it established the beginning of a theoretical and practical discussion about the relationship between on the one hand the (somewhat nebulous) notion of quality, and its containment within the discourse of 'experts', and on the other, diverse child care services and the communities they serve in contemporary multicultural societies.

As we outlined at the beginning of this chapter, the debate on quality in early childhood services and its measurement has been gathering momentum in the UK in recent years. This has partly been as a consequence of the domestic developments, such as the Children Act, which have already been mentioned. But also, the debate in the UK has been influenced by developments in this field in other parts of Europe (e.g. the work of the European Childcare Network, 1991) and further afield (e.g. in New Zealand, the Report of the Working Group on Early Childhood Care and Education (1988); and in North America the National Childcare Staffing Study (Whitebook, Howes and Phillips, 1989)).

In the light of our own multi-method study of one child care setting and the above literature, we would argue that four factors emerge as central to any discussion on quality. First and foremost, as our experience of using ECERS in one care environment demonstrates, any attempt at defining 'quality' is inherently a values-based exercise. Secondly, any definition of 'quality' is to an extent transitory and arriving at what may be called 'quality indicators' is a dynamic and continual process. Thirdly, a range of perspectives can be identified in looking at quality. Three major perspectives are: the views of the children; the views of the parents; and the views of staff providing care. Other views include those of the funding body. Relationships between these groups form an important focus in the contemporary debate on quality early childhood services in the UK and the ideal model for the development of pre-school services is frequently posited as the 'partnership' model (Wolfendale, 1984; Maxwell, 1985; Pugh, 1985).

Fourthly, equal opportunities policies and practices – covering access to services, their content and management and employment practices and procedures within them – are central features of quality in child care services and this means looking at 'quality' at two levels, individual services and service systems. We arrive at this conclusion on the basis of the children's rights perspective discussed in the guidance to the Children Act, that is that all children have the right to certain expectations of their social and economic environment. On the same basis, we would also argue that parents should have the right not only of access to services but also to choose between early childhood services.

What implications do we draw for the development of rating scales, from our experience and these conclusions? We have argued that any definition of quality must be values-based – a value judgement is always involved. Moreover, if the values underscoring a measurement do not reflect or insufficiently encapsulate the values and philosophy of a service, then how useful will any results be for the development of that service? How meaningful will the results be for parents, children and policy-makers? Measures of quality can be useful research tools but they can also contribute to a system of monitoring, evaluation and improvement of individual services. If measures are to have both a research and a service support function they must have *credibility* and *acceptability* with the service in which they are applied. To achieve this, an evaluative measure must state clearly its own values basis, and ensure it recognizes and covers the objectives that are important to the service.

This view of the process of redefining quality and making the values base of any definition explicit has clear implications for researchers and 'experts', who cannot hide behind the cloak of 'objectivity' and 'science' as a way of avoiding critical reflection of 'off-the-peg' measures. It means examining scales not simply in terms of the traditional tests (e.g. inter-rater reliability, internal consistency, scale assessment by nationally recognized experts and comparison of expert opinions), but in addition specifically addressing the question of the values which underscore the scale and making those values (both implicit and explicit) clear. It also means assessing the suitability of the scales for the particular service to be assessed. In effect an assessment must be made of the stated aims and philosophy of the service and how these are (or are not) reflected in those which underscore the scales. It is not simply a case of going beyond what Phillips (1988) called 'the Iron Triangle' (i.e. group size, ratio, qualifications) to look at issues of 'caregiving stability and continuity', 'structure of daily routines' and the 'adequacy of physical facilities' (Hayes, Palmer and Zaslow, 1990). It also means looking at the ways in which individual services and service systems meet the needs of, and reflect the constituency of, the communities which they serve.

An approach such as this indicates that there is a need for diversity of measures – some aspects of which might aspire to being general across all service provision, others being developed for more specific services. This should not be 'read' as a minimum standards approach. Rather it is an argument for 'opening up' the quality debate by recognizing that quality of services to young children has a societal element and is a public issue.

On this basis, it becomes possible to develop measures to evaluate performance of services in the achievement of specific sets of objectives. 'Quality' becomes operationalized through the identification of specific service objectives. As other contributors to the quality debate have identified (e.g. European Commission Childcare Network, 1991) that process – of defining service objectives, of including the rights and expectations of interests groups – is important in its own right. Moreover we would argue, such a process allows the examination of individual services and more broadly community and societal provision with the aim of ensuring that services are provided for all children regardless of race, gender, disability, parental income or geographical location.

REFERENCES

BJORKMAN M. S., POTEOT G. M. and SNOW, C. D. (1986) Environmental ratings and children's social behaviour: implications for the assessment of day care quality, *American Journal of Orthopsychiatry*, Vol. 56, no. 2, pp. 271–7.

BRITISH STANDARDS INSTITUTE (1990) *BS 5750 (Quality Systems)* British Standards Institute, London.

BROPHY, J. (1994) Parent management committees and preschool playgroups: the partnership model and future management policy, *Journal of Social Policy*, Vol. 23, no. 2, pp. 161–94.

BROPHY, J., STATHAM, J. and MOSS, P. (1992) *Playgroups in Practice: Self-Help and Public Policy*, HMSO, London.

BRYANT, D., CLIFFORD, R. and PEISNER, E. (1991) Best practices for beginners: developmental appropriateness in kindergarten, *American Educational Research Journal*, Vol. 28, no. 4, pp. 783–803.

CHILDREN ACT (1989), HMSO, London.

DAY, D. E., PHYFE-PERKINS, E. and WEINHALER, J. A. (1979) Naturalistic evaluation for program improvement, *Young Children*, Vol. 34, pp. 12–24.

DEPARTMENT OF EDUCATION AND SCIENCE (1990) *Starting with Quality: The Report of the Committee of Inquiry into the Quality of the Educational Experience offered to 3- and 4-year-olds*, HMSO, London.

DEPARTMENT OF HEALTH (1991) *The Children Act 1989 Guidance and Regulations Volume 2: Family Support, Daycare and Educational Provision for Young Children*, HMSO, London.

DUNN, L. (1993) Proximal and distal features of day care quality and children's development, *Early Childhood Research Quarterly*, Vol. 8, pp. 167–92.

ELFER, P. and WEDGE, D. (1992) Defining, measuring and supporting quality, in G. Pugh (ed.) *Contemporary Issues in the Early Years*, Paul Chapman, London.

EUROPEAN COMMISSION CHILDCARE NETWORK (1991) *Quality in Services for Young Children: a Discussion Paper*, European Commission Equal Opportunities Unit: Brussels.

FIENE, R., DOUGLAS, E. and KROH, K. (1979) *The Child Development Program Evaluation Centre Licensing Instrument*, Office of Children, Youth and Families, Hanisbury: PA

FIENE, R. and STEVEN, M. (1991) Quality assessment in early childhood programs: a multidimensional approach, Paper presented at the Annual Meeting of the American Educational Research Association, Chicago, Illinois, 3–6 April

GOELMAN, H. and PENCE, A. R. (1988), Children in three types of child care experience: quality of care and developmental outcomes, *Early Childhood Development and Care*, Vol. 33, pp. 67–76.

HARMS, T. and CLIFFORD, R. (1980) *Early Childhood Environment Rating Scale*, Teachers College Press, Columbia University, New York.

HAYES, C., PALMER, J. and ZASLOW, M. (eds.) (1990) *Who Cares for America's Children?* National Academic Press, Washington: DC.

KIDS CLUBS NETWORK (1989) *Guidelines of Good Practice for Out of School Care Schemes*, National Out of School Alliance (now Kids Clubs Network), London.

KONTOS, S. J. (1991) Child care quality, family background and children's development, *Early Childhood Research Quarterly*, Vol. 6, pp. 249–62.

MAXWELL, S. (1985) *Playgroups: The Parents as Parasite, Parody or Partner (Partnership Paper No. 7)*, National Children's Bureau, London.

MELNICK, S. and FIENE, R. (1990) Licensure and program quality in early childhood and child care programs, Paper presented at the Annual meeting of the American Educational Research Association, Boston, Massachusetts, 16–20 April.

MOSS, P. (1990) *Childcare in the European Communities, 1985-1990*, European Commission Women's Information Service, Brussels.

MOSS, P., BROPHY, J. and STATHAM, J. (1992) Parental involvement in playgroups, *Children and Society*, Vol. 6, no. 4, pp. 299–316.

NATIONAL CHILDMINDING ASSOCIATION (1991) *Setting the Standards*, NCMA, Bromley, Kent.

NATIONAL CHILDREN'S BUREAU (1991) *Young Children in Group Daycare: Guidelines for Good Practice*, Early Chilhood Unit (National Children's Bureau), London.

PHILLIPS, D. (ed.) (1987) *Quality in Child Care: What Does the Research Tell Us?* National Association for Young Children, Washington: DC.

PHILLIPS, D. (1988) Quality in child care: definitions of the A. L. Mainman Foundation Inc., Paper presented at symposium on the dimension of Quality in Programs for Children, White Plains, NY, June.

PHILLIPS, D., MCCARTNEY, K. and SCARR, S. (1987) Child care quality and children's social development, *Developmental Psychology*, Vol. 23, no. 4, pp. 537–43.

PRE-SCHOOL PLAYGROUPS ASSOCIATION (1989) *Submission on the Quality of Educational Experience for Under Fives to the DES Committee of Inquiry* (Unpublished), PPA, London.

PRE-SCHOOL PLAYGROUPS ASSOCIATION (1990) *Good Practice for Full Daycare Playgroups* and *Good Practice for Sessional Playgroups*, PPA, London.

PRESCOTT, E. KRITCHERSKY, S. and JONES, K. (1972) *The Day Care Environment Inventory*, US Dept of Health, Education and Welfare, Washington: DC.

PRESCOTT, E., KRITCHERSKY, S. and JONES, K. (1975) *Assessment of Child-rearing Environments: An Ecological Approach*, Pacific Oaks College, Pasadena: CA.

PUGH, G. (1985) *Parents and Professionals in Partnership – Issues and Implications (Partnership Paper No. 2)*, National Children's Bureau, London.

STATHAM, J. and BROPHY, J. (1992) The role of playgroups on a service for pre-school Children, *Early Child Development and Care*, Vol. 74, pp. 39–60.

STATHAM, J. LLOYD, E. and MOSS, P. (1990) *Playgroups in Three Countries (TCRU Occasional Working Paper No. 8)*, Thomas Coram Research Unit, London.

STATHAM, J., LLOYD, E., MOSS, P., MELHUISH, E. and OWEN, C. (1990) *Playgroups in a Changing World*, HMSO, London.

SYLVA, K. and MOSS, P. (1992) *Learning Before School (National Commission on Education Briefing No. 8)*, National Commission on Education, London.

WOLFENDALE, S. (1984) *A Framework for Action: Professionals and Parents as Partners (Partnership Paper No. 1)*, National Children's Bureau, London.

WHITEBOOK, M., HOWES, C. and PHILLIPS, D. (1989) *Who Cares? Childcare Teachers and the Quality of Care in America (Final Report, National Childcare Staffing Study)*, Childcare Employee Project, Oakland: CA.

CHAPTER 6

Quality in School-Age Child Care Services: An Inquiry About Values[1]

PAT PETRIE

School-age child care services are expanding in the United Kingdom and show considerable diversity, not only organizationally but also in terms of objectives and practice. As a researcher of these services, Pat Petrie has explicitly recognized that quality is a relative, values-based concept. Rather than impose her own concept of quality, she has sought to understand school-age child care services and their diversity through a participatory approach starting with the identification of the values of two key stakeholder groups – the providers of the services and the staff who work directly with the children.

INTRODUCTION

Who could be against the idea that child care services must be of high quality? Or, retreating somewhat, that at least children should spend their time in settings which are 'of acceptable standard'? Yet hidden within these laudable aspirations are a wealth of different meanings and value judgements. Briefly, people understand quality in different, sometimes divergent ways. For some, including the service providers, but not forgetting the social policy makers, high quality may be an ideal beyond attainment, needing resources quite outside their reach. Nevertheless, most of the people concerned would have some idea of what they would like to achieve: they would know a good child care service if they saw it and the difference between acceptable and non-acceptable standards would, generally, be clear. What might be less clear to any individual is that other people might have totally different understandings and make different judgements about the same service.

In the *Out-of-School Project*, I worked in one particular group of child care services – play and care services for school-age children (referred to below as 'school-age child care services'). I set out to bring some of these hidden differences in understanding quality to the surface and to examine them with two of the key stakeholder groups in these services – the providers and the staff who work directly with the children. The stance taken was that only they knew what they were aiming for and, therefore, their point of view and their understandings were paramount. Not that I do not have views of my own about 'high quality services', and the project helped to firm them up. But for the purposes of this undertaking, my views were irrelevant. This consultative approach is in the tradition of participatory research with its roots in the women's movement (Oakley, 1981) and its belief that 'a participatory model is essential if social investigation is to lead to citizens' knowledge, rather than people's data becoming experts' property' (Stanton, 1989, p. 23).

SETTING THE RESEARCH CONTEXT

School-age child care services in the UK

The context of the *Out-of-School Project* was social policy, so some background may be helpful, before returning to the research and how it was carried out. I was excited, as a researcher, to be able to examine and think about services which had hardly been studied before – certainly not in the United Kingdom. Unlike other provision for children, whether health services, schools or early childhood services, school-age child care services are still at an early, unprofessionalized stage of development. Compared with teaching or work in nurseries, there is little published material which discusses them, little training or education for staff, no professional body to set standards and no specific qualification required for working in them. Unlike countries where they are more highly developed, school-age child care services in the United Kingdom have no universally accepted curriculum. This lack of development says something about their low social status, but also that they are late arrivals, increasing in number when the streets are no longer places for children to play (Hillman, Adams and Whitelegg, 1990), when mothers are less home-based and when the school has been established for more than a century as a dominant institution in the lives of children and of their parents.

School-age child care services go under many different names: playschemes, after-school clubs, adventure playgrounds, homework clubs, out-of-school centres, day camps; and the names themselves speak of their variety. What they have in common is that adult staff take certain responsibilities for children outside school hours, and all of them come within the same regulatory framework; services for children up to the age of eight are regulated under the Children Act 1989. At the same time they have different types of *providers* – public, voluntary or 'for profit'; different *material resources* at their disposal – including income derived from fees, set at a high level, local government funding, and finance derived from small-scale grass-roots efforts; and different *organizational bases* – including local amateur, non-constituted management, business management, and management within local authority bureaucracies.

The research perspective

Given this diversity, school-age child care services are a rich field for uncovering ideas about quality and its values bases. To discuss provision in terms of values is to use the notion that there are systems of principles, implicit or declared, which inform human activity so that people's actions and judgements may be seen as values-based. Values are the basis of notions of right and wrong, of high quality and low quality, of what is preferred and what is rejected.

In the social sciences, researchers take what steps they can to be objective – it is one of the hallmarks of their trade – and to use 'objective measures'. Statements about 'quality' are based on a particular evaluative point of view, and many such are available. One is that of the 'expert', as exemplified in the British school inspectorate; or the art connoisseur, who speaks from experience and from a body of knowledge. 'Experts', including researchers, bring external criteria to bear on their subject, such as those drawn from child development and educational theory.

If a researcher wants to make judgements about 'quality', there is no shortage of ways in, but each has its own values base. One approach is to look at outcomes: that is to regard the service or an aspect of the service – staffing levels, perhaps – as a 'treatment'. Then, in the traditions of quasi-experimental psychology, to measure any 'effects' or correlations in the development or behaviour of children who have had the treatment and to compare them with children who have not had the treatment. Examples are: the extent to which nursery children leave – or do not leave – their mothers in a strange situation; their physical growth; their IQ and school attainment; whether they become pregnant as teenagers. All of these 'outcomes' are chosen in the light of specific values; they are chosen by researchers and used by policy makers and pressure groups, for the purposes of particular social agendas.

Another way in is with an instrument which measures what might be seen as input rather than outcome: for example the extent to which the organization and practice of services meet given criteria or evince quality indicators. Here again there are values underlying the chosen criteria, the values of the researcher and of the person who devised the instrument.

Both of these approaches, which have a long history, certainly have their uses. But they do not *explore* quality and do not set out to do so. Rather they presuppose a common understanding of what constitutes quality in the light of a common value system, on the part of the researcher, the research community and the research audience. Yet an examination of children's services from an historical point of view will find a divergent array of values and of notions about quality: educational, protectionist, authoritarian, romantic, self-expressionistic, and so on. What speaks of quality today, from the viewpoint of the late twentieth century educationist or child development expert, may not do so tomorrow and did not do so a century ago. Ideas about children and about services change, some develop and some of them, once held in high esteem are, in time, deplored or simply fade away. And while there are differences across time, there are also differences between different social groups.

The *Out-of-School Project* developed from this perspective. As I said earlier, I tried to set aside my own ideas about quality. The values which I consciously brought to the research sprang from curiosity and a search for a greater understanding of society and its institutions. I also used skills and an approach that I have used outside research, in particular my experience as a 'non-managerial supervisor'. The non-managerial supervisor is sometimes brought into organizations – it is fairly common in, for example, youth work – to support individual staff from a position outside the internal management structures. The idea is to help staff clarify what they are trying to achieve, within the aims of their organisation, and to support them in thinking about their task and finding ways forward – taking the larger aims and objectives of the organization as given. It has much in common with facilitating internal evaluation – of which, also, I have some experience – in which an outsider is brought in to facilitate staff and providers' evaluation in the light of their own aims. Underlying both of these is an understanding that the point of view of the client is paramount and only to be challenged from within its own framework. I tried to bring this general approach to the research project and studied services from a specific internal viewpoint: that of the providers and staff. Using external criteria based on an external viewpoint would have made it more difficult to elucidate what they were trying to achieve.

Another possible viewpoint, also internal, is that of the service user. In school-age child care services these are the children and parents who use the provision. They have their own points of view, their own values and notions of quality, and they are important. However, users are mostly in present circumstances *reactive* rather than *proactive*. They respond to what is on offer, rather than have any responsibility for shaping it as do providers and staff (although parental participation, children's councils, parents' co-operatives may all, of course, affect the users' position and influence). I hope to study parents' and children's views of quality in a forthcoming project, but it seemed important in this initial study to understand what was on offer before looking at how this might match users' requirements.

THE OUT-OF-SCHOOL RESEARCH PROJECT

The method adopted

The main task was to *characterize* services, to provide a taxonomy of provision by identifying the main differences between services, especially those relating to values, and to find economical and useful ways of describing them. The aim was to promote greater clarity and understanding about play and care provision for users, staff, service providers, regulating authorities and researchers.

The study examined fifteen different provisions, chosen for their variety. The *providers* included parents and other local community groups, private businesses, employers, churches, national charities and various local authority departments. The *venues* included schools, community centres, short-term housing, Portakabins, an adventure playground, employers' premises, purpose-built centres and a sports centre, in different parts of England, Scotland and Wales.

Each setting was studied with a view to answering the following questions: what are the *underlying values of this service*? what are the main *aims* connected with each value? what is the *organization and practice* employed to meet these aims and what *problems* arise? A qualitative approach was used. Answers were sought on the basis of conversations and informal observations during several visits – including normal opening hours, staff and management meetings, parents' evenings, celebrations and outings. I tried to be an unobtrusive observer and to be flexible about participating. For example, I might join in play with children, if they invited me to, or help supervise children on outings. Where necessary, managers and providers were interviewed in their offices, off-site, and I collected documentation such as brochures, the minutes of meetings and timetables.

The research was carried out in a consultative way. The providers and staff were seen as the experts and their views and experience were of prime importance. Nevertheless for the sake of the research these needed to be summarized, and I needed to check that my perceptions were accurate, in conversation as occasion arose, saying something like 'It seems to me that keeping the children occupied and amused is an important aim for your service.' When I had some understanding of the service from the point of view of management and staff, I presented them with a systematic written account in which each value was grouped together with its accompanying aims and related organization and practice. Problems in meeting aims were also recorded, and accompanying each set of values and aims were the typed field notes which related to it. Finally there was a discussion with staff and management (where these were distinct) so that any amendments and corrections could be noted.

For the most part it seemed to me that the participants quite enjoyed the process. Some did not want to read the written material, but were happy to be talked through it and to put me right on details or emphases. Participants were also sent a copy of the pages where they were mentioned, albeit under pseudonyms, in the project report, prior to its going to print.

In this way a range of different values, aims and the means of achieving these were identified *from the point of view of providers and staff*. As the study progressed, it became necessary to organize this material that was coming from the different cases in superordinate categories. It seemed useful to make a distinction between *provision values and aims* and *practice values and aims*, as well as whether or not there was coherence between these.

Provision values and aims

The people who provide school-age child care services may be motivated by many values: for example they may put commercialism and profit before all else, or they may believe in equality between all members of society, the importance of play or of child protection; they may be inspired by their religious faith, by Islam, Christianity or Judaism. All of these values and many more are held by different providers of school-age child care services. It is on the basis of these values, and to promote them, that provision is made. Linked to values, and developing from them, are the aims of providers – what they are hoping to achieve. In the research, aims could be as different as to run an efficient business (based on commercial values) or to promote equality between different groups of children (based on equality values). Logically subordinate to aims, come the objectives which providers decide must be put in place to meet their aims. For example here are some of the provision aims of a for-profit day camp (open during certain school holidays) with some of its linked objectives:

AIMS – to run an efficient business; to be competitive and corner the local market.

OBJECTIVES – to fix the level of fees so as to maximize profit and attract customers; to produce and place publicity material to attract customers.

Another example comes from an after-school club which placed a high value on equality between children:

AIM – to promote equality between children.

OBJECTIVES – to have a written policy about combatting racism; to provide training on the subject for staff and volunteers (these were just some of the objectives linked to promoting equality between children of different colour and different ethnic groups; other objectives were about equality between the sexes and about able-bodied children and children with disability).

In fact, the service providers who took part in the research had many different aims. Here are some of them, not listed in any order of priority:

- to improve the quality of life for children;
- to integrate children with disabilities into the community;
- to provide segregated play opportunities specifically for children with disabilities;
- to provide daycare for working parents;
- to retain employees;
- to provide respite care;
- child protection;
- prevention of children becoming 'at risk';
- profit;
- to facilitate children's play;
- to promote specific community cultures;
- to meet the religious needs of children and families;
- Christian outreach to the local community;
- equal opportunities;
- community building.

These aims are discussed at length elsewhere (Petric, 1984, which also provides a full account of all aspects of the Project). However, it should be noted that some of them are mutually contradictory because there are divergent philosophies and experiences, and different notions of quality, at work within them. Providers may place a different value, for example, on *empowerment* or on *protection*. The providers of one provision set out to integrate able-bodied children and children with disabilities, in more or less equal numbers within the same establishment:

> It's really important to integrate children from an early age. The schools and respite services segregate children and that means they are not at home in the community . . . Also it's good for able-bodied children to mix with children with disabilities.

A different view was put forward from the chairperson of another service which also catered for children with disabilities. For her, protection was more important than integrating children into the community:

> Here they are segregated from other children so that they can acquire skills and confidence . . . and play at their own pace. If they want to invite their brothers and sisters to join them here, that's OK. But if there are too many mainstream children, our children would be pushed aside.

Within their own framework of values, and given efficient and effective practice, both of these providers may furnish users with 'high quality' services. Their provision is based on beliefs about what is good for children. But these are beliefs not only about promoting optimum development – which is open to empirical research and ideas about what is desirable. They are also coloured by ways of thinking about children with disability.

Compare the following, from the same two providers, starting with the provider who runs a segregated play scheme:

> The disability activists say that the children need empowering. But it's parents who have a moral responsibility to bring children up as they see fit, and our children need protecting from others . . . yet the activists say that parents have too much choice and that the young people themselves don't have much choice. Our children are mutations, they're like four-leaved clover. Four-leaved clovers are not normal, but you keep them for luck because they're special.

The other provider stresses play and providing children with choice:

> Play to me has a very wide meaning. It's choice, making choices, flexibility, creativity – all the empowering words. Play is exploring your own environment, developing yourself mentally, physically and emotionally . . . so many choices are made for them in the rest of their lives.

There were many examples of such divergency between providers and between different practitioners. But it is important to notice that an outside observer cannot make any statement about the relative quality of either programme, except with reference to stated values, whether these are for 'empowerment' or 'protection' or something else. This is a point returned to later.

Targeting

To target a particular population of users is an objective for many providers. It distinguishes between them and allows inferences about values to be drawn. It is, therefore, useful to consider targeting and target groups as a component in the discussion of quality.

Targeting has different implications in different contexts. For example some local authorities and charities target children 'in need' in the light of their own values and priorities. They see what they have to offer as being of special use to certain parents and/or children. Reaching these populations is a way of putting what may be limited resources to best use. They do this in different ways, for example by setting up in an area where there is much poverty or by direct invitation to individual parents already known to them. Commercial providers, on the other hand, may target customers by advertising in districts where more parents can afford their services. For them, targeting is part of marketing rather than prioritizing scarce resources.

In current school-age child care provision in the UK targeted populations include:

- children with disabilities and their families;
- districts with a high level of children and parents 'in need';
- individual children and families 'in need', for example where families are in contact with social workers;
- parents who can afford services;
- the children of employees;
- families in certain ethnic minority groups;
- children attending a certain school or schools;
- single parent families;
- girls;
- young offenders.

These different targets manifest at local level (where they exist) that coherence and comprehensiveness have not been public-policy values in this field. This is apparent from the many central government departments which have an interest in school-age child care services, each department relating to public, voluntary and commercial providers in their own ways. The *Department of Health* has an interest in the protection of children by the regulation of services and by the provision, or development, of services for children 'in need'. The *Department of National Heritage* (Sport and Recreation Division) has an interest in children's play. The *Department of the Environment* is responsible for funding programmes aimed at urban regeneration, which may include grants for voluntary (non-profit) services. The *Department of Employ-*

ment is a newcomer to children's services and provides funding for the development of provision with an emphasis on employment issues, particularly the employment of women. The *Department for Education* encourages the use of school premises for provision, and is the department with concern for youth and community services which are also providers. The *Home Office* too has an interest, in that play and leisure activities are seen as preventing juvenile crime and are provided by some police authorities.

These interests in school-age child care services are, in practice, separate. They are seen by the different departments as means towards their own distinct ends so that, at the level of central government, different stakeholders focus on the child in different ways, each in the light of their own value systems. For each department, a slightly different 'child' comes into the frame: the child who needs protection or, by contrast, the child from whom society needs protection; the child as the customer of leisure and recreation; the child as the offspring of employees, who needs child care in the interests of the employer, the labour market and female equality; the child as a member of society with a claim on its recreational resources. These different views, their associated values and notions of quality, are played through in provision at local level.

In order to evaluate these different services and to make statements about their quality, it is necessary to consider their different provision aims and to ask to what extent they are fulfilled by targeting. Do they keep offenders out of trouble? Do they avert children being taken into local authority care? Do they enable mothers to participate in the labour market? Answers to these questions would provide at least part of any evaluation of their quality from the point of view of their providers.

But effectiveness is not the only consideration. At the same time it is important to remember that while they may have these desired results, there may be other unintended outcomes which provide material for a different consideration of quality, and one which may have no relevance for the provider. An example would be the extent to which targeted services segregate groups of children and parents. An outside observer who valued social cohesion might prefer universal services and might therefore find the quality of expensive day camps, which segregate the children of the well-to-do, as questionable as those provisions which segregate children 'in need'. From this viewpoint, also, there are problems about any service which leads to the possible stigmatizing of its users.

Some providers who took part in the research had decided to target local populations where there were high levels of poverty. They were keen to stress that individual children using the services were not necessarily 'in need', and that they would not want them to be labelled in that way. A senior member of management in a local authority said she wanted the services to be open to all sections of the community – not just 'as a repository for "poor things"'. A mother who used a similar service located in a decaying housing estate with very high unemployment, pointed to the problems: 'a lot of them (other parents) think it's for . . . single mothers, so they won't use it, they won't come on the trips, they think they're for deprived children and that their children are not deprived enough'.

On the other hand, in one local authority, some holiday playschemes were reserved solely for families who were in contact with social workers. The account of the senior worker suggests something of the working atmosphere of the playscheme:

> We have a social worker who I get in touch with when we have problems. We banned four children . . . All of us have to accept we can't solve the children's problems . . . One twelve-year-old we had was leading younger children astray . . . There was an eleven-year-old whose attitude to us was awful. We've got forty children every day but this girl needed one member of staff for herself. She hit one child in the face. We banned her. Her mother was very good about it. Dealing with parents is the worst part of the job. They say things like 'Is my child going to get thrown out for what someone else did?' The problem . . . is telling parents about children being bad. You worry about what the parent might do . . . One boy was shaking and in tears when I told his father about something he had done wrong. The staff were very upset but I was acting on the advice of his social worker. I've got to carry out their instructions. We're here to give them a good time. One child came in tears saying that his mother was ill. She was doing odd things, we knew she was schizophrenic.

The additional stress for staff may be one unintended result of a segregated scheme of this sort and one which – quite apart from any desire for social cohesion – may influence the effectiveness of the provision and thus its quality, even when judged from within the values system of the provider.

Before turning to quality at the level of day-to-day practice within any service, there is another aspect which I can only indicate here but which can be amplified by the reader in the light of the earlier examples and discussion. Quality does not reside only in the practice and organization of any particular service, such as its programme, the interaction between staff and children, the adequacy of its premises and equipment. There are social policy considerations also which relate to the objectives, aims and values of the providers. Pertinent questions with implications for quality may be posed about the *general* impact of any provision – not only on those who use it and work in it, but upon the wider society. For example, what is the effect for able-bodied children and their parents of not sharing play schemes with children with disability?

Practice values and aims

At this point *staff* must be brought into the picture alongside *providers*, because they can have notions of quality, legitimately distinct from the interests and aims of the provider. Perhaps this needs some explanation. At the daily level, the practice of staff often followed through from the aims and objectives of the providers. For example, in a service where a *provision* aim was to supply play facilities for children, then facilitating a social environment to support children's play was, not surprisingly, a major *practice* aim. Again, where a major provision aim was to promote equality between children, staff were appointed, trained and supported to share this aim in their everyday work with the children.

However, there was not always coherence between the values and aims of staff and those of providers. The extent to which there is, or is not, coherence is one of the characteristics of school-age child care services. Incoherence may arise because of inefficient management procedures, poor communication or supervision; but there are other, more fundamental reasons for incoherence. Some providers had little interest in practice, seeing this as the domain of staff. This is not to say that they had no concern for the children; they might certainly intervene if something were to 'go wrong'. But for these providers, the provision of a service is seen as an end in itself; how it operated is less important. They might be concerned with some aspects of quality, especially those required for registration under the Children Act, but have no strongly formed opinion about daily practice. Where there is a low level of cohesion between the main practice values and provision values, staff act as the agents of the provider, operating with relative autonomy within the provision. They provide, for example, child care for working parents or protection for children in need on behalf of the provider. What might be called the curriculum of the provision is, largely, left to staff and to whatever experience, skills and training they have been able to obtain.

Some of the main examples of practice aims identified in the research, in no particular order of priority, were:

- to engage children in arts, crafts, educational and sports activities;
- to ensure that children have 'fun' and amusement;
- to facilitate children's play and choice, to encourage friendships;
- to integrate children with disabilities;
- to foster children's awareness of the natural world and beauty;
- to give children experience of a variety of arts and crafts;
- to promote equal opportunities;
- to encourage self reliance;
- to promote obedience and good manners;
- to give value to some of the cultural activities of local ethnic minority groups;
- to safeguard children's health and safety;
- to observe an anti-racist and anti-sexist approach;
- to integrate the child's day;
- to relate to the school and the community;
- to provide support for parents;
- to provide supplementary education.

Again, as with the providers, divergence can be detected between some of these aims. Categories which I developed in the course of the Project included whether the bias was towards play, amusement or work and whether work was chosen by the child or not. These are broad categories. *Play* is defined as involving activities which children choose, whose processes they direct and where external constraints are relatively low. Play activities are enjoyable and intrinsically motivated. Here are field notes, used as an illustration of the play approach:

Children come and go from the various play activities as they please. Two children start off at a table which has been set up with collage materials. They make 'cakes' by gluing lentils to the bottom of the paper cake-cups, and then take them off to a play kitchen/shop corner, to bake and sell them.

In other services which had a *work* approach, children would have been encouraged – or obliged – to persevere making a collage, rather than 'playing' with the materials.

Amusement does not necessitate an initial choice of activity on the part of children: although their participation may be willing, the choice of activity is made by the staff. Also the direction of the process is less in the hands of children and more in the hands of staff but, as with play, children's enjoyment is seen as important. Children may have an intrinsic motivation to continue an 'amusement' activity for its own sake, or there may be extrinsic motivation such as prizes or competition provided or generated by staff.

Where amusement ranked high, workers did not place a high value on play. Their concern was that children should not be bored, that they should have enough to do or – as some put it – that they should have fun. Staff devised and led activities such as sports, karaoke, arts and crafts, party games, discos and video shows. The children were less active in generating their own activities, creating their own play environments or making use of time in their own way. Often children were given commercial art kits, with much of the preparation already complete, so that within a short time they had something described as 'professional' to show for very little effort and with little opportunity for creative choices. This activity could be called a pastime, rather than art or craft – nevertheless the children seemed to enjoy it.

There were also examples of provision based more on work, rather than play or amusement. Two sorts of work were distinguished: willing and unwilling. *Willing work* is seen as a chosen activity; the child may direct the process, according to his or her level of expertise, or it may be adult directed; there are external constraints on the process because it sets out to achieve an end – it is extrinsically motivated. Such work can include arts and crafts, sports and school work. *Unwilling work* shares the characteristics of willing work except, significantly, it is not a chosen activity but done under compulsion.

Examples of both were found in the services studied. In one after-school club, once children had chosen a craft-activity, staff expected them to complete it evening after evening, in spite of protest. In another, the children did 'lessons', every evening – not in every case willingly – and staff followed parents' requests to hear children read and tested their spelling in preparation for school the next day.

Relating in some respects to play, amusement and work, was whether the emphasis was on the *individual* child or on the *group*. Children were more likely to be organized in a group, rather than as individuals, where practice was oriented towards amusement or work (especially unwilling work) than when play was highly valued. There were also values-based differences in the methods of control which staff used and how they reacted towards 'unacceptable' behaviour including a *democratic*, a *punitive* and a *group control* approach. These too were often tied in with the curriculum so that, for example, the democratic approach went hand in hand with a high value on children's play, self-reliance and freedom of choice. It was as though different staff and providers were construing 'childhood' in different ways.

DISCUSSION

The preceding pages should make it clear that in the *Out-of-school Project* I was not concerned with 'inadequacies' or 'high standards' whether with regard to premises, space, staff:child ratios, resources or anything else which goes towards the delivery of a service. I see these as logically subordinate to questions of quality and relating rather to effectiveness: are they sufficient, or of such a kind to facilitate the particular service which providers and staff intend?

Instead I was interested in exploring different notions of quality within the framework of public policy. The most striking aspect of the study was the enormous diversity and often divergence of these notions. The factors, in particular the values, which underlie these differences need some discussion. They arise from the different sectors involved in provision, differences between sub-cultures in the wider society and the effect of public policy.

First, there are the different *sectors* to which UK providers belong: the public, commercial and voluntary sectors. Although there is not necessarily homogeneity within any one of these, nevertheless each sector has its own particular history, its own aims and its own interaction with social policy. These are examined elsewhere (Petrie, 1984).

Second, there are the *sub-cultures*, whether commercial, religious, social class or ethnic, to be found within the larger society. These sub-cultures have their own value systems, some of which are mutually exclusive. Providers and staff are drawn from these different groupings and construe quality in their own ways. As a result, different staff and different providers may not agree as to what is a 'high quality' service, what it is that children 'need', what are suitable activities for them and suitable ways of interacting with them.

Thirdly, and importantly, there is *public policy*. While providers and staff are influential, they nevertheless exist within a context of public policy and its values. Until the late 1980s, public policy in the UK towards school-age child care services was largely a position of 'no policy'. Child care (for any age) has never been universally provided or subsidized – unlike health and education services. Recreation and play services had been supplied at the discretion of the local authority and their private and voluntary sector successors, without regulation. Any state or charitable provision of child care or play was targeted mainly at children 'at risk' or 'in need'.

As I argued earlier, coherence has never been a public policy value in the field of play and daycare for school-age children. Most recently, the Children Act 1989 has placed some obligations on local government to regulate child care services and to provide for children 'in need' – but not necessarily directly. Indeed, current policy in all fields is away from direct provision by local authorities. They are permitted to provide child care services directly, and in some cases do so, but within the financial constraints of public spending policy. The public sector, in particular social services, is seen by the Children Act as the facilitator of voluntary provision, working in partnership with other agencies, rather than as the direct provider. So public policy admits diverse understandings of quality – as many as there are potential providers. These understandings are tempered in their execution by the local authority whose duty it is to register and inspect services and see that they meet certain minimum requirements. It remains to be seen whether the new regulatory framework resulting from the Children Act will produce greater uniformity or coherence.

In conclusion, questions about quality must be explored not only with regard to individual services, but with regard to national public policy towards child care and play as a whole. In the UK the values of public policy may be expressed, in broad terms, as those of a market economy, regulated and modified for the sake of child protection, affected by a history of voluntaryism and of public recreational facilities within a generally democratic framework. This has something in common with, for example, the situation in the United States (except, especially, for the regulation of school-age child care services). It should be possible therefore to make broad comparisons between the effectiveness of public policy in these two countries, within their own similar frameworks, and to compare the concomitants of the policy within the two countries. It would not be possible, however, to make similar judgements about the quality of public policy in, say, Denmark compared with the UK because the two sets of public policy values are so disparate. Danish aims include a system of universal public provision for all children and parents who need it: it is not possible to assess the effectiveness of UK policy from within the same values framework – although it is perfectly possible to judge one framework against another.

This raises the subject of relativism. Is taking the stance described above to say, in effect, that there is no such thing as a 'good' provision or 'bad' provision, 'good' public policy or 'bad'? That there is only provision or policy that is effective or otherwise, with regard to specific values and aims on which individuals, groups and external evaluators differ? Thus, if members of a religious group do not wish their daughters to play active games, but prefer them to do needlework, in what sense is their provision 'good' or 'poor' in this respect? Is it best to be descriptive and say that this provision is low with regard to promoting physical health and equality of opportunity for females but high with respect to observing parents' wishes? This stance, attempting to describe provision within its own value system, was adopted purposely in the research reported above.

I think that it was an appropriate approach because it allowed a more sophisticated understanding of a new area both for research and for public policy, than would have been possible if I had attempted to study them with a uniform quality assessment measure, or a battery of developmental tests. It also showed some of the problems which providers and staff face in trying to meet their aims, although I have not reported these here. In addition it was possible to examine how services might set about achieving similar aims in quite different ways.

But while the approach was appropriate for the Project, a less relativistic viewpoint is necessary for other, non-research, activities. Indeed, in order to develop policy and services, rather than carry out research, choices between competing values have to be made. I hope that the Project made some of these choices and their concomitants clearer, so that there can be further debate about school-age child care services and their development.

The Project's acknowledgement of pluralism does not preclude change at the level of either practice or social policy. The pluralism described exists within the context of a democratic society. In a democracy, ideally, an important premise is that there is social cohesion, equality and shared interests – these form the non-negotiable values base from which other values evolve. Another understanding is that rationality has a high status. So in a democracy it is understood that people debate, negotiate values and seek to persuade others. They do this privately as well as through the media, in the courts, in local councils and in Parliament. From time to time they vote. Dissatisfaction with the status quo can be expressed through these varied democratic processes and be a source of development.

However, complete social cohesion and agreement is almost certainly unattainable, and conflict and divergence remain. Individuals or groups find aspects of public policy repugnant, even though they are the results of the democratic process. They see their own values expressed more perfectly elsewhere – whether in a religious faith, notions of a national past or in the statements of international documents such as the United Nations Convention on the Rights of the Child. Sometimes these other values become paramount, not only in terms of hierarchies of belief but also in terms of action. For some dissidents, beliefs, reasoning and feelings run so strong, and so contrary to what is prevalent, that they place themselves outside the democratic framework and they break the law: setting laboratory animals free, impeding women seeking abortion, or attacking the headquarters of racist groups.

Such extreme actions are, axiomatically, rare. Most dissidents remain within the law, whether out of pragmatism or because they hold to the democratic value: legislation and common law draw the bottom-line as to what is permitted. And if this is true for the law-abiding dissident then it has implications for others. The law prohibits, but it also permits. Within the law, service providers may certainly embrace whatever values and promote whatever practice they wish. This acceptance, within the democratic framework, is about legality. It does not imply either equivalence between different ways of bringing up children or between different policy models within this framework. Given the democratic ideal, public debate about the system of child care provision, and the day-to-day practice within it, must look at what furthers that ideal and what impedes it. It should look at issues concerning equality for parents, children and staff and make hard choices when these are in competition. Such debate should be the basis of development; what society permits today can be illegal tomorrow, what is frowned on now may be promoted in ten years' time.

Development is a process which would be more perfectly rational, more transparent to the reader, listener or voter, if any statement about 'quality' were to be accompanied by a statement of the values on which it is based, and the aims it wishes to fulfil – democratic or otherwise. I hope that the *Out-of-*

School Project provides some impetus towards this, at any rate in the field of children's services.

REFERENCES

HILLMAN, M., ADAMS, J. and WHITELEGG, J. (1990) *One False Move: a Study of Childrens Independent Mobility*, London: Policy Studies Institute.

MAYALL, B. and PETRIE, P. (1983) *Childminding and Day Nurseries: What Kind of Care?* Heinneman Education, London.

OAKLEY, A. (1981) Interviewing women: a contradiction in terms, in M. Roberts, (ed.) *Doing Feminist Research*, Routledge, London.

PETRIE, P. (1984) *Play and Care, Out-of-School: Diversity of Practice and Provision*, HMSO, London.

STANTON, A. (1989) *Invitation to Self Management*, Dab Hand Press, Ruislip, Middlesex.

NOTE

1 The research reported in this chapter has been supported by the Department of Health.

CHAPTER 7

No Equality, No Quality

CAROL JOSEPH, JANE LANE AND SUDESH SHARMA

Quality in early childhood services may be recognized as a values-based and relative concept, but does this mean that in practice a completely relativistic approach to quality is acceptable? Drawing on experience from Britain, Carol Joseph, Jane Lane and Sudesh Sharma propose that limits do need to be applied and that equality should be a non-negotiable core value that is integral to all definitions of quality on the basis that it is a fundamental human right. They discuss how this value can be applied in early childhood services with respect to racial equality through the adoption of anti-racist strategy and practice, and emphasize that this needs to be a process including all stakeholders.

INTRODUCTION

An early childhood service that values children must value all children equally. A society that believes in justice and equality for all its citizens must address not only any existing inequalities but also the mechanisms by which such inequalities are reproduced and perpetuated. Tackling these issues in the early years is vital. But a service based on principles of equality will not just happen by chance. It must be planned for, strategically.

Equality means equality of gender/sex, social class, disability, sexual orientation – and 'race' (although the word 'race' is in common usage it is in quotation marks here as an indicator of its questionability as a term: it derives from historical, pseudo-scientific attempts to categorize people according to their skin colours and physical characteristics, and there is no scientific basis for this division into biologically determined groups, with their presupposed differences). Although we believe all inequalities, all oppressions, are interconnected, and that equality needs to be viewed holistically, this chapter addresses the issue of racial equality specifically. It suggests that the principles of racial justice and equality, aspects of human rights, are integral to the quality of services and that they are non-negotiable. There is, as yet, no shared understanding of what they mean in practice. We must, therefore, lay down clear parameters, policies, procedures and practices for this component of quality of early childhood services.

THE CASE FOR CORE VALUES

Equality is non-negotiable

While it is not relevant here to determine all the components of quality in early childhood services, even if that could be done, it is important to identify some of the objectives. The process of determining these objectives is influenced by a range of factors, including the basic values or principles held by those determining them. Personal attitudes and beliefs contribute to these values, thus influencing the way quality is assessed and informing the objectives of the service. It cannot be assumed that there are shared understandings of what constitutes quality because the values bases of people depend on so many variables.

Should an entirely relativistic approach towards the quality of early childhood services be adopted? Should outcomes and practice depend entirely on whatever values and beliefs are held by the stakeholders in particular services? Should those involved in providing particular early childhood services have the right to decide what they want for the children attending those services? Or should there be some values which are regarded as so critical to the well-being of all children and their families that they are defined as a core and non-negotiable part of all definitions of quality? If so, who determines what these values should be and on what basis are they determined? Should it be possible to negotiate quality or should some values be imposed on others, even when they are reluctant to accept them? These are important questions and should be considered seriously, because whatever is decided must be founded on a clear analysis of what is involved.

We believe that part of the definition of quality should be common across all services, and based on certain common core values. One of these core and non-negotiable values is equality, which we would define minimally as follows:

> All children must be treated as individuals, given equality of opportunity and treated equally as they grow (taking positive account of any barriers that impede their progress) and any factors that discriminate against them must be removed.

We would base our case on equality being a fundamental human right, and that the concept of human rights, including racial equality, should lie at the heart of definitions of quality in early childhood services. There are a range of stakeholders involved in early childhood services – organizers, politicians, advisers, trainers, policy makers, lawyers, local communities, governors–managers, practitioners, families and, of course, children. Some of these stakeholders may have agendas other than the implementation of equality. But the need of every child to be treated with equality and to see all other children also treated with equality is too important to be left to individual stakeholders.

Because of their vulnerability, the rights of children should be seen as a priority and protected by others. In a society where racism (which we define as constituting all those practices and procedures that historically and in the present have the effect of disadvantaging and discriminating against people because of their culture and/or ethnicity) is so widespread or, perhaps, even more important *because* it is so, the attitudes and beliefs of individuals cannot be permitted to undermine the values of racial equality and justice. It is important to resist the argument that, somehow, equality is a matter for democratic discussion and decision. There can be no negotiation as to whether or not human rights are respected: any other approach to quality is unlikely to deliver a service founded on such fundamental rights. What is needed is an approach that ensures that these fundamental rights are not negotiable, together with a clear understanding of why this is so and why without equality there cannot be quality.

A starting point for defining those human rights which should form the values base for a common core definition of quality in early childhood services is the Articles of the Universal Declaration of Human Rights, adopted by the United Nations in 1948, and the UN Convention on the Rights of the Child. The 54 Articles of the Convention lay down the basis for treating all children equally, although this does not mean that Britain itself (or indeed any other country) fulfils every criterion of the Convention in its existing laws or practice. It does, however, define a universal parameter of good practice.

We believe the issue is not as controversial as it might at first appear and that there are, in fact, some common shared values which inform ideas about quality in early childhood services. Certain values, and the objectives they give rise to, are widely shared and do not need to be imposed. They include a belief that children should respect and value each other – a belief that is of fundamental significance to all children when it is translated into practice. In short, most people would be likely to agree with our minimal statement defining equality.

Practice not perfect

What is *not* shared is an understanding of the implications of what this means, the present and historical impediments to its implementation and the way that other attitudes and beliefs of those apparently sharing common values about equality may prevent that translation into practice. Services must be based *explicitly* on principles of equality, but they also need appropriate policies and strategies devised for their implementation. Misinformation, misunderstandings, ignorance and prejudice stand in the way of building on commonalities.

So while most people would say that the quality of early childhood services must ensure that equality is put into practice and many people in Britain, perhaps the majority, may believe that that is exactly what is being done at present, the reality is that this is not so. There are organizations, services and individuals whose practices are based on principles of racial equality. But there exist many nurseries, schools, playgroups, creches and family day care situations where black and minority ethnic children do not see themselves or their cultures reflected in the resources, do not see people similar to themselves as their carers/educators and do not hear or see their home languages spoken or written. This may make them feel devalued and not accepted. There are many facilities where racial prejudice is not addressed and where white children are not helped to understand and accept that they are part of a multiracial society. There are young children who are recipients of overt or covert harassment based on their skin colour, physical features, culture, religion and language.

There is early childhood provision that does not widely advertise its vacancies for children or staff, thus excluding applications for such vacancies from those who do not know about them. There are methods of arranging admissions, waiting lists and job selection procedures that, for various reasons, disadvantage and discriminate against particular racial groups. There is a whole range of personal and institutional practices and procedures involved in the development, organization and provision of early childhood services, none of which may be *intentionally* disadvantageous or discriminatory but which have the *effect* of being so. Some of this may result from a failure to take account of the presence of black and minority ethnic communities living here. Changed circumstances have consequences, in terms of addressing the effects of 'traditional' practices on particular groups of people. It may also result from a deliberate wish to keep things as they are – with or without the specific intention of excluding some other people. Overall, it cannot be said that all children are treated equally.

There are likely to be significant differences in attitudes and beliefs between people about their perceptions of others, based on their perceptions of differences of 'race'. The quality of early childhood services will thus vary according to who determines what goes on. In terms of racial equality, this ad hoc method is totally inadequate. It leaves each service at the mercy of the whims of those responsible, whether the issues and their practical implications have been considered, or whether they have not been considered through ignorance or reluctance to change practice.

Furthermore early childhood services are not situated outside society – they are part of it. As such they are subject to its wider influences. Racist attitudes and beliefs are deeply embedded in British society. For many, if not most, black and minority ethnic communities and individuals this *affects* their everyday experiences. But perhaps, more significantly, what *determines* their life chances, their educational opportunities, the jobs they have, where they live and what they do in their spare time to a far greater degree are those institutional practices and procedures that disadvantage and discriminate against them. This is because racist attitudes and beliefs have become systematized into institutional practice, such institutionalization being a component of racism. So, addressing equality issues in early childhood services is much more than what people *think* or how they *behave* as individuals. We need to address every practice and procedure, every facet of decision-making in the whole organization of the service to ensure that nothing, consciously or unconsciously, disadvantages or discriminates against black and minority ethnic children or their families.

In predominately white areas of Britain and in early childhood services where there are only white children, the situation is further compounded by the absence of black and minority ethnic groups of people as users or staff. Isolation from personal contacts means that attitudes and practices are less susceptible to change. The need for action, therefore, is as great in such areas as in multiracial areas. Whether children live in largely white or multiracial areas, the objectives are the same. The influences on their learning processes may vary but the power of their environment to induce racist, non-racist or anti-racist attitudes remains. The acceptance of the premise that equality is integral to quality has real consequences – undoubtedly, this is a massive task.

While the principle of equality is not negotiable, the mechanisms and processes to ensure its implementation clearly are. As will be seen later, we only have to look back over the last fifteen years or so in Britain and identify various approaches to racial equality that have been practised in early childhood services to see that some were more successful, more appropriate, than others in attaining or working towards that objective. Processes change, offering scope for reviewing policies and practices and everyone involved with services should always be seeking methods of improving them.

RACISM IN BRITISH SOCIETY

Historical roots of racism

Why, or how, does racism exist? What are its roots? How is it manifested today? Why is it relevant to early years services? Historically some groups of people have been subjected to racism and have remained so; with others the racism appears to lapse but retains the ability to be revitalised, for example the racism towards Irish people in the nineteenth century has been reactivated by current IRA campaigns, while racism towards Muslims in the Crusades was revitalised in anti-Muslim attitudes during the Gulf War.

Exploitation of the labour of people has existed for a long time, indeed still exists. In the early Middle Ages and earlier, slaves were largely treated as a class within the society, a 'necessary' though lowest order, with some basic rights and with opportunities to gain freedom. This form of slavery was distinct from that of the enslavement of non-European peoples practised later. From the middle of the seventeenth century the trade in black slaves from Africa to work in North and South America and the West Indies grew enormously. These slaves had no legal rights and were bought and sold as if they were commodities, thus breaking up family life.

The belief in racial superiority, the justification for such inhumane and cruel treatment, manifested itself in Christian Europe's attacks on the Jews and in an assumption of the inferiority of Africans, based on their physical, cultural, linguistic and religious differences. Quasi-biological theories of the racial superiority of white people were developed to justify the slave system and eventually to justify the exploitation of people through colonization. It was often used to divide and rule, resulting in hierarchies of privilege in those colonized, for example, in India or in parts of Africa where Indian migrants/ settlers were recruited as indentured labour and denoted of 'higher class' than Africans.

So although racism is a set of ideas and beliefs, it also had (and has) a very important *economic* function – enriching Europe at the cost of using the labour, raw materials and natural resources of colonized countries to supply industry and trade. White racial superiority made itself felt in all walks of life through white culture, history, literature and language. At the same time the history of civilizations in South America and Africa were almost ignored, leaving an impression of 'barbarism' and 'primitive' life-styles. When overt colonialism ended there was little attempt to address its legacy. These notions of superiority remained, unchallenged and not really recognized; for example, there are still instances where black children are described as having 'no language' or 'no culture'. They remained entrenched in the general belief system and were passed from generation to generation, in the same way that many other beliefs are passed on.

We have only to look at books and other resources produced in Britain from colonial times onwards to see how endemic these ideas were, reinforcing the perceptions of people colonized as being 'childlike'. This was especially true of Africans who were perceived as having no history until the British came and 'civilized' them. Asians (originating from the Indian subcontinent), in contrast, were perceived as being 'exotic' and more 'developed' – though less so than the British. Some of these stereotypes and misrepresentations persist, for example where African/Caribbean children are seen as 'aggressive' and Asian children as 'passive'.

Right up to the 1950s and 1960s (and occasionally more recently) there were overtly racist sentiments expressed by government ministers and other people in positions of influence and power (Fryer, 1988). Since then, although legislation against racial discrimination has been enacted, racially discriminatory laws about nationality, immigration and asylum have been passed.

Although some black and minority ethnic people have migrated to and lived in Britain for centuries, it is only since the 1950s that they have been actively recruited to work here and, more recently, have come to live as British citizens. What they found when they arrived was much hostility and overt and covert discrimination in all walks of their lives. Painful and humiliating racism was a common experience. Evidence (Brown, 1984; Jones, 1993) shows that there is *still* widespread discrimination against black and minority ethnic people – in fields of employment, housing, health, social services, education and access to services. Some of this is due to stereotyped and racist attitudes, for example, where a black applicant is told there is no job or accommodation available and a little while later a white applicant is offered it. Much, however, is the result of institutional practices and procedures.

When the facts of discrimination have been known so long and are so well documented and when the processes for identifying and eliminating it are so clearly defined and yet it still remains, we can only deduce that reluctance and/or hostility to deal with it are the real obstacles to change. It is the everyday insidiousness of the way racism is perpetuated that is so often difficult to grasp. At the same time, there is also increasing activity from overtly fascist and racist organizations and an increasing number of attacks on black and minority ethnic people. The links between the past and the present are being maintained; racism is still alive and well.

Racism and children

Black and minority ethnic families for a long time have had serious concerns that their children faced discrimination and did not enjoy equality of opportunity in the education system. Such concerns include admissions, exclusions, attainment levels and racial harassment. Evidence of discrimination is difficult to ascertain because it often takes place in private situations, with few witnesses present, is hidden by institutional procedures or the perpetrators are not covered by the law, because they are children; there is also no systematic monitoring on an ethnic basis to identify discrimination or disadvantage. Nevertheless, evidence of discrimination and racial harassment in the educational system is beginning to be identified (Commission for Racial Equality (CRE), 1985, 1986, 1988a, 1988b, 1991, 1992).

In early childhood services we need to be aware of what is happening to older children. We need to see if unequal treatment and harassment in these services based on stereotypes is beginning to get a hold with potentially dire consequences for children as they grow older. For example, what, if any, are the links between the commonly-held stereotype that young African/Caribbean boys cannot concentrate and their over-representation among those excluded from primary and secondary schools (Department for Education, 1991)?

The effects of racism on young children have already been documented. Research (Milner, 1983) shows that children as young as the age of three can distinguish between various skin colours and physical features. Indeed this is not surprising: we would expect them to recognize the difference between a red and a yellow flower and, of course, we encourage them to do so. How often though do we even *mention* skin colours, thus passing on subtle messages of what is acceptable to discuss: skin colour differences, so obviously recognizable, are perhaps not discussed because of the misguided idea that drawing attention to differences (differences that are ranked in a racial hierarchy) is unkind and the differences best ignored.

Yet the research also shows that young children can ascribe hierarchical values to various skin colours and physical features. They learn their attitudes and beliefs from their whole environment – including toys, books, posters, the media, their peers, their families and other adults around them. They learn from what and who they see (and do not see), what and who they hear (and do not hear) and what they do (and do not do). If one thinks about and examines what children would learn about black and minority ethnic people from their environments (i.e. what the world looks like to *them*), it is easy to recognize the distorted view of the world as it is likely to be portrayed to them. Even where parents have a very positive input to a child's life and thought, it is often surprising (and dismaying) to realize what opposing information they have taken in, and may appear to believe and endorse, from other elements in their world, especially when they meet other children in group situations. They learn very soon who is seen as important in society, who is included and who is omitted and what roles different people are expected to play; this process is, of course, similar to the way they learn their attitudes to men and women.

We can no longer pretend that either the world at large or the environment of the children for whom we are responsible is racially 'neutral', neither discriminating against nor favouring children on racial grounds. Yet while it may be easy to accept that racism is rife generally, it may be more difficult to accept its effects on young children. Finding out what children think and believe in the presence of adults, with whom they may be reluctant to say what they *really* think, is difficult; children often know what they are expected to say, especially to adults. But there are many descriptions by individuals (mostly not officially recorded) of what young children say and do that give extreme cause for concern that they are learning to be racially prejudiced, for example, instances of young white children refusing to sit next to black children, making negative remarks about their appearance and ridiculing languages that are not English.

If people continue to claim that children are 'innocent' and do not learn attitudes from what is around them, then it can be denied that the issue of equality in early childhood services – so far as what the children themselves are learning – is important. The tabloid media in Britain maintains a relentless vilification of any group or individual who suggests otherwise, as witness the many newspaper 'stories', often fabricated or blown out of all proportion, ridiculing and distorting those trying to present children with a balanced view of the world. Such media are likely to oppose direct racial discrimination against children in, say, admission to a nursery, yet remain resolute and powerful in belittling the role of history on the way young children form their attitudes.

ADDRESSING RACISM AND PROMOTING RACIAL EQUALITY

From multiculturalism to anti-racism

What has been done to promote equality and remove inequality in early years services? In compulsory schooling (from 5 to 16) issues of racial equality have been addressed in some form or other, however inappropriately or inadequately, since the 1960s. In early years services, apart from the provision of learning English as a second language, the issue has only been really widely considered since the late 1970s/early 1980s. There were, of course, individuals and groups beavering away, by writing, by practice and by discussion much earlier than this, and these pioneers were behind the changes that were later instituted.

Briefly, the processes – whether they could be described as theories or philosophies is difficult to say, because of their ad hoc implementation and nature – started off as forms of assimilation. Newly-arrived people were expected to adopt British ways of life, leaving their own ways of living at home. Even what they did at home was often criticized. This clearly failed – very few 'migratory peoples' leave their cultures, customs, languages and traditions behind them.

Cultural pluralism or multiculturalism, variously defined, replaced these earlier ideas. However defined, it usually included only issues around the curriculum and its ethos – introducing aspects of 'culture' to each other and sharing common experiences across cultures, for example, foods, festivals and music. It tended to reinforce the exotic and, in reality, the culture of white people was seldom discussed. White teachers and carers were usually responsible for deciding what they considered relevant to develop concepts of cultural pluralism, decisions which often conflicted with the children's own cultural experiences. These were small steps forward but, in themselves, peripheral at best and counterproductive at worst. In understanding the historical role and the present consequent reality where notions of racial superiority are steeped in society, it is likely that to discuss ideas of 'culture' or of 'multiculturalism' may only serve to reinforce racist ideology. Recognizing that racism means *ranking* of cultures in a racial hierarchy makes the link. Talking about 'people's cultures', without recognizing this differential ranking, may merely provide more ammunition to devalue them. Encouraging children to 'share' their cultures by, for example, demonstrating Indian dancing, Arabic cooking or Chinese writing, without dealing with this underlying racism is likely to reinforce it. But, if this is done in a context where the culture, language and dress of all children are equally valued through everyday acknowledgement, their self-esteem is likely to increase, leading to greater confidence and achievement.

For many years there have been consistent criticisms of 'multiculturalism', by black and white people, as a diversion from educational attainment objectives. It is now largely accepted that, although it is important (i.e. all cultures *should* be equally valued) in British society, multiculturalism is not, of itself, sufficient to ensure equality. The basic obstacle to equality is racism and it is not possible to remove racism without confronting it; to ignore racism or to try to deal with it by stealth (for example, by multicultural education) is doomed to fail. What is needed is 'anti-racism' - a strategy combining socio-political policy and practice to counter racism in all its forms, cultural, institutional and structural, as the major obstacle to racial equality.

The role of legislation in promoting racial equality

More than principles of good practice are needed to ensure racial equality. British legislation acknowledges the need to address elements of racism, regarding the elimination of racial discrimination, in the Race Relations Act 1976 and, regarding the care of young children, in the Children Act 1989 (for relevant details of both these Acts see CRE, 1989, 1991, 1994; Lane, 1993). The Race Relations Act 1976 lays down what constitutes unlawful discrimination in the fields of employment, housing, education and goods, facilities and services, defines other unlawful acts and exceptions and establishes the Commission for Racial Equality, defining its duties and powers. While overt acts of discrimination (defined as direct discrimination) in early childhood services are rare, they are not unknown. For example, there have been incidents where Romany Gypsy children have been refused playgroup places and family day carers have refused to accept African/Caribbean or Asian children into their homes; both of these are unlawful and constitute direct discrimination. And if the stereotype about black boys' inability to concentrate results in them not being provided with the full range of learning experiences offered to other children, then this too could be unlawful discrimination.

Less obvious acts of discrimination, defined as indirect discrimination, are far more common. This occurs where a requirement or condition, applied equally to everyone, has a disproportionately adverse impact on a particular racial group because they cannot comply with it and it cannot be justified on other than racial grounds. Indirect discrimination often reveals customs or institutional practices or procedures that may have been in place for some time but were not, necessarily, ever intended to discriminate. For example, operating a 'first come, first served' nursery waiting list (rather than just being a list to provide information about potential applicants) might disproportionately affect particular racial groups of families who have recently arrived in Britain and are unfamiliar with the system of nurseries and waiting lists. Similarly, requiring a specific qualification or experience for a job might disproportionately affect a group who do not have that particular qualification or experience, even though they have other qualifications or experience that would be equally relevant for the job.

The Race Relations Act sets legal parameters from a firm values-base. For early childhood services to be of good quality, they must not be in breach of the Act. What the Race Relations Act cannot do, however, is to determine what specific practices should be *present*. The Commission for Racial Equality, however, has a statutory duty 'to promote equality of opportunity and good relations between persons of different racial groups generally', which enables it to recommend and advise on the most appropriate ways to achieve this objective (CRE, 1994).

In contrast to the Race Relations Act, the Children Act 1989 *does* address the issue of equality by requiring local authorities to take account of a child's religious persuasion, racial origin and cultural and linguistic background in the registration and inspection of private 'day care' services (in Britain, day care providers of early childhood services for children under eight have to be initially registered by the local authority as 'fit' persons, with follow-up inspections at least annually). It also requires local authorities to conduct a three-yearly review of all 'day care' services and, in providing 'day care' and other services for children defined as 'in need' (a duty imposed on local authorities by the Act) to have regard to the different racial groups to which these children belong.

The guidance that accompanies the Act (Department of Health, 1991) goes further and makes explicit what is expected of the services and why issues of racial equality are important to consider. It refers to the need for those working with young children to value and respect different racial origins, religions, cultures and languages, free of racial stereotyping, drawing attention to the early age that children learn about such differences and their capacity to assign different values to them. It identifies the need to have equal opportunities policies with monitoring and reviewing arrangements, using ethnic data, to assess how far 'day care' and education services are operating in a non-discriminatory way. It cites the right of children to be free of discrimination such as racism and to be cared for as part of a community which values their diversity, to facilitate their development and to foster a sense of identity. With regard to whether a person is fit to look after children aged under eight, it requires local authorities to consider that person's 'knowledge of and attitude to multicultural issues and people of different racial origins' and 'commitment and knowledge to treat all children as individuals and with equal concern' (para. 7.32). In conducting the three-yearly Review, local authority Social Services and Education Departments (in consultation with health authorities, other departments and agencies and all local communities) are required to collect basic data on all 'day care' provision, as well as school provision for young children, so that they can analyze the information, including policy objectives, the curriculum and 'multicultural and equal opportunities aspects'.

In practice, the Race Relations Act is particularly important in identifying racial discrimination in employment recruitment and selection procedures, in admissions to early childhood provision and in the way all children are provided with opportunities to benefit from the full range of activities and learning experiences. In order to be able to identify any discrimination it is essential that relevant data on the ethnic origins of everyone involved is collected, monitored and analyzed at every stage of the procedures. This is not a difficult task in employment and admission procedures and should be easily and routinely done, after consultation and agreement with local communities involved in the services. Regarding the actual curricular practice, it is perhaps more appropriate to monitor what is going on by close observation and assessment rather than formal ethnic data collection which could be time consuming and perhaps less insightful.

The Children Act, while requiring the issue of racial equality to be addressed by local authorities, does not cover education department services which depend on the curriculum devised locally and the commitment of those involved. But the three-yearly Review covers *all* early years provision and, together with the guidance recommending consideration be given to a range of racial equality issues, the Act should provide a mechanism to examine the effectiveness of practices and procedures already in place.

While these two pieces of legislation cannot be described as anti-racist in the way defined above, they do address some of those factors comprising racism. Together they provide a framework in which early childhood services should operate – the Race Relations Act providing for the elimination of racial discrimination, the Children Act providing for the promotion of equality of opportunity and the accompanying guidance addressing a range of issues, including that of countering the learning of racist attitudes by young children. They are clear examples of legislation having a clear value base of equality.

Beyond legislation, to countering the perpetuation of racial inequality

But we need to go further than implementing legislation. Even if it were possible to eliminate discrimination and to ensure that positive account was taken of every child's religious persuasion, racial origin and cultural and linguistic background, the cycle of learning racist attitudes is likely to go on, which in turn leads to racist behaviour (individual or institutional – by intent or neglect) as children grow up. Anti-racism must include a comprehensive strategy to counter this process, to provide all children with accurate and balanced information about the wider world we live in and its multilingual, multiracial, multicultural and multifaith (or no faith) nature. Children need to know that making adverse judgements about each other on the basis of skin colour, physical features, dress, language, accent, dialect, religion or culture means denying our shared humanity. Differences are just that. On educational grounds alone, prejudice interferes with the process whereby children consider information objectively. It denies them the skills of collecting information from a range of sources and critically evaluating each item on its merits – scientific tools which they need for effective learning.

All children have a right to be provided with an environment where racial prejudice is not learnt. They have a right to use the information they are given to make up their own minds about the way things are, to discuss concepts of fairness and justice and to learn that being proud of one's culture is not the same as believing it to be superior to others. Being able to empathize with people is also important. If we do not know what children are thinking, what their attitudes are, what *their* values bases are, we cannot possibly know if they are learning to be racially prejudiced. Only when we know this can we know what needs to be done to counter the process. So we need to be acutely aware, at all times, of any indications about what children's attitudes are; we need to talk with children and provide resources and a forum for raising issues.

If we wish to intervene in the cycle of racist attitudes being perpetuated from generation to generation, we need to take positive action in early childhood services, for if we fail to do this, many children may grow up manifesting racist behaviour and fail to address institutional racist practices and procedures. In working with children in this context, it is important to discuss what they may say or do in a supportive, caring way, never attacking them personally or making them feel guilty about themselves. Indoctrination is not the issue, unlearning negative prejudices and encouraging positive racial attitudes and beliefs is. Ways of countering the learning of racist attitudes include:

- 'circle time', to share ideas and ask questions;
- opportunities to discuss and reflect on the world outside early childhood provision, as children see it and in a way that they can understand;
- discussions and practice (painting and cut-out paper work) to raise issues of the variety of skin colours, physical features and hair textures positively;
- opportunities to provide information to correct prejudiced ideas about such things as crime, Africa, the Middle East, differences in intellectual capacity, where it is 'appropriate'/'right' for various people to live, what sort of jobs various people do;
- opportunities for discussing issues in calm and stress-reducing ways – especially where children disagree among themselves – to develop constructive ways of resolving conflicts.

Practising anti-racism is a process, not a one-off activity. It is not about doing a few things in an ad hoc way. It requires a systematic analysis of every aspect of early childhood services and then devising practices and procedures to ensure that they deliver equality to all children and their families. Some people may feel that models of good practice would be helpful. We believe that, although sharing ideas can be useful, going through the whole process of examining existing practices and procedures is critical to a real understanding of what needs to be done. It is part and parcel of a strategy for implementation, in which learning how to communicate with others, including all the other stakeholders in the service, is a prerequisite to success.

We offer the following broad guidelines to the process of developing anti-racism in early childhood services, covering employment and service delivery issues:

- identify the stakeholders in the service;
- ensure that the stakeholders are able to communicate effectively with one another. If they are unable to do this the process of discussion and analysis is likely to be difficult.
- devise a 'value-statement', to be agreed by all the stakeholders, stating what principles are believed to be the core of an equality policy;
- outline a programme for action, to be agreed by all the stakeholders, covering the processes involved in developing a policy, time constraints and personal responsibilities for action;
- develop an explicit stated policy, with wide consultation with all stakeholders, which defines the objectives, implementation (including monitoring and analysis) and resources;
- where parts of the policy are developed by different groups, ensure continual liaison and opportunities to comment on work done;
- consult continually with identified interested parties;
- examine continually all the structures, procedures and practices of the organization, in employment and service delivery (including admissions, resources, curriculum, behaviour, teaching styles and dealing with racist incidents and harassment);
- collect, monitor and analyze by ethnic origin all those practices and procedures where decision-making or assessment is involved, on a regular basis;
- record, monitor and analyze all racial incidents, for example, harassment or name calling and including any action taken;
- develop strategies to counter the learning of racist attitudes by young children and provide a framework where such attitudes can be unlearnt as part of regular curricular practice;
- consider a contract of good practice between each parent, child and the service.

Some of this is being done in some places. Issues are being addressed and written about. There have been real shifts in the last ten years, including the emergence of: supportive funding intiatives; carefully thought-out policies in education; successful Parliamentary lobbies for changes in legislation; black/minority ethnic support and pressure groups (for example, the Black Childcare Network); national anti-racist networks and pressure groups for early childhood services (for example, the Working Group against Racism in Children's Resources and the Early Years Trainers Anti-Racist Network) and for teacher education (for example, the Anti-Racist Teacher Education Network); and good practice guidelines that address racial equality (for example, by the Pre-School Playgroups Association, National Childminding

Association, Early Childhood Unit of the National Children's Bureau and Save The Children Fund). In addition, many individuals have taken the issue of racial equality forward, the pioneers of change referred to earlier.

But there is still a long way to go. Despite a clear commitment among national organizations responsible for early childhood services and widely available and disseminated information, it is likely that the majority of practice remains largely unaffected; there has even been a backlash, orchestrated by the 'New Right', against those tackling racial discrimination and disadvantage. There is no overall anti-racist strategy, no comprehensive national commitment and implementation programme to provide racial equality in early childhood services. This indicates first and foremost that the issue of racism and its relevance to early childhood services has yet to be incorporated into the planning and organization of the services *as a whole*.

To change this is a tough agenda. Power is seldom given up without a struggle. There will inevitably be conflicts between the various individuals and groups involved; the process of change in the field of racial equality can be exceedingly fraught. This is because it is seldom about additions and bolting on. It is more about structural changes – dismantling something and replacing it by something else – which would be threatening in any situation. Add to this, resentment, reluctance and overt racial hostility and the mixture may be explosive.

There is one specific aspect of equality, however, that must be paramount – the way racism affects black and minority ethnic children and their families. For adults, being subjected to racism is very painful. For young children it is likely to be even more hurtful and damaging because they are not yet able to understand its origins and so may see themselves as the cause of it.

This takes us directly back to the concept of quality and the non-negotiability of equality. Structures to implement racial equality must be put in place. Changes will not just happen by osmosis, and staff cannot be expected to just 'pick up' concepts in the absence of a clear forum. Within that forum continual sharing of ideas is important and understanding is critical – involving so far as possible all the stakeholders in the service.

Assessing the equality components of quality

Do we need to measure quality in terms of equality? If so, how do we do it? Perhaps quality, the best quality, is finite but ever unattainable. In terms of what we see as 'measurable', over periods of time it is likely to change – it is dynamic. So, as time progresses, there will always be new horizons to consider. But we need to assess how far equality is being implemented at any one moment in time because if we do not, there will be no means to identify progress or what advice and support may be needed or helpful.

When we think about equality we can perhaps only *describe* a range of aspects that do, or do not, contribute to quality. If quality consists of various components including resources, health, safety, food, 'curriculum', admissions, policies, procedures and practices, knowledge of child development, behaviour, 'ethos' – it is obvious that some of these are more readily measurable in terms of equality than others. Perhaps all are best assessed by descriptions rather than formal measurement, which may preclude recognition of their complexity and richness.

It may be useful to develop a 'chart' of assessment, describing a range of possibilities for each component that is relevant to the equality dimension in quality – a range which can be changed over time. For example, regarding resources, descriptions could range from: a *refusal* to have black dolls and books reflecting our multicultural society (when refusal to register should be considered); through the provision of good resources but no real under-standing of how to use them; to the use of a range of resources as part of a strategy to positively reflect diversity and counter the learning of racist attitudes. Such an assessment could be the result of self-evaluation on the part of the service provider, negotiated with the registration officer as part of the annual inspection procedure. This process would identify training and support needs in a positive way to improve the quality of practice.

In the end the crucial question may really be *not* how we assess the quality of early childhood services (and equality) but how we ensure that those doing the assessing (registration and inspection officers in local authority social services departments, the government's Social Services Inspectorate, and inspectors from local authority departments and the national Office for Standards in Education) have the skills, knowledge and commitment to assess equality issues as integral to quality. This takes us back to training and education and the *explicit* inclusion of equality issues in all organization, procedures, practice and assessment.

CONCLUSION

How far have we really got in assessing the quality of care/education with regard to racial equality? The answer must be, not far. Until we understand and know what quality means in terms of equality we cannot begin to assess how successful we have been in implementing it. Legislation has helped to define it and, compared with a decade ago, there are a lot more organizations and individuals who, at the very least, know that equality should be addressed specifically. The how (and the why) are perhaps less well known. But there are some education and social services departments who are beginning to know what is needed and are developing assessment tools. Others are nowhere near this process and may not even believe it is necessary. But change has always been like this – slowly lurching forwards (and occasionally backwards) in the process. The historical stain of racism is only now beginning to be washed out.

REFERENCES

BROWN, C. (1984) *Black and White Britain: The Third PSI Study*, PSI Heineman, London.
COMMISSION FOR RACIAL EQUALITY (1985) *Birmingham LEA and Schools: Referral and Suspension of Pupils*, CRE, London.
COMMISSION FOR RACIAL EQUALITY (1986) *Teaching English as a Second Language: Report of a Formal Investigation in Calderdale LEA*, CRE, London.
COMMISSION FOR RACIAL EQUALITY (1988a) *Learning in Terror: A Survey of Racial Harassment in Schools and Colleges*, CRE, London.

COMMISSION FOR RACIAL EQUALITY (1988b) *Medical School Admissions: Report of a Formal Investigation into St. George's Hospital Medical School*, CRE, London.

COMMISSION FOR RACIAL EQUALITY (1989) *Code of Practice for the Elimination of Racial Discrimination in Education*, CRE, London.

COMMISSION FOR RACIAL EQUALITY (1991) *The Lessons of the Law: A Casebook of Racial Discrimination in Education*, CRE, London.

COMMISSION FOR RACIAL EQUALITY (1992) *Secondary School Admissions: Report of a Formal Investigation into Hertfordshire County Council*, CRE, London.

COMMISSION FOR RACIAL EQUALITY (1994) *From Cradle to School: a Practical Guide to Racial Equality in Early Childhood Services* (4th edition), CRE, London.

DEPARTMENT FOR EDUCATION (1991) *National Exclusions Reporting System (NERS)*, HMSO, London

DEPARTMENT OF HEALTH (1991) *The Children Act 1989, Guidance and Regulations: Volume 2, Family Support, Day Care and Educational Provision for Young Children*, HMSO, London.

FRYER, P. (1988) *Black People in the British Empire: An Introduction*, Pluto Press, London.

JONES, T. (1993) *Britain's Ethnic Minorities: An Analysis of the Labour Force Survey*, Policy Studies Institute, London.

LANE, J. (1993) What role has the law played in getting rid of racism in the lives of children? in G. Pugh (ed.) *Thirty Years of Change for Children*, National Children's Bureau, London.

MILNER, D. (1983) *Children and Race: Ten Years On*, Ward Lock Educational, London.

CHAPTER 8

Developing Cross-Cultural Partnerships: Implications for Child Care Quality Research and Practice

ALAN PENCE AND MARIE MCCALLUM

Working across cultural and institutional differences is a significant challenge within early childhood services. In this chapter Alan Pence, with the University of Victoria, and Marie McCallum, with the Meadow Lake Tribal Council, describe the evolution of a collaborative post-secondary educational Project that resulted not only in the development of an innovative, cross-cultural, curriculum model but also in the establishment of a caring and respectful partnership. It is argued that such partnership approaches contain broader implications for the study and advancement of quality child care.

INTRODUCTION

This chapter recounts the evolution of an unusual partnership in North American post-secondary education for work in early childhood services. It is a partnership between a university degree programme located on Canada's west coast (British Columbia) and an Aboriginal Tribal Council representing nine First Nations (individual reserves) in the north-central area of Canada (north-west Saskatchewan). Although separated by over 2,000 kilometres, and vast cultural and institutional differences as well, the partnership has thrived over the five-year period of its existence. The survival and development of the partnership has meant stepping outside expected and typical institutional relationships to identify a common ground of caring, respect and an interest in innovation upon which the collaborative project could be built.

While the impetus for the partnership was the development of a post-secondary child care curriculum, the implications of the partnership move beyond curriculum to address issues at the core of quality care regardless of culture. Both the specific elements of this university/First Nations partnership, and the broader implications of its partnership approach for child care research will be explored in this chapter.

THE MEADOW LAKE TRIBAL COUNCIL AND CANADIAN FIRST NATIONS EARLY CHILDHOOD CARE AND EDUCATION

The Meadow Lake Tribal Council of Saskatchewan (MLTC) and the School of Child and Youth Care (SCYC) at the University of Victoria commenced their partnership in 1989. The initiative was Meadow Lake's.

> The First Nations of the Meadow Lake Tribal Council believe that a child care program developed, administered, and operated by their own people is a vital component to their vision of sustainable growth and development. It impacts every sector of their long term plans as they prepare to enter the twenty-first century. It will be children who inherit the struggle to retain and enhance the people's culture, language, and history; who continue the quest for economic progress for a better quality of life; and who move forward with a strengthened resolve to plan their own destiny.
>
> (MLTC, 1989, p. 1.)

MLTC's stated interest in supporting its children and families through child care programmes emerged in the mid-1980s as part of Tribal Council economic development consultation with each of the nine Meadow Lake First Nation communities (MLFN). In the period 1985-1988 the Meadow Lake Tribal Council had developed and expanded its training and economic development ventures to a significant degree. However, a number of the participants in the training programmes were dropping out due to a lack of reliable, good quality child care services. In addition, small business developments were also struggling; many of these business initiatives depended on single parents both as individual entrepreneurs and as employees. Without reliable child care services, parents were often forced to drop their employment to care for their children. The result of an MLTC economic development assessment, completed in 1987, was that almost all of the nine First Nations communities within MLTC identified child care as a specific requirement in their community.

Although child care had emerged as a key economic and educational support for development within the nine MLFNs, resources to develop services were blocked by inter-governmental disagreements over jurisdictional authority for such services. Throughout Canada, child care services are designated as a provincial responsibility; however, on-reserve social services for First Nations individuals are provided through agreements with the federal government. With the exception of the Province of Ontario, all of the other nine Canadian provinces had been unable to resolve the dispute over which level of government was responsible for child care services on-reserve. The result was that virtually no First Nations communities in Canada (except for Ontario) had funded, on-reserve child care services.

MLTC was well aware of these problems in the development of services to on-reserve First Nations people and was prepared to move quickly when it learned of a new federal government initiative that was to be made available for the establishment of innovative demonstration and development projects through the Canadian Department of Health and Welfare Child Care Initiatives Fund (CCIF) established in 1988. The Meadow Lake Tribal Council submitted an initial proposal to CCIF in 1988 for Phase 1 planning dollars. The plan that emerged contained an on-reserves services development component (family day cares and a centre-based child care programme) and a training and education component designed to support the services aspect of the plan.

A PARTNERSHIP IS ESTABLISHED

In order to fulfil their fuller vision, MLTC required a post-secondary institution partner. Early in 1989 the leadership of MLTC approached several institutions, but were disappointed with the responses they received. A number of colleges and universities already had established programmes which those institutions felt would be able to meet MLTC's needs, but none was enthusiastic in accepting MLTC's vision as the starting point for a new and unique programme. The School of Child and Youth Care did not have an established First Nations degree programme, but did possess a strong interest in First Nations child and family issues and in community-based education.

While other post-secondary institutions with established programmes appeared to be in a more suitable position to respond to the MLTC overture, paradoxically those institutions' prior developments had introduced a degree of institutional rigidity, inhibiting their ability to respond flexibly and creatively to a new initiative. The paradox of knowledge and experience as an impediment to development, rather than an asset, is a thread that weaves throughout the MLTC/SCYC project and is, it will be argued later in this chapter, a component of current limitations in the more global study and development of child care quality as well.

Having virtually no institutional experience in developing curriculum partnerships with First Nations communities (although a number of individual faculty members had First Nations' and other cross-cultural experiences), the SCYC's child day care specialist approached the first meeting with the MLTC Executive Director with hesitant interest. That hesitation was quickly eased, however, as the vitality of the MLTC Executive Director and the strength of his commitment to the Project became evident. A partnership in principle was established at the first meeting in May 1989 between Ray Ahenakew, Executive Director of MLTC, and Alan Pence, child day care specialist at SCYC.

The first stage of the newly established partnership involved the undertaking of a literature review of First Nations early childhood curriculum work by SCYC on behalf of MLTC (Greenwood-Church and Pence, 1990). That work led to the submission of a jointly developed proposal to the federal government by MLTC late in 1989 (MLTC/SCYC, 1989). The proposal received funding approval in the summer of 1990 and the MLTC/SCYC Child Care Career and Educational Ladder Project officially commenced work on 1 September 1990.

A MODEL EMERGES

The autumn of 1990 was an extremely busy and challenging period for the newly established partnership. The CCIF grant was for a three-year period during which a full two years of Early Childhood Care and Education (ECCE) curriculum had not only to be developed, but delivered at a site remote from the curriculum development team based at the University of Victoria. The Project team felt it was critical to avoid the temptation, given the tight timeline, to just take existing ECCE curricula and add a few cultural artifacts to make it 'culturally appropriate'. Such practices of superficial 'add-ons' had, in the eyes of the curriculum development team and MLTC, been justifiably criticized in the literature.

The question of how to proceed in this largely uncharted domain was the major challenge to the curriculum development team, and it was at this point that the partnership began to move from an agreement on paper and in principle to a true test of reliance, one on the other. The nature of the partnership was forged in the early months of the Project as the curriculum development team, in co-operation with and support from the MLTC, sought to define the nature of what would become a unique curriculum design and process; the quality of the partnership and the product were tempered through the partners' combined efforts to operationalize the new model. Through the process of development and application numerous personal and professional commitments as well as friendships were established between the two organizations extending from administrative through to delivery levels. These commitments proved to be critical to the unification of the two organizations into a strong and meaningful partnership.

As a result of these significant, and often personally felt commitments, it became increasingly less adequate, over time, to describe the Model and the Partnership in dispassionate and objective terms; such a description would exclude the 'spirit' of the partnership which had become so central to its character and success. When approaching the federal government for extended financial support for the Project, beyond its initial three-year period, the words of the academic partner in describing the Project came out in non-academic images and in a story form – the story of an odyssey, an image of a little boat on a big sea. That story follows to provide both a description, and some of the flavour, of the Project as viewed by the lead author.

Presentation to Federal Departments' Representatives, February 1993

As we co-operatively began our planning work for the education and training aspect of the Project, and as we considered our review of the literature on First Nations post-secondary education and child care training, it increasingly seemed that the Project must enter uncharted waters if we were to accomplish our objectives. We knew that there were many challenges ahead. We knew that we would encounter times of rough seas, times where some of us would not be paddling in unison with the others, times where fog would obscure our vision. We also knew that we needed to come up with some way that we could stay on course, despite the challenges that lay ahead.

Meadow Lake and UVic (SCYC) decided to bring together a small group of advisers who were not a part of the boat, but who might be able to help us identify how we could prepare for the journey. We all (MLTC, SCYC and Advisory members) met on two occasions late in 1990 and once early in 1991; what emerged from those meetings was a set of guiding principles which we would come to use as 'stars' to guide our way. Some of the principles were integral aspects of either UVic, MLTC or the collaboration. Others followed from discussions with the consultative group. The seventh, *The Generative Curriculum Model*, was the conceptual structure and process plan designed to give life to the principles and the curriculum.

Those principles became the guide for our curriculum work. We believed that if we stayed true to them, no matter where we ended up, it would be a better place than what we had found in the First Nations early childhood literature and what we had found in post-secondary education practice. The principles are:

1. *The Community Initiated/Community Based Approach:*

The first principle was largely established by the nature of our coming together and confirmed in our early discussions. The initiative was MLTC's, and we both considered community-based education as the way to proceed.

2. *The SCYC Scope of Child and Youth Care Services:*

The professional scope of the School of Child and Youth Care was part of the appeal of our program to MLTC. Although child day care was the immediate focus of the Project, the broader range of services to children, youth and their families within the scope of Child and Youth Care was of great interest and relevance to MLTC.

3. *The Educational and Career Ladder:*

The education and career ladder was also of great interest to MLTC. The Council did not want their community members to pursue 1 or 2 year programs that might lead to an academic dead-end of non-transferable credits. Ours was a step-on/step-off, four-year degree, education and career ladder (see Figure 8.1).

A CHILD AND YOUTH CARE CAREER AND EDUCATIONAL LADDER		
COURSE WORK	PROFESSIONAL	RESPONSIBILITY
A 40 hour Introduction to becoming a Family Day Care Provider	**Pre-Professional**	Daily operation of a FDC program under central agency supervision
10 month, Certificate level, ECCE educational course work and supervised practica	**Para-Professional** ECCE – Level 1	Assist, under supervision, in child care group program (day care centre)
10 month, Diploma level, ECCE educational course work and supervised practica	**Professional** ECCE – Level 2	Lead the delivery of daily activities and care for normative 2 to 5 year olds
3rd year Child and Youth Care Courses	**Professional** ECCE – CYC/Level 3	Planning, funding, and supervision activities for normative or specialized child populations
4 year, Baccalaureate Degree in Child and Youth Care	**Professional** ECCE – CYC/Level 4	Planning, funding, and supervision activities for various child and youth care programs

FIGURE 8.1

4. Bi-Culturalism:

Bi-cultural respect and learning was fully supported by both partners. One of the Elders described it as two sides of a feather – an understanding of majority culture, values and practices, and First Nations culture, values and practices.

5. Empowerment:

This principle reflected the desire to move away from a deficit oriented, 'sickness' perspective, to a strengths identification approach using *strengths* as the building blocks for child, family and community development.

6. *The Child as an Ecological Focus:*

An ecological framework of interactive systems and system levels is central to much of the work of the Project. The framework sees children and children's well-being as central to the well-being of families and of communities.

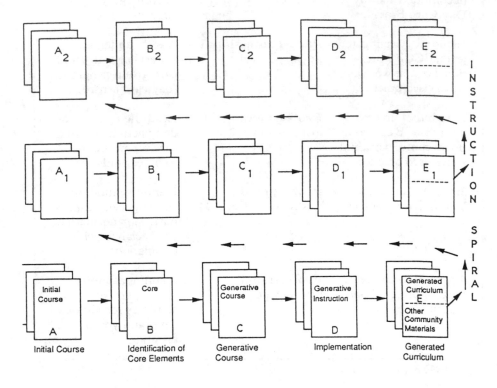

FIGURE 8.2: *Generative Curriculum: The Spiral Model*

7. The Generative Curriculum Model:

The seventh component of the principles work was a conceptual model to operationalize the principles-driven curriculum. The basic structure is a spiralling model that successively builds on culturally appropriate information generated in the preceding deliveries of the courses. The spiral structure rests on the foundation of the seven principles (see Figure 8.2).

I will come back to the principles and the Generative Curriculum Model a little later on in our agenda, but right now what I'd like to do is to 'fast forward' our little boat on the big sea: through all of the storms of operationalizing the principles; past the doldrums when new people would arrive and need to be oriented to the boat and its mission; and through the static of miscommunications that inevitably occur, to where we are today, two and a half years into the Project.

I am very excited by the place we have come to. It appears to be nothing less than a new shore: a new approach to First Nations post-secondary education and to the preparation of students to work with young children, their families and communities. It is an exciting place to find ourselves, but we need your help to go ashore. Not all of the mountains, valleys and shoreline are clearly visible from our vantage point in the boat, but here are some characteristics that *do* exist and which we *can* describe:

- It is a place where students are allowed to remain rooted in or near their communities and are not required to move far away for months or years at a time.
- It is a place where students can apply what they learn, on a daily basis, with their own people and in their own communities.
- It is a place where students can step off a career ladder to pursue professional employment and step back on to pursue degree work.
- It is a place where both majority and First Nations information is valued.
- It is a place where a mainstream University and a First Nations Tribal Council work in co-operation, harmony and trust.
- It is a place where Elders play a key role in contributing to curriculum, to students and to children's and communities' development.
- It is a place where students, Elders and teachers are all instructors and are all learners.
- It is a place where communities take the responsibility for defining and describing the caregiving practices and standards that they will follow.
- It is a place where strengths, rather than weaknesses, are considered the appropriate starting place for developing strong children, strong families and strong communities.
- It is a place that provides many new things to learn, not just for First Nations and Universities, but more broadly for 'any community' and any post-secondary institution.

In short, what we have discovered thus far on our shared voyage is the outline of an alternative landscape – a land form influenced by a different set of principles than those we typically experience. It is a landscape that, in my opinion, offers great promise at a time when we need promising alternatives.

(Pence, 1993)

The opening comments on the Project contained in the story recounted above were augmented later in the day with details of the Generative Curriculum Model. Those comments have been paraphrased below to provide the reader with a sense of the process entailed in the Generative Curriculum Model.

The saga of the Project, conveyed in the boat story, contains parallels for an understanding of the Generative Curriculum Model (GCM) as well: both the Project and the Model can be understood in terms of the 'mechanics': of meeting, of planning – of writing, of teaching; and both can be understood at the level of a journey, the meta-level accomplishment of performing the 'mechanics'.

The initial mechanics of the Generative Curriculum Model are reasonably straightforward: Step 1, an identification of certain courses that have been identified by institutions and authorities as requirements to receive academic and professional credentials; Step 2, an analysis of these courses to identify key concepts and content that must be included in the curriculum to receive the credentials. (Thus far the GCM does not deviate from mainstream curriculum orthodoxy, however . . .). Step 3 acknowledges that these key concepts and content are culturally embedded and that other cultures may have similar or dissimilar concepts and learnings. For example, in the team's research for a child development course, course writers came across a Navajo developmental chart, showing an ages and stages structure not unlike a chart for Erikson or Piaget, but emphasizing the child's development of spirituality and a sense of community-belonging, both important issues in a Navajo child's development. Such a chart did not exist in writing within the MLFNs, but all partners felt that the 'generation' of such information was of critical concern. Step 4 addressed the question of how the Generative Curriculum Model would work within the class. Clearly the traditional didactic learning structure of instructor as fount of all learning and students as passive receptacles was inappropriate for, in this course, students *and* instructors had much to learn. The appropriate source of community-specific information for the MLFN were the Elders, and in some cases other community members. In the Generative Curriculum Model Elders are an integral part of the weekly course structure; their knowledge, experience and wisdom is a critically important and respected part of the curriculum, as is learning from 'mainstream' western sources.

The final 'mechanism' of the Generative Curriculum Model, Step 5, is the collection of the generated material that comes from the Elders, from the communities, and from the students in forms (videos, tapes and print) that can be passed on into the next iteration of the course and become a part of an ever evolving and growing curriculum that includes valued and useful information from both mainstream and community perspectives. The result of the Generative Curriculum process was the outcome desired by the MLTC programme graduates as they were prepared to work either on- or off-reserve, with children and families from either aboriginal or non-aboriginal heritage.

Descriptively, the mechanics and processes of the GCM are fairly straightforward; operationally, putting that description into practice, is challenging. Almost a year and a half of the Project had passed, with a number of courses tested in the field, before the curriculum team felt it had a solid, consistent approach to operationalizing the principles. Instructors, students and course writers as well wrestled with this new approach to post-secondary learning.

The end result of the challenges: the challenge to break with the typical, the known, the secure; the challenge to identify principles that could chart and guide a new approach; the challenge to devise a model that could incorporate the identified principles; the challenge to operationalize the model both in curriculum and instruction; the challenge to hear from the community and to understand its strengths; and the challenge to learn while doing, resulted in a Model that transcended its mechanics, that became more than the sum of its parts. What emerged from the MLTC Project and the Generative Curriculum Model was an evaluation and a contextualization of western practice: for example, information in the valuable and influential document *Developmentally Appropriate Practice* (Bredekamp, 1987) was balanced by what the GCM team members referred to as 'Community Appropriate Practice' (Mulligan, 1993). Curricula that are not respectful of cultural diversity, that do not acknowledge that there are many trails that lead up the mountain, cannot expect to generate the pride and self-respect necessary to develop caring caregivers. In the words of one of the students for an assignment on professional values:

> Respecting the dignity and worth of each individual will reflect who you are as a person . . . A caregiver will build trust and good working relationships among co-workers and parents if she treats them with care, understanding, and with great respect.

As identified in summative evaluations (Cook, 1993; Jette, 1993a), the process of the Generative Curriculum Model had a ripple effect that spread well beyond the students, the courses and those immediately involved, to touch the lives of children, families and other community members, in ways that were not fully foreseen. In a manner reminiscent of the eloquent words of the National Grand Chief of the Assembly of First Nations, Ovide Mercredi, this Project moved beyond the lives of those immediately involved:

> When you heal a child, you heal a family;
> When you heal a family, you heal a community;
> When you heal a community, you heal a nation.
>
> (Mercredi, 1991)

The overtures to the federal government to provide additional funds to further develop and understand the Model were successful, and an additional nineteen months of funding were made available to the MLTC/SCYC partnership. In addition, the Province of British Columbia became interested in the Project in late 1991. The province provided community needs assessment dollars in

1992, and in 1993 provided funds for a second pilot with the First Nations of the Cowichan Tribes located on Vancouver Island in British Columbia. This second pilot was a critical next step in the evolution of the Model, a test of its transferability to a culturally dissimilar First Nations community and a test of the ability of the partnership model to extend to a three-way collaboration among: a First Nations community, a College course-delivery partner, and the University curriculum development partner. While it is too early for a full evaluation of this three-way partnership, the early signs are positive. Given those positive signs, and the prior success of the original partnership with MLTC, the stage is set for a national, multi-site pilot involving First Nations and post-secondary delivery institutions in various parts of the country, working in a series of three-way partnerships with the curriculum team at the School of Child and Youth Care, University of Victoria.

REFLECTIONS ON NOT KNOWING AND ON THE PARTNERSHIP

Returning to the original partnership between MLTC and SCYC which laid the groundwork for that which followed, a central paradox emerges: that the success of the Project is based as much, or more, on the partners' awareness and appreciation of what is not known, as on what is known. Neither the Tribal Council nor the School had an awareness of the issues the other faced on a day-to-day basis, nor of the knowledge that was necessary to operate effectively in the other's milieu. That knowledge came to the Project by way of the partnership. It was this *acknowledged lack of knowledge* that was essential to the formation of a strong partnership – a partnership based as firmly on necessity as on desire.

Just as firmly, each respected that the other partner did know its own environment, was effective in that other environment, and would utilize that knowledge and effectiveness in support of the partnership and the overarching objectives of the Project. Such trust is not a given, it is both gained and learned. Gained over time through small but consequential acts; learned over time as one sees, hears and learns about the other and the environment of the other. Slowly a fuller picture of the partner and its environment emerged, and slowly trust was tested and established.

Early in the Project's history a pooling of the partners' knowledge bases indicated that there were relatively few successful experiences that could guide the development of this particular initiative. The review of the literature by SCYC produced little in the way of exemplary early childhood and child and youth care post-secondary programmes. Likewise, MLTC's collective experience of post-secondary educational programmes produced little that was deemed exemplary and some that had been problematic.

Somewhat surprisingly, the effect of this infertile search of the literature and recollection of experience was not restricting, but freeing! What both reviews suggested, was the need for new and innovative approaches to First Nations post-secondary education. Furthermore, both the MLTC experience and the review of the literature suggested that little would be lost, and potentially much gained, through trying new approaches.

The effect of that awareness was to reinforce to an even greater degree the reliance that each partner must place in the other. If there were no existing maps to use as guides, each was all the more dependent on the resources and the resourcefulness of the partner. Our freedom to explore would be limited only by our collective creativity, our vision, and our ability to support the other.

We had by that time begun to forge another characteristic of the Project, a willingness to take risks and to depend on the support of our partner in doing so. For the SCYC team this risk-taking involved a 'realigning' of the Project's primary allegiances away from the university institutional structure and mores, which it was felt would inevitably prove too inflexible and slow-moving if we were to be able to follow smoothly the requirements of the new partnership. Such a realignment of allegiances carries the potential of institutional wrath, but the review work that had been undertaken provided a solid argument against orthodoxy and for innovation. Such a decision to turn from traditional, institutional responses to pursue new and untested approaches to meeting a community's needs could not have been undertaken without a growing sense of trust and a belief in the combined strength of the partnership.

The MLTC also took risks in working with their new academic partner. The experience of many First Nations in attempting to work with academic institutions has been problematic, and in many cases there is a distrust of non-aboriginally controlled institutions. MLTC was not exempt from voices of concern, both from within and external to their organization. At a number of points along the way, critics of the partnership emerged. Time was needed to show the merits and the potential of the partnership, and the cost of buying that time was shouldered by the MLTC and SCYC Project leaders.

In the early months of the three-year funding period instructors were hired, students commenced studies, and course writers developed curricula, not on the basis of a full and informed plan, but on the basis of a willingness to take risks in pursuit of the Project's objectives, and a commitment to engage in on-going evaluation in pursuit of better and clearer processes and products. Risk, trust, error and evolving support were the essence of the early period of the Project.

As noted earlier, a Project does not develop on a foundation of risk and trust without moving beyond the rational to embrace the emotional. A high level of personal caring emerged to join the project objective of 'quality care', imbuing the latter with personal sentiment and commitment. The Project became more than a partnership effort to develop a culturally relevant curriculum, it became itself a caring environment. In that transformation the traditional separation between researcher and subject, university and community began to dissolve. As it dissolved it became easier to see, to understand, and to be in the other's world, and to appreciate more fully what quality truly meant both to oneself and to the other. Quality had to do with a state of mind and a state of being. It had much more to do with ways of measuring things internally and subjectively, than externally and objectively. As noted by Ms Debbie Jette, Commencement Speaker at the student graduation ceremony in June 1993, quality was not just a moment in time, measurable, replicable and quantifiable, but rather what that moment meant 'looking ahead seven generations and back seven generations' (Jette, 1993b). If the quality of that moment could meet that test, then the quality was good. These are tests of quality not found in western academic literature. The School would not have looked for them, nor seen or felt them, without our partner's guidance.

Clearly this Project and Partnership have significant personal meaning to the principal author and to other members of the SCYC and MLTC teams, and the partnership approach and the Generative Curriculum Model are of potential value in a variety of cross-cultural, post-secondary education applications. But there is another dimension to this experience, one which has much broader relevance to child care researchers in their understanding of quality child care. That other dimension, a missing element in most western child care research, lies at the heart of caring.

REFLECTIONS ON PARTNERSHIPS AND QUALITY CARE RESEARCH

The single greatest value of partnership research to the study of quality child care is the opportunity that partnerships provide for caring to occur within the research enterprise itself. That component is critical, for without the light of caring, that which is sought may well be lost. This 'finding' of the MLTC/SCYC Project cannot be found in the 'data' of the Project. Its accuracy cannot be tested, its understanding is elusive. Its 'truth' is as indefinable as caring itself – its presence must be felt, for it cannot be objectively observed or measured.

Entry into the world of 'caring research' is a step through the looking glass of 'research on caring'. The tools, the rules and the 'way things are', are different on the two sides. It is a place that, like the MLTC/SCYC partnership, is largely uncharted. And like that partnership, it requires a leap of faith to enter and explore it. But even at this very early stage of exploration, there is a strong sense that in order to understand quality caring, one must possess the 'quality of caring'.

Undertaking 'caring research', possessed of a 'quality of caring', is not a traditional value within research and academic communities. Such perspectives and positions are not a part of western science, western objectivity, and western rationality. They speak of mysticism, faith and the immeasurable. But then again, is caring measurable? Is it not, at least in part, transcendant? Is using scientific instruments and methodologies to understand caring, not, in some way, akin to searching for God with a telescope?

Clearly there is a land beyond the looking glass of western rationality and science that has yet to be explored in our search for understanding quality care. And also, quite clearly, there are dangers there for those who make their living as academics and researchers. But even on the 'safe side' of the mirror, the world of western science, there is much that research has yet to learn about quality care, and this research too could be facilitated by partnership activities.

LIMITATIONS OF RESEARCH ON QUALITY CARE

The limitations that exist in research on quality care stem largely from researchers' failure to appreciate the broader ecology of child care – to place themselves outside the micro-system of the child's immediate environment. Early in the field's history, child care science became monopolized by a psychologically oriented, positivist model of research. While extremely valuable, the information resulting from this approach tends to be narrowly child-centred, micro-system focused, outcomes oriented and contextually limited. The broader social, cultural and historical elements of quality care research have been and continue to be underdeveloped in the western literature and in particular the North American literature. The self-contained, scientifically controlled model of western positivist empirical study is restricted in its ability to perceive and understand social and cultural assumptions, values and mores outside its practitioners' own traditions and orientations. Such research is problematic not so much for its generation of wrong answers, as for limitations in its posing of questions. The current literature on quality care is problematic both in its assumptions of what constitutes desirable developmental universals, and in its restricted understandings of diverse environments, social change and cultural diversity.

The compelling questions that relate to the realization of quality care in contemporary North American society cannot be adequately understood without shifting from a search for 'quality universals' to a search for 'quality perspectives'. Such a transition requires movement away from the ever finer measurement of micro-system environmental variables to an awareness and appreciation of quality care perspectives as held by an expanded reference group, including not only caregivers, parents and children, but also employers, elected officials, licensing officers, opinion leaders and others in the meso-, exo- and macro-systems of the child care ecology. Many of these perspectives are at present lacking in the research literature on quality care, and while these broader perspectives remain absent, those who wish to develop a campaign for improved care quality will be at a profound disadvantage as they lack critical information regarding the socio-political environment in which they must act.

The points made above can be seen as one potential form of partnership research, an intra-cultural research approach that would seek to include a diversity of perspectives. There is much that child care research has to learn from the broad circle of child care stakeholders. However, the expanded list of stakeholders provided is clearly western in its conceptualization. In order to generate a relevant cross-cultural list of stakeholders, the MLTC/SCYC Project would suggest that an inter-cultural partnership is required. While at one level one could argue that a cultural informant would be able to generate such a list, at another level the realization of a caring project requires much more than information. It was largely through the realization of vulnerability, the *need for* and not just the *desire for* a partner, that established the critical ingredients of risk, trust, faith and ultimately, caring, to occur within the MLTC/SCYC Project itself. And it was through the realization of caring within the partnership that the manifestation of caring through the partnership became possible.

This paper would argue that in cross-cultural child care projects, where the objective is culturally appropriate quality care, the means of developing care and the ends of achieving care must be understood as one. Indeed, in both inter- and intra-cultural quality care projects the means and ends of caring must be evidenced.

CONCLUSION

The partnership work of the MLTC/SCYC Project has opened many doors previously not noticed by those involved. Each door required a level of awareness, faith, trust and commitment that would not have been possible outside a partnership model. Through the dynamic of the partnership, caring itself entered the Project and an activity that had begun, in part, as research on caring, became caring research.

The transformation was a profound one that lies beyond the pale of western scientific traditions. Yet, how can we come to know caring, a most powerful and delicate phenomenon, without bringing its quality into our work? How can we measure caring, when we do not know it?

Caring relationships present great challenges to western science and western ways of understanding: for they cannot be built, they must be nurtured; they cannot be imposed, they must be desired; they cannot be seen, they must be felt. They are in opposition to many tenets of western science and culture, but without them our understanding of caring will be forever elusive and fragmentary.

REFERENCES

BREDEKAMP, S. (1987) *Developmentally Appropriate Practice in Early Childhood Programs*, National Association for the Education of Young Children, Washington: DC.

COOK, P. (1993) *Curriculum Evaluation for the MLTC/SCYC Career Ladder Project*, Unpublished manuscript, School of Child and Youth Care, University of Victoria.

GREENWOOD-CHURCH, M. and PENCE, A. R. (1990) *A Curriculum Review of Native Indian Early Childhood and Child and Youth Care Education and Training Materials*, Unpublished manuscript, School of Child and Youth Care, University of Victoria.

JETTE, D. I. (1993a) *Meadow Lake Tribal Council Indian Child Care Program Evaluation*, Unpublished manuscript, Meadow Lake Tribal Council.

JETTE, D. I. (1993b) *Address to the Graduating Class*, Unpublished manuscript, Meadow Lake Tribal Council.

MEADOW LAKE TRIBAL COUNCIL (1989) *MLTC Program Report*, Unpublished manuscript, Meadow Lake Tribal Council.

MEADOW LAKE TRIBAL COUNCIL and SCHOOL OF CHILD AND YOUTH CARE (1989) *Indian Child Care Education and Career Ladder Proposal*, Unpublished manuscript, Meadow Lake Tribal Council.

MERCREDI, O. (1991) Assembly of First Nations meeting, *Vancouver Sun*, 20 June.

MULLIGAN, V. (1993) *Cross-Cultural Program Planning*, Workshop presented at the North-West Territories Day Care Symposium, September 1993, Yellowknife: NWT.

PENCE, A. R. (1993) *Presentation to Federal Departments' Representatives: A Boat Story*, Unpublished manuscript, School of Child and Youth Care, University of Victoria.

PENCE, A. R., KEUHNE, V., GREENWOOD-CHURCH, M. and OPEKOKEW, M. R. (1993) Generative curriculum: a model of university and first nations co-operative post-secondary education, *International Journal of Educational Development*, Vol. 13, no. 4, pp. 339–49.

CHAPTER 9

The New Zealand Experience of Charter Development in Early Childhood Services

ANNE B. SMITH AND SARAH-EVE FARQUHAR

In the late 1980s, New Zealand embarked on a significant reform to its provision and regulation of early childhood services. A major element in that reform was the initiation of a system of charters designed to recognize the diversity of programmes, philosophies and cultures within New Zealand while balancing support for that diversity with certain national values and objectives. Anne Smith and Sarah-Eve Farquhar describe the history and implementation of the chartering system, highlighting the key dynamic of how a change in government can fundamentally alter the nature and direction of reform.

INTRODUCTION

Chartering is a process where various stakeholders (parents, staff and the community) are given the opportunity to define quality at the individual centre level in negotiation with a government agency. The intent of the process is to strike a balance between centrally determined criteria of quality and the philosophy and local needs of centres. The government agency retains its right to insist on certain aspects of quality while encouraging the individual services to codify their own values and goals. The charter forms the basis for accountability procedures which determine whether centres meet their stated goals.

New Zealand has experienced a transformation in its early childhood services in the 1980s and 1990s (Dalli, 1990; Dalli, 1992; Meade and Dalli, 1991; Smith, 1992). One of the toughest issues faced was how to improve the general quality of early childhood services while at the same time retaining New Zealand's strong tradition of cultural and philosophical diversity among different early childhood groups. This chapter evaluates the New Zealand early childhood experience of charters in the light of how successful they have been in balancing local centre and service values against administrative definitions of quality.

REFORMS TO EARLY CHILDHOOD SERVICES IN NEW ZEALAND

The charter is one aspect of a recent series of administrative changes to the education system in New Zealand. In order to understand these changes it is necessary to provide the reader with some brief historical background.

Early childhood services in New Zealand have had a long history of state funding and are numerous, comprising more than 25 varieties which have been developed in an ad hoc manner. Centres and services were set up in response to local needs but a few strong national movements provide a network of organization and support. Development has been based on community initiatives, in a context of a bewildering and inequitable variety of funding and monitoring mechanisms (Meade, 1988); and administration by two government departments, Education and Social Welfare. A consensus developed in the 1970s that there was a need for a more integrated system of care and education and a necessity for an educational component in child care centres. It was argued that children had a right to good quality, well-funded early childhood education no matter which type of centre they attended (Cook, 1985; Smith and Swain, 1988).

Education came on to the political agenda of the 1980s, despite the strengthening ideology of free-market thinking which influenced developments at the time (Meade, 1991a). Anne Meade argued that the new government policy which developed for early childhood was the result of an 'accumulated discourse' from the years of previous reports and discussions which were for the first time influencing bureaucratic government structures. Two very important changes towards a more integrated system were the transfer of administrative responsibility for child care from the Social Welfare Department to the Education Department in 1986, and the introduction of three-year training for early childhood staff in colleges of education in 1987.

In what has been called a 'quiet revolution' (Burns, 1989) New Zealand education in the late 1980s and early 1990s was radically restructured, as had been the case in other areas such as agriculture, defence and taxation. The release of the Meade Report, entitled *Education to be More*, in 1988 followed a similar report (the Picot Report) on the restructuring of primary and secondary schools. There were aspects to Meade's recommendations which were constrained by reforms to the school system, particularly the move towards a devolved administrative structure. The government response to the Meade Report was entitled *Before Five* (Lange, 1988). *Before Five* followed a widespread and serious attempt to consult with all early childhood organizations to produce the best and most acceptable decisions possible.

Changes to early childhood education implemented in October 1989 with the adoption of *Before Five* were to structure, funding, control over quality and training. The Ministry of Education provides funding and overall policy for early childhood education, the Education Review Office monitors centres (and schools) and ensures accountability, and the Early Childhood Development Unit provides advice and in-service training.

New Zealand, like many other countries, has been influenced by the literature on the importance of quality early childhood centre environments (e.g. Caldwell, 1986; Holloway and Reichart-Erickson, 1989; Phillips, McCartney and Scarr, 1987; Vandell and Corasaniti, 1990; Whitebook, Howes and Phillips, 1989) for ensuring optimal child development outcomes. Yet the early childhood constituency in New Zealand has a strong and divergent value base which has been articulated in documents such as the Meade Report and *Te Whariki*, the recently released Early Childhood Curriculum Guidelines (Carr and May, 1992). The Meade Report acknowledges the importance of research-based criteria of quality such as staff: child ratios, group size and caregiver qualifications, but in addition has a section on 'The Value Base of the Working Group'. Amongst the values mentioned are the importance of implementing the Treaty of Waitangi[1] and cultural survival and transmission to succeeding generations. Other values outlined in the report included improved social and economic status for women, enhancement of the family, safeguarding of human rights and freedoms, and supporting and recognizing Pacific Island and other minority cultures.

THE CHARTER

A 'charter' is defined as a contract between the Ministry of Education and the individual centre, drawn up through consultation with parents and the community. Charter documents contain an outline of centre policies, philosophies, and characteristics. They are required to specify in what ways and how the individual centre intends to work towards standards of higher quality than the minimum licensing level. The charter is a quality assurance mechanism for the government. The funding of individual centres from Vote: Education is linked to the development and approval of charters with the Ministry according to the level of quality the government is prepared to support.

(Farquhar, 1991a, p. 526)

Meade (1991b) saw the charter as an opportunity for staff, managers and parents to reflect on the goals of the early childhood centre and the way that those goals could be achieved. It was hoped that the philosophy and local needs of each centre would be written into its charter. A pamphlet (1990) about charter development published by the *Before Five* committee suggested that the charter was unique to each individual centre and that parents' input was an important part of the charter. Centres were told that charters would not be approved without evidence that parents, staff and the community were consulted.

The charter requires that you have a say in the quality and style of care and education being provided ... Each centre will develop its own charter through meetings and discussions between the management, staff, parents and whanau[2] of the children who attend.

(*Before Five* pamphlet, 1990, p. 1)

Initially the charter had to meet National Guidelines as set out in a Management Handbook which was distributed to all centres. The Handbook noted that nine topics were to be addressed in charters: Charter and Review Procedures; The Learner; Special Needs Children; Health, Safety and Environment; Relationships with Parents/Whanau; Treaty of Waitangi; Equity; Staff Development and Advisory Support; Land and Buildings. Each topic started with a non-negotiable principle and description of what should be included in management plans in order to achieve each principle. The requirements for quality which had to be incorporated into centre charters were greater than previous requirements. Centres which met minimum standards and had a charter committing themselves to higher standards of quality were eligible for government funding. (Minimum standards had to be met to acquire a licence but did not guarantee funding.)

When the policy was first introduced, National Guidelines in the Management Handbook set out standards of staffing, curriculum, advisory support and minimum physical plant requirements. The guidelines suggested a ratio of 1:3 for under-2-year-olds, 1:5 for 2-year-olds and 1:8 for 3- to 5-year-olds in child care or 1:10 for sessional centres. Group size was to be no greater than 25. A trained staff member was required to be with any group of children at all times. Although the final charter requirements fell short of the ideal they were a genuine attempt to move centres towards better quality standards.

Since the *Before Five* changes came into effect, the state has funded about 50 per cent of the upfront costs of early childhood centres (the level varying with the particular service) (Gardiner, 1991). Funding is on the basis of child contact hours and funds are paid in bulk to each centre by the Ministry. Funding in 1990 was $7.25 per hour per child under two and $2.25 per child over two (up to a maximum of 30 hours). Funding increases in child care were to some extent reflected in lower fees for parents, but also in greatly improved salaries and working conditions for staff. In effect there was a substantial increase of funding – a 65 per cent increase in funding between 1989 ($73.8 million) and 1990 ($112.8 million).

Further funding increases were promised by the government to be phased in bringing other early childhood centres to the same level as kindergarten by 1994. By 1994 all early childhood services were to be on the same hourly rate as the funding level for kindergartens (about $3.40 an hour). Funding subsidies were (and still are) available for low income families through the Social Welfare Department.

While the Ministry of Education is responsible for checking that centres meet minimum standards, the Educational Review Office monitors whether centres are meeting their charter commitments. The Review Office visits centres every two years (for approximately two days) and then prepares a report on the centre, which is available to the public. In the case of criticisms there is no automatic triggering of any action (such as visits from advisory support agencies). If, however, the ERO report shows that there are serious problems with a centre it is the Ministry of Education's responsibility to follow this up or withdraw the centre's licence until the problems are remedied.

Since the *Before Five* reforms of 1989 the Labour government has been succeeded by a National government. Although the essentials of the reforms have been retained, there have been some major losses, all of which impact on the achievement of higher quality. Not long (about a month) after centres had completed the laborious process of negotiating charters under the Management Handbook guidelines, the Handbook was superseded by another document called *The Statement of Desirable Objectives and Practices* (known as DOPS). The introduction of this much less stringent and vaguer document removed the necessity for quality to be higher than minimum standards. Also reference to various value issues (such as the Treaty of Waitangi) were removed. An example of how DOPS drew back from encouraging higher quality (and higher cost) programmes was the lack of mention of staff/child ratios in DOPS. Hence there is now no necessity for ratios to be better than the 1:5 for under 2s set out in the minimum standards. Secondly the phased increase of funding which was outlined in 1990 was frozen. The 1990 budget cut $18 million from funding for under-2-year-olds so that the hourly funding for this age group is now $4.50 (rather than $7.25). There was also some watering down of requirements for training and an increase in fee subsidies through the Department of Social Welfare for parents who could not afford the full cost of child care fees. These moves all signalled less commitment to high quality early childhood education (Dalli, 1993) and sparked fears of a return to Social Welfare based funding for child care.

RESEARCH ON CHARTER DEVELOPMENT

The chartering process has been the subject of very little empirical research but a great deal of theoretical analysis by policy researchers. Most of this theoretical work relates to primary and secondary schools (e.g. Codd and Gordon, 1991; Dale and Jesson, 1992; Middleton, 1992; Nash, 1989). Most analysts argue that the motivation for the reforms, including the charter, came from the domination of New Right ideas (mainly from Treasury and the State Services Commission) in contemporary educational politics. Nash (1989) believes that the restructuring of educational administration generally had the clear objective 'to achieve greater control of essential functions and to withdraw from intervention when it cannot be successful' (p. 119).

Nash saw the reforms as having a dual function of both state control and community participation which enabled central government to concentrate on the essential functions of policy-making and fiscal and managerial control while throwing back the problems of the school on to the community. Codd and Gordon (1991) also saw the reforms as designed to 'produce a decentralization of responsibility for resource allocation while maintaining centrally determined regulation of supply' (p. 22). They cite a number of late changes in the legal basis for the charter which removed the government's responsibility to fund schools: (this became an 'undertaking' rather than an 'agreement'). Dale and Jesson (1992) saw the reforms as a drive towards management efficiency and accountability rather than solving education issues. They describe a lack of educational vision and a system where educational decisions were made by 'non educationally-informed' people. Policy analysts seem agreed that the charter process used the rhetoric of partnership and community involvement to increase the regulatory power of the state.

It is unclear to what extent the critical policy analysis carried out in relation to schools applies to the very different policy context of early childhood education. The school system within New Zealand had been a relatively homogeneous, centrally controlled system which had received substantial government support. In contrast early childhood centres received much less government support, were subject to minimal government control and were heterogeneous. The context of early childhood education was also one in which there was some degree of consensus that changes towards a more fair and equitable system and higher overall standards of quality were required. Also early childhood centres on the whole (except for the private sector) were much more accustomed to a degree of community and parent participation and responsibility in decision-making.

A further factor which supported a climate for change was that the Early Childhood Working Party was chaired by Anne Meade, a person who had wide credibility and acceptance from early childhood educators and who was known to be committed to the needs of early childhood in New Zealand. According to May (1991) the ticket of entry for early childhood to receive its share of newly apportioned educational cake had been the acceptance of restructuring and devolution on the Picot model. Nevertheless she argues that the thrust of the Meade Report was towards supporting policies that had been fought for by many women for decades:

> The Meade Report incorporated and coalesced many of the strands and dreams early childhood advocates had lobbied for over the years and which had been documented and developed in numerous working groups and abandoned reports.
>
> (ibid., p. 8)

The Meade Report was a thorough attempt to provide real solutions to the many problems of the early childhood education system.

Farquhar's research (1991, 1993) constitutes one of the few studies which looked at the impact of the chartering process on centres from the perspective of parents and staff in early childhood centres. Sarah Farquhar's doctoral study of the charter development process in early childhood centres in Dunedin in 1990 coincided very fortuitously with the time when early childhood centres were involved in drafting their charters. A brief description of the main types of centres in New Zealand is necessary in order to explain the sample selection and composition for Sarah's study.

New Zealand has a very diverse early childhood system which has one of the highest participation rates in the world. Ninety-three per cent of 4-year-olds, 73 per cent of 3-year-olds, 38 per cent of 2-year-olds and 17 per cent of 1-year-olds were enrolled in early childhood centres in 1992 (Ministry of Education, 1993). Most centres (86 per cent) are community non-profit centres, with 13 per cent commercial centres and 1.5 per cent provided directly by the state (Gardiner, 1991). The four largest early childhood centre types are briefly described here.

The service with the longest history is kindergarten which began in 1889 out of a background of charitable provision for the poor during a time of depression, added to by the ideas of Froebel and moral regeneration through pre-school education. Kindergartens are free early childhood services offering sessional part-time programmes for 3- and 4-year-olds, which cater for the largest percentage (34 per cent in 1989) of New Zealand children below compulsory school age. Kindergartens are virtually free to parents and until the 1989 reforms received the lion's share (about 70 per cent) of government expenditure on early childhood education.

Child care centres, a term for a broad array of types of centres, cater for the second largest number of children (27 per cent in 1990). They differ from playcentres and kindergartens because they include infants and toddlers and offer all-day sessions, but not all child care centres take infants and not all are all-day programmes. Government funding for child care centres gradually increased through the 1970s but in 1988/89 they still only received 15 per cent of government early childhood funding. Until 1986 child care centres were administered by the Social Welfare department but after that they were administered by the Education Department.

Playcentres cater for the third largest group of children, mainly over 2 ½-year-olds (23 per cent in 1990). Playcentres are parent run co-operatives with a strong philosophy of play-oriented progressive education. They are run on a voluntary self-help basis for up to three sessions a week. Playcentres are not regarded primarily as a service for children but as a parent education and support group. Playcentres received a small amount (4.5 per cent) of government funding for training, liaison and programmes before the 1989 reforms. Both playcentres and kindergartens have always been administered and funded by the Education Department.

The fourth main type of New Zealand early childhood centre is Nga Kohanga Reo or Maori language nests which catered for about 10 per cent of children in 1989. Unfortunately, kohanga reo could not be included in this part of the study because they were not required at that time to develop a charter.

There were four kindergartens, three child care centres and two playcentres in the sample. A small sample was chosen so that the charter development process could be looked at in depth in a diverse group of centres. The main method of data collection was participant observation during regular consultation processes and during meetings organized by the researcher. Three meetings of committee/management and staff representatives from nine centres were organized by Sarah. Committee, parent and staff meetings as well as informal functions (such as social evenings or family meals) were attended in order to observe the process of charter development for each centre. On three occasions this involved meetings in parents' homes. Mostly Sarah listened, watched and recorded at such occasions but participated whenever she was asked for assistance or had information which she felt was useful and relevant.

The three meetings of centre representatives to discuss charter development were organized by Sarah and held at a room in the university at strategic points in the process of charter development. The first was in early March when centres were beginning to develop their charters, the second was in May which was close to the Ministry of Education's deadline and a third in November after the draft charters had been negotiated with the Ministry. At the final meeting Sarah gave participants a written transcript of tape-recorded discussions of the previous meetings and a summary of the process of charter development in order that they could read, check, correct and add to

Sarah's record. This provided confirmatory evidence of the validity of the data collected through participant observation. Centres seemed motivated to attend these voluntary meetings even though they were held in the evening after a day's work. Although the purpose was in part to assist Sarah with her research, the meetings were also perceived by centres to be valuable to them in developing their charters, a process which was then quite new.

The charter writers

There were variations in who wrote the charters among and between early childhood services. At the child care centres, the management (committees or owners), director and staff had the major responsibility for writing the charter. Two of the three child care centres belonged to the New Zealand Childcare Association which provided them with useful information to guide them in writing their charter. These two centres also sought substantial parent input. The community child care centre wrote its own charter through seven fortnightly meetings of the director, staff and parents. By the time the final meeting arrived the one parent attending volunteered to incorporate notes from previous charters into the final copy which was then passed on to the director and executive committee for approval. The director and supervisor of a second (institution-based) community child care centre drafted the charter based on early consultations through a meeting and a survey of parent views. Staff worked on the drafts at regular staff meetings and this was made available and displayed for parents to read and approve. The owner of the only private child care centre wrote a draft charter which was circulated to staff and parents. She made minor revisions based on their feedback.

At kindergartens and playcentres charter preparation was treated as a combined staff, subcommittee or parent council responsibility. Because both kindergartens and playcentres belonged to umbrella organizations they received considerable input from their national organization (the Otago Playcentre Association and the Dunedin Kindergarten Association). This input consisted of a skeleton charter or framework to which individual centres could add additional components. The frameworks consisted of programme, philosophical and administrative statements. Kindergarten committees (consisting of parents) met regularly and took responsibility for shaping the charter with the association framework as the basis for their own documents. At one playcentre (an urban centre) four parents took most of the responsibility for writing the charter but checked regularly with parents at meetings. At the rural playcentre a wider group of parents participated in the writing, with most parents accepting responsibility for writing different sections. Everyone then got together to discuss ideas and drafts at a single meeting and the president and secretary later tidied up the drafts to produce their charter document.

The process of consultation

There were many variations in the methods of consultation and the number of people who participated in consultation and discussion in different centres.

These methods included written procedures such as displaying the charter on noticeboards, notices or newsletters sent home with children; more systematic data gathering procedures such as the use of questionnaires or telephone interviews; and more interactive procedures varying in formality from small subcommittees intensively working together and public meetings to informal conversations and social events. Formal meetings tended to evoke low turnouts despite advertising in local newspapers, shopping malls and community areas. Social events such as family teas, fish and chip evenings, parent lunches, and barbecues were also used. These tended to draw greater participation but sometimes lower task involvement as in the case of one family tea where the centre owner waved around a copy of the charter and asked people to sign that they had been consulted when they had not even read the final version. The evening was entirely devoted to social interaction without any discussion of the charter! Subgroups tended to be more effective but did involve more responsibility for a smaller group of parents and/or staff.

Many centres did not find it easy to get parents interested or involved in writing the charter. All centres experienced some difficulty in getting parents to participate and many lowered their expectations after an initial failed attempt. One teacher commented that parents had to be continually jollied along. Where centres held regular meetings, as in one centre that had seven meetings altogether, the attendance declined markedly with time. There were many meetings with a low attendance. The process of charter development was perceived as making large physical and emotional demands on staff and parent time. Parents had many other time commitments which influenced their willingness to take part, especially at child care centres where most parents (mainly mothers) were working full-time. Parents who had children at school were also being asked to participate in charter writing for their school. The most effective methods of consultation were those which were realistic in terms of the time that people could give, chose meeting times and formats which suited parents, and where the charter content was meaningful to parents (e.g. avoided bureaucratic or professional jargon).

Attitudes to the charter

The views expressed by centre supervisors at various points in the study certainly did not provide evidence of overwhelming enthusiasm for the charter. The view that this was 'just another piece of bureaucracy' and a requirement imposed from above was not uncommon. For example one staff member said:

> We were virtually told everything we had to do to develop and write in the charter. We were given so much information from the Association, the Ministry and the ECDU. In the end I felt I was just involved in a bureaucratic exercise.

Many people disliked the fact that there were major chunks of the charter (from the National Guidelines) which were non-negotiable and had to be incorporated. Most centres appeared to see the main motivation for writing the charter as to gain government funding. Indeed this was one argument which centres used to cajole parents to participate.

Some positive points did emerge. One centre saw the charter-development process as a useful exercise which was helpful for staff professional development and programme improvement. The playcentres not surprisingly, as they use a parent co-operative approach, were quite successful in involving parents in the process of charter writing, although they were not particularly keen on following requirements set down by a government department. Despite the difficulties and complaints, at all centres the charter had been a major topic of conversation at formal and informal meetings and in written communication for five months. It would be difficult for this not to have had some lasting effect on parent/staff relationships and understanding as well as practices and programmes.

Parents and staff (especially new staff) did learn more about the centre's philosophy and practices and staff learned more about parent and community views. Centres which had not really thought through or articulated their philosophy were forced to carry out this important task. In many cases the process of consulting over the charter raised awareness of the need for communication between parents and staff. Parent feedback resulted in the staff questioning some of their own views and practices or at least realizing that parents did not accept or understand aspects of the programme. Receiving feedback from parents sometimes had aversive results for staff as is illustrated by the response of one staff member to parent comments.

> They thought that we didn't talk to the fathers, only the mothers. And silly comments, like we had nowhere to welcome them or nowhere for them to sit. Well we've got a sofa.

In other cases parent comments led to staff giving parents a rationale about why they did certain things. For example, when a parent complained about sand clogging up the washing machine and questioned the need for a sandpit, teachers explained why they thought sand play was important for their programme and children's development. In some cases a major change of procedure emerged out of parent feedback. For example, in one kindergarten parents indicated that they did not feel that home visits were necessary so the centre adopted the policy of only home-visiting when the parents requested it.

The content

There were two main areas of contention about the content of charters – the Treaty of Waitangi and Special Needs sections. The Management Handbook required that there be acceptance of Maori values, customs and practices and that staff and parents/whanau should participate in courses on cross-cultural understanding so that they would know more about Maori language and culture. In the area of Special Needs, centres were required to make provision for children with special needs in a mainstreamed setting alongside other children. The playcentres did not disagree with these principles but at some of the kindergartens and childcare centres the Treaty of Waitangi and Special

Needs sections were debated. Generally the professional staff in centres showed more acceptance and understanding of the National Guidelines than the parents. A number of parents expressed reluctance to incorporate Maori culture giving such reasons as the lack of Maori children attending centres. One kindergarten had a partially separate 'special needs group' and preferred this system to full mainstreaming. Many of the kindergartens argued that they did not have the resources for mainstreaming because of their inadequate teacher/child ratios. The centres which argued that they did not have the resources for mainstreaming added sections to their charters saying that they would only accept special needs children if ancillary resources were available.

Changes to quality

The development of the charters did necessitate changes in practice to meet charter standards. For example, kindergartens had to greatly increase their drive to get parents involved. Kindergartens in New Zealand have either 2 or 3 teachers and 40 children per session so in order to meet the charter standards of 1:10 for sessional programmes parents had to be involved. Teachers were able to use the change in requirements to persuade parents that they had to take seriously the responsibility of parent helping or else be prepared to pay fees to hire additional staff. (Kindergartens did not receive any increase in funding with the reforms but they are virtually free to parents.) There was a move towards hiring qualified staff on the part of the child care centres. (This resulted nationally in a shortage of trained staff and considerable pressure on training organizations.) Sarah noted in 1991 that:

> The most obvious change has been a movement towards some te reo Maori and tikanga Maori. Consultation and discussion on the requirements in the Treaty of Waitangi section appears to have resulted in a growing acceptance of biculturalism in all centres (for example, Maori posters on walls and Maori language by staff in their interactions with the children). Two centres have now established links with the whanau of a Kohanga Reo in their community.
>
> (Farquhar, 1991b, p. 13)

After the stress of writing the charter was over it often came to be viewed as potentially useful as a reference document, a resource document and a tool for self-evaluation. It was a record of where the centre was coming from philosophically. One staff member said:

> Sometimes things get lost with changes in people and supervisors. We forget what has been done.

Charters are therefore seen by many as useful written documents which can help solve philosophical disputes between parents and staff. There is a general awareness that the charter is a legal document on which centres will be monitored and judged. One supervisor said:

It's made us accountable. We live with the expectation that one day ERO will walk in the door and we had better be doing what we state we are doing.

Follow-up

In August 1993, four years after the original study began, we conducted a small follow-up study by sending out questionnaires to the nine centres who participated in the original study. All centres returned the questionnaire. The questionnaire focused on the extent and nature of changes to charters since 1990 and of staff, parent and community involvement in any modifications. All of the responses except two indicated that the charter had been changed relatively recently (within the last twelve months). One playcentre and the one private child care centre in the study said that their charters were quite unchanged since the original study.

Centres were asked to rate on a 1 to 4 scale how major the charter changes had been (1 was minor and 4 was major). Two centres rated the changes made as minor (1) and the other five centres rated the changes made as fairly minor (2). The areas of change were reported to be child abuse (four out of six centres), health policies (four centres), buildings and maintenance (one centre), special needs children (one centre) and equity (one centre). It is not surprising that many centres have added sections on child abuse to their charters since there has been a major scandal recently in Christchurch involving child care centre staff in the sexual abuse of children. National organizations as well as the Ministry of Education have also been involved in helping implement abuse prevention programmes in early childhood centres.

When asked to rate the extent of staff involvement in changes (1 being very little involvement and 4 being a great deal) centres' responses were spread across the continuum. Three centres (one rating of 1 and two ratings of 2) said that there had been very little or a little staff involvement, two centres rated it as moderately high (3) while two centres (both kindergartens) rated the involvement as very high (4). Management committees (usually a group of parents) were rated by three centres as having very high involvement, by one as having moderate involvement, by two as having relatively little involvement and by one as having very little involvement. The general involvement of parents and the community was rated as very high by three centres, moderately high by two, relatively low by one and very little by another. The comments from five out of the six centres who changed their charters suggested that the way that most centres consulted parents was to give them the opportunity to read and comment on the redrafted charter. One centre said:

After each section was discussed by the charter committee a summary was displayed for parents to read and comment upon in an exercise book. Newsletters to parents reminded them of the topics for discussion and comment.

The impression gained from the questionnaires is that while parents were given the opportunity to comment, few were interested. Charter committees, on the other hand, were small groups of parents who were highly involved and responsible for changes. One centre commented:

> Generally most parents are apathetic and don't really involve themselves with the kindergarten in any way unless they are on the management committee.

We asked whether centres regarded the charter as a living document which related to the operation of the centre and was discussed by staff or parents. Seven out of the nine centres responded to this question in the affirmative while one centre said that it *was* in theory (the implication being that in practice it was not) and the other centre said that it was potentially a living document. This centre said:

> Somehow the whole thing has a very low priority amongst all the many other things which need to be done at playcentre.

It is clear, however, from the answers that most centres see the charter as an explicit statement of the centre's current policies. Staff refer to the charter on issues like employing staff, emergency procedures, parent education policies. One centre said:

> Yes, it is referred to, sets guidelines for decision making and is something we all feel we have 'ownership' of.

While another centre said:

> Staff discuss some areas of the charter but are always aware of needing to meet the requirements.

The theme of being held accountable to the charter was raised by other centres. For example:

> The Education Review Office are quite pedantic and check that individual kindergartens are actually involving parents within the running of their kindergartens.

Very strong dissatisfaction with the administrative changes since the original charter development process was expressed by one centre in relation to the Ministry of Education:

> When we originally wrote the charter and got it in *with a great deal of effort* by the required date, it then took a year before we heard back and what we heard was all the new Desirable Objectives and Practices, not even any indication that they had read what we had taken such time and effort over. We felt the whole thing was a big farce and were very put off. It has taken a whole new 'generation' of parents in the centre to get rid of this feeling.

We asked each centre how many parents consulted the charter before and after they enrolled their child at the centre. Centres estimated that between zero and 80 per cent of parents consulted the charter before enrolling their child. The mean estimated number of parents consulting the charter *before* children enrolled was 12 per cent. From zero to 85 per cent of parents were estimated to consult the charter *after* children were enrolled with a mean of 28 per cent.

Another recent study (Westaway and Wheeler, 1993) asked a group of forty parents using either kindergartens or childcare centres, about the information they used to select an early childhood centre for their child. About half of the parents said they viewed some sort of written information about the centre before enrolling their child. The written information included both the charter and parent booklets. Fifty-nine per cent of the parents who viewed written information referred to the charter. Hence about a third of this sample of parents said that they looked at the charter. This study, using parent reports, suggests that a somewhat larger number of parents were using the charter than was indicated by our follow-up study.

The charter is part of a policy which is designed to increase the amount of parental choice, yet only between a fifth and a third of parents consult the charter. It does not therefore seem to play a major role in the choices of most parents. Some centres had a much larger number of parents consulting the charter than others. Possibly these centres draw the charter to the attention of parents either before or after children are enrolled. The centres' attitude to and use of the charter clearly has a considerable influence on the parents who visit.

The follow-up study suggests that the charter is now an accepted part of the procedure of running an early childhood centre. Most centres review and change their charter frequently but with a moderate degree of staff and parent involvement. The major responsibility for charters seems to lie with small committees of parents assisted by supervisors or head teachers. The charter is generally regarded as a centre's statement of goals and objectives, a useful ongoing guideline for programme and policy, but which is used more by staff than parents. There is however a minority of concerned and interested parents who do use the charter before enrolment as a means to help them choose a centre and after enrolment to clarify centre policy and objectives.

CONCLUSIONS

There was some positive impact of the charter on early childhood centre quality – it had the immediate effect of upgrading some structural features of quality (such as ratio), it heightened awareness on the value issues advocated by the Meade Report (such as biculturalism and equity), it encouraged centres to articulate their own values and goals and their obligation to practise according to these. Staff have been forced to clarify and codify their practices and they have had to think through their philosophy and values. In this they have made varying degrees of effort and with varying degrees of success in involving parents. Parents have been rather less interested and involved than might have been expected in the whole process.

On the negative side the necessity of writing a charter was ill understood and thought to be daunting and time-consuming by many centres. Instead of seeing the charter as a chance for parents and staff to participate jointly in articulating policies for their own centres, many perceived it as an empty bureaucratic requirement. There was undoubtedly some bungling on the part of the administrators which reduced the credibility of the new policies. Centres were confused by several changes to deadlines and of ground rules (for example the total withdrawal of the National Guidelines after centres had spent half a year accommodating to them). The charters might have been more positively received if centres had perceived the link between them and the introduction of policies that had been long awaited (mainly better funding and support for early childhood centres).

The charter should have provided an opportunity for centres to retain control over the policy and practice in their own centres and for early childhood services to maintain the diversity and autonomy they prized, but it was not perceived in this way. Despite the widespread consultation over the Meade Report implementation, centres were simply unprepared for the nuts and bolts of the new policies. Possibly the consultation reached the level of national organizations but not the centres who were the members of these organizations. While there had been a 'shared discourse' about the need for change to early childhood funding and administration such details as the charter were not seen to be a part of that discourse. Some of the difficulties may be ironed out with time but if the charter is to be a living document some information and communication by early childhood leaders and Ministry policy makers will be required.

Unfortunately, the framework of quality guidelines for early childhood charters was an extremely short-lived phenomenon. It was only a short time after the charters had been approved that a new government was voted in. It immediately decided that centres would be required only to meet the minimum standards and have a charter (with reduced requirements) to obtain funding. The incentive to upgrade quality to a higher quality than minimum standards was largely removed with the introduction of the *Desirable Objectives and Practices*, although some centres retained their commitment to higher quality. Centres were no longer constrained to meet equity requirements in relation to gender or the Treaty of Waitangi. Hence restraints upon centres to write centrally defined views of quality (which stemmed from early childhood leaders) into charters were greatly diminished. Centres are now free to include anything they want in the charters. They can, on the other hand, simply put DOPS into their own words without bothering with consultation or value statements of their own.

In the new deregulated climate the main ingredient in policy designed to improve quality is parent choice. The idea is that parents will choose the type of centre which best fits their own needs and values. Thus market forces will determine whether a centre attracts sufficient parents and children to keep the operation viable. If parents have some knowledge and understanding of the things which make up good quality care and education and they have access to centres which offer these things, then there is no problem with this theory. However, parents may not have such knowledge and understanding and even if they do they may not be able to afford or may not have available in their area the type of centres desired. Indeed there is some evidence (e.g. Howes and

Stewart, 1987) to suggest that parents with the most financial and educational resources choose the best quality centres. Hence the revised chartering process can be seen as an adjunct of New Right educational policies rather than a way of encouraging parent participation and involvement.

Although the early childhood reforms are typically seen within the New Right educational reform framework, it needs to be emphasized that there were many items in the package of reforms which had been long fought for by the early childhood sector. Because the historical and current socio-political context is so different for early childhood education than for primary and secondary education, we argue that it needs to be seen and analyzed differently. Little attention has so far been given by policy theorists to the early childhood sector.

The current situation where centres only have to meet minimum standards and write a charter based on DOPS to qualify for government funding means that many of the aspects of the charter which were intended to promote quality have disappeared. The charter can now include more or less what the parents and staff want it to include, within the limits of DOPS and of the resources available to them. The Ministry and the Educational Review Office in their monitoring role concentrate on whether the centres are meeting DOPS. The reality of the situation is that this aids conservatism and moves the field backwards from progress in reducing inequalities in early childhood education. This can be illustrated by the equivocal attitudes of many parents to such issues as biculturalism and mainstreaming. Had the National Guidelines stayed in place increasing dialogue could well have led to the acceptance of the moves towards reducing inequalities. Values which have become part of the accumulated discourse of early childhood education in New Zealand are now quite vulnerable and can be easily lost. They will survive in the centres which accept them but they probably would have regardless of the charter.

The pendulum has swung too far in the direction of lack of accountability and low requirements for quality. It is possible for centres to abuse their greatly increased funding since the accountability procedures are so weak. There is nothing to stop centres spending on items unrelated to quality, and the incentive for this may be somewhat higher in private centres. Even where the Education Review Office identifies poor practice there is no mechanism to require improvement, except in the case of serious physical harm being caused to children, and even then response seems to be slow. There has been an abdication of government responsibility for protecting vulnerable children and providing the best education possible. Other changes which occurred during the reforms have conspired to allow this to happen. The most notable is the total restructuring of the Ministry of Education. The Early Childhood Division was abolished and the people who worked there dispersed into other areas like Policy, Curriculum or Buildings. Hence there is a distinct lack of visibility of the early childhood perspective within this public service, policy-making institution. The reforms originally came about through a consensus of early childhood people inside and outside government departments, parliament, the Labour Party, unions and other groups (Meade, 1991a). Government early childhood education officials, who had been relatively impartial advocates towards better quality, are no longer there. (Unions can always be accused of professional self-interest and 'provider capture'.) There is currently a lack of informed advice to government by knowledgeable early childhood specialist officials in the Ministry of Education.

The government has succeeded in disengaging from the day-to-day issues of early childhood education, particularly the concern to maintain high quality care. This is left to the centres themselves and means high variability in the quality of provision and reliance on parent choice to recognize and reward it. The reality is that only a minority of parents make an active, deliberate and reflective choice of early childhood centre. Hence, inequalities are likely to remain in our early childhood system between the parents with cultural capital who know how to seek out quality and those who don't.

The charter does have the potential to be an effective living document which encourages centres to develop their own views of quality in consultation with their local communities. At present it does not fulfil that function and is merely a means for the government to devolve responsibility for quality to the local community with reliance on an ineffective means of parental choice to ensure quality. It seems that politically we are unlikely to move away from a devolved administrative structure, therefore it is increasingly important for the early childhood community to turn its attention to making the procedures work. Without appropriate funding the charter is an empty document, thus the field must hang on to what funding it has and fight for improvements. The charter also loses its point if there is a low level of awareness and understanding of its purpose. Hence in-service training is needed to help staff and parents in early childhood centres to use the chartering process effectively. In addition more effective and frequent monitoring procedures are urgently needed.

There have been major problems with the implementation of chartering in New Zealand. Some of the difficulties experienced may be avoidable by other countries. The aim of chartering is to include various stakeholders in the process of defining quality for a particular service. Clearly most parents and staff in this study did not perceive the process to be one which empowered them to contribute their own values about quality. Staff generally took much of the initiative, were only partially successful in involving parents, and generally perceived the process to be an empty exercise. The major problem was that there was a change of government before the reforms were fully implemented. The new government was much less committed to the general goal of increasing quality and more concerned to keep costs to a minimum. For the chartering process to work, there has to be a government which is genuinely concerned in order to protect values and ideals about quality which have emerged from the cumulative discourse of the country's history and tradition of early childhood education. Without such a commitment it is not possible for there to be a genuine balance between central and local perspectives and chartering merely becomes a way for governments to abdicate their responsibility for young children.

REFERENCES

BURNS, V. (1989) Early childhood education in New Zealand: the quiet revolution. The voice of the child: Who speaks? Who cares? Who listens? Paper given at the OMEP XIX World Assembly and Congress, University of London.

CALDWELL, B. M. (1986) Day care and early environmental adequacy, in W. Fowler (ed.) *Early Experience and the Development of Competence*, Jossey-Bass, San Francisco.

CARR, M. and MAY, H. (1992) *National Early Childhood Curriculum Guidelines in New Zealand*, Waikato University.

CODD, J. and GORDON, L. (1991) School charters: the contractualist state and education policy, *New Zealand Journal of Educational Studies*, Vol. 26, no. 1 pp. 21–34.

COOK, H. (1985) *Mind That Child: Childcare as a Social and Political Issue in New Zealand*, Blackberry Press, Wellington.

DALE, R. and JESSON, J. (1992) Mainstreaming education: the role of the State Services Commission, in H. Manson (ed.) *New Zealand Annual Review of Education (Vol. 2)*, Victoria University, Wellington.

DALLI, C. (1990) Early childhood education in New Zealand: current issues and policy developments, *Early Child Development and Care*, Vol. 64, pp. 61–70.

DALLI, C. (1992). Policy agendas for children's lives, *New Zealand Journal of Educational Studies*, Vol. 27 no. 1, pp. 53–69.

DALLI, C. (1993). Young children are vulnerable. Paper given at launch of CECUA-NZEI campaign on quality education in the early years, Wellington.

FARQUHAR, S.-E. (1991a) A 'Purple People–Eater' or quality assurance mechanism? The 1989/90 early childhood centre charter requirements, in M. Gold, L. Foote and A. Smith (eds.) *The Impact of Policy Change: Proceedings of the Fifth Early Childhood Convention*.

FARQUHAR, S.-E. (1991b) *Quality in Early Childhood Centres: Experiences of Charter Development in Early Childhood Centres in 1990 (Report One)*, Ministry of Education Research and Statistics Division, Wellington.

FARQUHAR, S.-E. (1993) Constructions of quality in early childhood centres, Ph.D. thesis, Otago University.

GARDINER, C. W. (1991) *Review of Early Childhood Funding – Independent Report*, Waikato University.

HOLLOWAY, S. D., and REICHART-ERICKSON, M. (1989) Child-care quality, family structure, and maternal expectations: relationship to preschool children's peer relations, *Journal of Applied Developmental Psychology*, Vol. 10, pp. 281–98.

HOWES, C. and STEWART, P. (1987) Child's play with adults, toys and peers: an examination of family and child-care influences, *Developmental Psychology*, Vol. 23, pp. 423–30.

LANGE, D. (1988) *Before Five*, New Zealand Government Education Department, Wellington.

MAY, H. (1991) 'From a floor to a drawer' – a story of administrative upheaval: a post Meade reflection on early childhood policy, *Te Timatanga*, Vol. 9, no. 2, pp. 3–11.

MEADE, A. (1988) *Education to be More (Report of the Early Childhood Education and Care Working Group)*, Government Printer, Wellington.

MEADE, A. (1991a) Women and young children gain a foot in the door, *Te Timatanga*, Vol. 9, no. 2, pp. 12–21.

MEADE, A. (1991b) What is quality early childhood education and care? Address given to the Assessment and Evaluation in Early Childhood Teachers Refresher Course, Hawkes Bay.

MEADE, A. and DALLI, C. (1991) Review of the early childhood sector, in *New Zealand Annual Review of Education*, Department of Education, Victoria University, Wellington.

MIDDLETON, S. (1992) Gender equity and school charters: theoretical and political questions for the 1990s, *Women and Education in Aotearoa (Vol. 2)* Bridget Williams Books, Wellington.

MINISTRY OF EDUCATION (1993) *Growth in Early Childhood Sector Enrolments*, Ministry of Education Research and Statistics Division, Wellington.

MINISTRY OF EDUCATION (1990) *The Ministry's Guidelines for Negotiating Early Childhood Charters*, Ministry of Education, Wellington.

NASH, R. (1989) Tomorrow's schools: state power and parent participation, *New Zealand Journal of Educational Studies*, Vol. 24, no. 2, pp. 113–38.

PHILLIPS, D., MCCARTNEY, K. and SCARR, S. (1987) Child-care quality and children's social development, *Developmental Psychology*, Vol. 23, no. 4, pp. 537–43.

SMITH, A. B. (1992) Early childhood education in New Zealand: the winds of change, in G. A. Woodill, J. Bernhard, and L. Prochner (eds.) *International Handbook of Early Childhood Education*, Garland Publishing, New York.

SMITH, A. B. and SWAIN, D. A. (1988) *Childcare in New Zealand: People, Programmes, Politics*, Allen and Unwin, Wellington.

VANDELL, D. L. and CORASANITI, M. A. (1990) Variations in early child care: do they predict subsequent social, emotional, and cognitive differences? *Early Childhood Research Quarterly*, Vol. 5, pp. 555–72.

WESTAWAY, F. and WHEELER, P. (1993) *How Parents Select an Early Childhood Centre* (*Paper Educ 316, Early Childhood Research and Policy*), report of a research project carried out for the University of Otago.

WHITEBOOK, M., HOWES, C. and PHILLIPS, D. (1989) *Who Cares? Child Care Teachers and the Quality of Care in America* (*Final Report of the National Child Care Staffing Study*), Child Care Employee Project, Oakland: CA.

NOTES

1. The Treaty of Waitangi was signed in 1840 by the British Crown and Maori chiefs. It granted the British Crown sovereignty in return for Maori authority over land, resources and other taonga or treasures (including language).

2. Whanau is a Maori word meaning extended family or a group of people who care for one another. It is also a Maori social structure, incorporating all age ranges, interests and experiences which makes decisions by a consensus method, where control is vested in the whanau, not in any individual member.

CHAPTER 10

Fragments for a Discussion About Quality

CLAUS JENSEN

Ideas about quality change over time and Claus Jensen illustrates this process of change through the recent history of the Danish extensive, diverse and publicly funded system of early childhood services. Ideas of quality are discussed, implemented and reviewed at the level of individual centres, which have great autonomy and where the process increasingly includes parents and children as well as workers. While there is little state regulation of services, the government provides support for this decentralized system through public funding of services, high levels of training for child care workers and encouragement of child and parent influence on the operation of centres.

INTRODUCTION

An exhibition of what are claimed to be paintings has just opened at Durand-Ruel. I visited this exhibition, and my horrified eyes beheld terrible things. Five or six mentally deranged individuals (one of them a woman) are showing a joint exhibition of their work. I saw people collapse in laughter in front of some of the paintings, but *my* heart bled. These so-called artists describe themselves as revolutionary 'Impressionists'. They take a piece of canvas, paint and brush, then they apply a few blotches of colour at random, and finally they sign the whole thing with their name. They are poor, deluded individuals – like inhabitants of a madhouse who collect cobblestones and call them diamonds.

(Gombrich, 1973, p. 411)

This is how one apparently highly regarded Parisian art critic described an encounter with the Impressionists in 1876. But in 1993 people are prepared to stand in long queues to admire the very same artists – which only goes to show how much our views on quality have changed in the last hundred years! One hundred years of hindsight make it easy to see how much the concept of quality can change, but noticeable changes also take place over the course of a much shorter period of time. Quality reflects not only today's standards (the way I understand the world today), but also historical fact (the way I am influenced by the theories, traditions and events of the past).

This chapter is based on twenty years of personal experience of Danish early childhood centres. It illustrates the changes that have taken place in Denmark, including views on quality, and also how quality is an issue for individual centres and for children, parents and workers in each centre. But first I should like to provide an introduction to the types of child care centre found in Denmark, presenting a good number of dry facts which are necessary for the subsequent discussion.

THE STRUCTURE OF DANISH CHILD CARE

The basic system

If you know nothing about the Danish child care system, the structure of Danish child care may seem somewhat muddled. But for the majority of Danish parents the system is completely familiar. Many of the parents sending their children to centres today used to attend such centres themselves or know about them from brothers and sisters. So despite some local variations, the system is familiar and quite straightforward for Danes.

The Danish child care system caters for children aged from six months to eighteen years (until recently maternity leave and parental leave lasted for five months after birth; recently parental leave has been extended, so that parents now have at least seventeen months of post-natal leave available). It should be mentioned that Denmark also has a public system of family day care, which is used most for children under one to three years. However, most parents prefer to send their young children to centres (see Chapter 3 for levels of attendance by children of different ages at centres and family day care).

Three types of child care centre have dominated developments in Denmark during the twentieth century. The *vuggestue* (day nursery) is for children under the age of three years, and the *børnehave* (kindergarten) is for children from the age of three until they start school between the age of six and seven (most Danish children go to a nursery class at school in the year before compulsory school begins, which is age seven). The start of school marks a sea change after which the life of children is divided into school time and spare time. The centre provided for children after school hours is the *fritidshjem* (centre for school-age children), which is distinct from the school both physically and in terms of content; traditionally, Danish children are welcome to attend such centres from the age of seven until the age of about fourteen. These three types of child care centre are not the only ones in Denmark (see below), but they do represent the great majority.

The vast majority of centres are located in housing areas. From the very early days, the importance of the link between home and centre has determined this location. There are some centres located close to workplaces, but they are few and far between.

Danish kindergartens and centres for school-age children normally cater for about sixty children, but day nurseries only have room for about thirty-five children. There is a good deal of variation (owing among other things to local conditions), and in some cases centres cater for fewer children than the norm.

Similarly, a typical Danish child care centre has three group rooms with about twenty children in each, or twelve in each in the case of day nurseries. In addition to these group rooms there are often a number of smaller rooms or one big common room. The great majority of centres have an outdoor area of varying size for use as a playground, offering many different activities. The children often spend a good deal of their time outdoors.

Private, religious and political organizations have always been active in establishing and running centres in Denmark, although they receive public funding to do so. A large number of centres (about a third overall) are still run by such organizations, but many have now been handed over to be run by the local authorities (communes) in which they are located, and overall communes provide most centres directly. However, it is worth pointing out that it hardly matters to the children or parents *who* runs a centre. In the case of centres run by private organizations, an agreement is drawn up between the centre and the commune concerned before public funding is granted; this means that in practice there is little difference between the various types of centre. As a result, I shall make no distinction between privately-run and commune-run centres.

Danish legislation stipulates a number of guidelines in connection with the way centres are run. But the majority of issues (e.g. staff:children ratios, budgets) are the responsibility of the commune concerned. This means that there are differences in the way centres are run, although viewed from outside Denmark there is a large degree of homogeneity. After all, Denmark is not one of the largest countries in Europe. There are 5.6 million inhabitants living in 273 communes.

New types of centres

The three types of centre mentioned above (day nursery, kindergarten and centre for school-age children) have always been the most common in Denmark. But alternative types have also been opened, adding to the diversity of the Danish system. These newer types of centre should be mentioned here, partly because they will have a big impact in future and partly because some of them provide valuable insight into early childhood services in Denmark.

Adventure playgrounds

The first adventure playground in Denmark (indeed the first in the world) was established as long ago as 1943. Today there are many such playgrounds in Denmark, but unfortunately (in my view) there are still far too few. These playgrounds provide for children mainly between the ages of six and fourteen years. Most of the activities take place outdoors, and the children have a great influence on creating, changing and providing new ideas. There is continuous construction activity going on in such playgrounds: the children build the most amazing houses for themselves out of recycled materials. Once such houses are finished they have to be properly fitted out and the group with responsibility for the project experiment with aesthetic forms of expression. It is never boring to walk round such playgrounds and knock on a door when you want to visit one of the houses. Outside their houses the children often lay out a small garden or build a terrace where they can sit and admire their months of hard work. Or they can sit and make new plans. Should they add a second floor? Or would a good basement be a better idea? As they work, the children learn to use tools, and their buildings become increasingly complex and impressive. There are also a great number of animals at most adventure playgrounds: horses, donkeys, goats, sheep, pigs, chickens, geese, and last but not least, rabbits, which are the personal pets of the children who have to look after them and build suitable hutches.

Our modern cities are often deserts of houses and tarmac, and in such an environment adventure playgrounds seem like oases. There are plenty of plants, including fruit trees, bushes and shrubs. There are also many quiet corners where children can hide away to ponder the meaning of life. Hopefully, public awareness of the environment these days may lead to increasing numbers of adventure playgrounds. Once you have visited such a playground, it is impossible to view the suburbs and desolate centres of our modern cities without considering the possibility of turning part of a car park or disused patch of grass into an area of waterholes, earth banks, wooden houses, animals and activity in which 'Please keep off the grass' signs are banned.

Outdoor child care centres or 'forest kindergartens'

These centres are a much more recent development. At the end of the 1980s various steps were taken to find out whether alternative child care centres were possible. Outdoor child care centres have proved to be one of the most successful of these alternatives, and they are being set up with increasing frequency. There are many different kinds, but as a rule they are associated with more traditional centres where parents bring their children in the mornings and pick them up in the afternoons. However, the children attending the outdoor centre spend most of their day in the woods – not only in the summer when the sun shines, but all year round.

Many of these centres have their own bus for transport from the pick-up point in town to journey out to the woods. These buses are fully equipped with a toilet, wardrobe, and for those children who require them, sleeping facilities. Outdoor centres normally visit the same area most days, and the children get to know these areas so well that they can continue games and activities from previous days. The built-in mobility of an outdoor centre with its own bus also makes it possible to visit other places. If the weather is bad, or if the children simply need a change of scene, it is easy to do something else (e.g. visit an ordinary child care centre, workshop, farm, museum – or family and friends).

There is a limit to the number of outdoor centres that can be established in Denmark, in view of the wear and tear caused in the woods concerned! But there is no doubt that such centres are a valuable alternative – not only as an option for parents, but also as a general source of inspiration for other child care centres.

Centres on school premises

Centres on school premises are another new type of centre which deserves mention, because they have become so widespread in Denmark in recent years. Since the mid-1980s, more centres on school premises have been set up than any other type of centre. Such centres provide child care for school-age children, just like the centres *off* school premises mentioned above (*fritidsh-jem*). This new school-based type of centre has given rise to considerable debate among both child care workers and politicians, and many aspects of this debate are of interest to people outside Denmark. Consequently, I shall deal with the subject in greater detail below.

Child care centres for mixed ages or 'age-integrated institutions'

In Denmark and the rest of Western Europe, the number of children in each family has declined significantly in recent years as the birth rate has fallen. This means that increasing numbers of children now grow up with only one or two brothers and sisters – or with none at all. Centres for mixed ages (six months to fourteen years) are one way of compensating for this trend. The first of these centres was set up in Denmark in the early 1970s, since when many have been opened. The concept of 'mixed ages' is interpreted in many different ways. Some centres favour complete integration of all children aged six months to fourteen years, while others provide a separate area for the youngest children.

In such centres, children have the opportunity to spend part of their day with children of other ages. This does not necessarily mean that the children are together in all their activities, but the close proximity of older children enables younger children to watch what they do, learn how they play, see how they communicate with each other, and so on. This provides a direct opportunity to copy and obtain inspiration about how to behave, and this is exactly what happens. But the younger children are not the only ones to benefit. Centres for mixed ages allow older children to behave childishly and regress if they like without worrying about pressure from peer groups. Friendships can arise across age barriers, and the older children receive active training in the importance of being tolerant, since there are clear differences in the abilities and needs of the children in such centres. Brothers and sisters can spend time together without necessarily being in the same room as each other, which benefits parents because the children are more relaxed with each other. What is more, parents also benefit enormously from the fact that they can pick up all their children from the same centre and relate to one group of child care workers only.

The idea of centres for mixed ages has had a big impact on early childhood services in Denmark. Other centres used to be divided according to age, but this is no longer common. Virtually all centres are now mixed within the age groups catered for: groups divided according to age are only found in some centres for the youngest children (six months to one year). It is also worth mentioning that there has been comprehensive restructuring of many day nurseries and kindergartens during the past five years, to produce centres for mixed groups aged 6 months to six years.

Summarizing the system

Ole Langsted's chapter (Chapter 3) has already shown that the Danish system is very extensive in terms of coverage by publicly funded services. Moreover, the system is still being developed. Many communes have made commitments that child care places (either with family day carers or in centres) will be available for all children in the near future, and the Danish Government has recently (in 1993) made a national commitment to provide publicly funded places for all children over the age of twelve months by 1996.

The system also has considerable diversity. Many communes and private organizations are involved in running services, and for very differing communities. There are many types of services, and variations within each type. At the same time, the system has considerable coherence. The strong emphasis on community-based services providing for their local areas has already been mentioned. All centres (except those that are school-based) are the responsibility of one department, social affairs, at local and national levels and subject to social legislation. The high level of public funding provides a secure financial framework for services and reflects a high and sustained level of public commitment and support. There is a common emphasis on parent involvement and listening to children (discussed already in Chapter 3), and a number of widely shared values. Last, but not least, all staff in early childhood centres (whether working with babies or school-age children) have the same basic training, and pay and conditions; overall, about 60 per cent of workers in the system have the basic three and a half years training and many untrained workers go on to take this training having gained work experience first. Of course each worker has her or his own special area of interest, and there is scope for some specialization during training. But in countless cases, staff need to be able to cope with issues which are relevant for children of all ages.

CHANGING IDEAS ABOUT QUALITY

Enormous changes have taken place in child care services in Denmark in less than thirty years; the present widespread system only began to develop from 1964. Before that date, when legislation was passed which laid the foundations for a generally available service, child care centres used to be available to the few and carried a social stigma. But today the vast majority of Danish parents regard them as a natural part of daily life – a vital prerequisite for their own working lives and a qualitative improvement in the lives of their children.

This all might sound too good to be true for readers outside Denmark. But as in all fairy-tales, conflicts are unavoidable! There have been (and still are) many conflicts at all levels of Danish child care. For instance, the role of the welfare state has been widely criticized recently, not for the first time. There are a relatively large number of political parties in Denmark and several of these parties wish to dismantle the welfare state, favouring rapid privatization to solve Denmark's problems and 'set the wheels in motion again' (as they put it). But such views are currently expressed by a political minority, and in general the Danish people are extremely satisfied with the child care system.

But that is enough about the political situation and the types of child care provision in Denmark. It is time to take a look at child care centres in terms of quality. The fact that Denmark has widespread child care services says nothing about the quality of life for children using such facilities. Quantity is not the same as quality.

The 1970s: a decade of change

It is often hard to evaluate the current situation. A few years of hindsight generally provide a clearer view of the issues at stake in public discussion or debate. So I intend to start by going back a couple of decades to the beginning of the 1970s, when a debate began which was to have an enormous impact on child care in Denmark.

The 1970s witnessed great expansion in Denmark. Large numbers of women entered the labour market for the first time, and as a result there was rapid expansion of child care services. A great number of new centres were built and capacity in colleges to train workers for these centres was increased. Competition for places at these colleges quickly became fierce, and working with children became increasingly popular.

Women were not the only ones keen to gain new child care qualifications. A large group of men were also interested, and the spirit of the decade allowed them to become involved in what had traditionally been an area dominated by women. Changes were inevitable. The new students were inspired by the spirit of 1968, and full of the wish to challenge the authoritarian system. They had often gained other qualifications or job experience before starting their child care training, and their average age was in the mid-twenties. In other words, child care students were relatively mature and often had their own children; this is still the case today and is a great benefit to the Danish system.

Actually, the system was not as authoritarian as many people believed. But it certainly needed modernization in terms of both content and tone. Until the 1970s, children under three attending day nurseries were brought up to be quiet, orderly and clean; they were cared for but the pedagogical approach was limited. The centres were equipped with rows of cots, and children were handed back to parents at the door since parents were not allowed to enter (this was to reduce the risk of infection).

A revolution in ideas and practice changed all this in the 1970s. The use of cots was discontinued, which gave the children far more freedom, both physical and psychological. The general health of small children was also much improved by this time, which opened the way to an understanding that this youngest age group had a lot of other needs: hygiene is of course an important aspect but it had become too dominant. Nurses were no longer needed, and white coats symbolizing a clinical attitude to child care disappeared. Experiments were carried out which quickly revealed that very young children were capable of far more than anyone believed possible, as long as they were given sufficient space and time. They wasted time at first when learning to pour milk from the jug into the cup, but their joy and pride as they learned to do so reduced the amount of clearing up required in the long run.

The centres for children over three years changed in a different way. They were part of another tradition where the physical care and hygiene perspective was less dominant; for example, no nurses were employed in these centres. Their tradition was greatly influenced by Fröbel and Montessori. For a great number of centres and colleges this was combined with pedagogical ideas developing since the 1930s and based, among others, on the theories of Sigmund Freud. Children's autonomy was of central importance to this movement: 'It should come from the children themselves' is the title of an interview given a few years ago by a *pedagog* (child care worker) who had worked in the field from 1938 to 1976.

With the expansion of services in the 1970s, a third approach emerged. In a very short period, new elements were introduced such as the so-called 'children's meetings' and 'project work'. The idea was to teach children at an early age about the society to which they belonged. Children's meetings enabled them to play a democratic part in the discussion of various relevant topics. Practical chores (setting the table, preparing meals, etc.) became part of the daily routine, and at children's meetings the work required was shared out once a week and everyone was made a member of a working group.

> We do not wish to mollycoddle children in order to protect them. We wish to teach them to evaluate their own situation and reactions critically against the framework of society. Like adults, children have the right to learn the truth about the world they live in. They must not grow up with the same biased perception of reality, full of prejudice and fear of communism, which unfortunately seems to pervade the ideas of many adults these days.
>
> (Poulsgaard, 1975, p. 88)

Some people were far more revolutionary than this. Much was at stake, and the level of ambition was extremely high. 'Structured child care' was the order of the day. The theoretical inspiration for the new system came largely from Soviet psychology, and a number of theorists adapted Soviet ideas to Danish society and had a great influence on the theories used in Danish child care for a number of years. To be fair, it should be said that not all child care centres contributed to the revolution. But they were all affected by it, and very many changes were made. Even boxes of dressing-up clothes were replaced! No more kings and princesses: no more tutus and crazy hats. The boxes were filled with overalls instead.

Naturally, the press and politicians realized what was going on, and child care workers were criticized strongly. No distinctions were made – *all* child care workers were condemned as a dangerous group which was undermining society. With the benefit of hindsight it now seems that both parties over-reacted, but the result was that child care workers were given an image problem which it took years to change.

At the same time, child care workers started to view their role as salaried employees in a much more radical light. In the past, child care work had been regarded as a vocation, but in the 1970s it became a job from which a decent salary was expected. The role of the trade union also evolved, to play an important part in the professional life of its members. Membership of trade unions is high in Denmark compared with other countries, and 94 per cent of all child care workers are now members of their trade union. During the 1970s, the union for trained workers became (and still is) the organization which undertakes most continuous training. Likewise the weekly trade union paper became a central source for pedagogical information and discussion.

The great debate

A reaction against structured child care by centre workers themselves was inevitable, since in practice structured child care was often far more restrictive and humourless than the system it replaced. Initial attempts to rebel failed, however, owing to the fact that structured child care was the dominant theory in the organizations and magazines which were the mouthpieces of the profession.

Subsequently, the 1970s have been described as the period of the great debate. This is not an entirely accurate description. What happened was that increasing numbers of child care workers left the debate about theories of working with children to its own devices, since they found it barren and non-productive. Structured child care did not help child care workers to understand and improve the quality of the time they spent with children. Structures and systems had become more important than individuals meeting each other every morning; the energy and enthusiasm had disappeared; what was supposed to be progressive was regarded by many as authoritarian. So the structured child care approach did not fall apart due to any concerted movement of opposition: rather it withered away – just as it is difficult to continue a war if the soldiers do not show up.

However, few of the child care workers who experienced the changes at first hand would deny the importance of the period. Many of the declarations made in the 1970s now seem ridiculous. Despite this, though, the decade undoubtedly saw the start of a necessary process of child care modernization that is still far from complete.

The emergence of current practice

The focus of child care shifted. Gradually child care workers started considering their daily routines more carefully. At first, the new movement was against all theories, in the belief that theories were like trees, preventing you from seeing the wood. This may be a rough generalization, but it does say something about how child care centres viewed the situation. The focus of attention became the centre itself, with a view to creating a better balance for the parties directly concerned (children, parents and staff).

Experiments, large-scale and small-scale, were initiated to discover new systems to replace the divided and highly organized routines resulting from structured child care. For instance, many centres carried everything down into the basement at the weekend to see what would happen on Monday morning when the children arrived to be greeted by empty rooms. How would the children react? How would the adults react? What kind of activity would arise within the four walls?

Sometimes centres went to jumble sales to buy old sofas and armchairs. Why should children always listen to stories sitting in rigid, upright chairs? It is actually much more pleasant to listen to a story if the story-teller and children all sit in the same old battered sofa. The result of these experiments was that child care workers discovered (or perhaps rediscovered) that children use their bodies far better when they are allowed to use the entire floor, and that sitting too long on a chair might actually be unhealthy!

Child care centres were very cautious at first, but gradually they became more adventurous. They changed into more pleasant places: there was more room for life and more room for differences. More experiments were called for; and rules were analyzed carefully. It was discovered that far too many rules were the result of adults' fear of chaos or the need felt by adults to ensure orderly conditions. Are the children allowed to crawl on the roof of the shed? 'No' say the rules, because Karen (one of the child care workers) gets too nervous when they do so. But the rest of the staff are not so nervous, so crawling on the roof is allowed except when Karen is in the playground. This example (and many others like it) proved that children are perfectly capable of making allowances, as long as they are given a sensible explanation.

Can the children eat when they are hungry? Can the children's big construction play with bricks, started in the late afternoon, remain out for the next morning? Two examples (again among many others) where there has been an increasing willingness to follow the children's demands when possible. The number of rules was reduced considerably, and more flexible solutions were found.

A great proportion of communication is indirect, and this also applies to the world of child care. Child care workers with experience of alternative therapy started applying this knowledge in order to gain greater understanding of the complexity of human relations. The goal was not to change child care centres into therapeutic treatment centres, but to utilize personal experience in order to evaluate relationships critically.

Games, wishes, sex roles, friendships and much else were discussed at great length, and curiosity and openness became a far more integrated feature of activities. The box of dressing-up clothes was filled again with tutus, skirts and Batman capes. Fairy-tales were not only allowed but even encouraged. Instead of using their fingers to point accusingly at children, child care workers started using them to write the children's own stories, including their poems and the latest naughty joke told by their older brother at home. Boys were allowed to play with toy pistols and rifles, instead of playing such games only when staff had their backs turned. Children were also allowed to bring their own teddy bears, cars or dolls with them. Such objects were no longer regarded as threats to orderliness, but became a useful way for children to connect their two worlds of home and child care centre.

Danish child care centres did not discuss all of these ideas at exactly the same time or in the same order. But the vast majority have considered the issues raised to some extent, and they have learnt a lot from this process.

Conflict with schools

In the mid-1980s a conflict arose between schools and child care centres. This is worth mentioning here because it presented Danish child care with a serious problem, and also says a lot about how quality is currently perceived in the child care system. In order to understand what follows, the reader must remember that in Denmark virtually all child care centres are under the auspices of the Ministry of Social Affairs, while schools are under the Ministry of Education. Despite the contact between these two systems of services, there is no doubt about which of the two has the greatest influence.

In the mid-1980s there was a great demand for reform of the Danish school system. Many new teaching methods and structures were proposed, in particular related to the transition from child care centres to reception classes. During this process, the idea of extending teaching hours from three to four hours a day for the youngest school children (or even better to six hours a day) was put forward. The arguments in favour were often based on what was known as the 'total school system'. Under this approach, children should remain in school all day, rather than dividing their time between school in the morning and school-age child care centres in the afternoon; the activities of the afternoon should be closely connected with the teaching of the morning to ensure that children regarded school as a total experience instead of having a daily routine influenced by different objectives and ideas.

Such a radical change would have had major consequences for child care centres for school-age children, not only with regard to their structure but also in terms of content and the way children and adults related to each other. The Minister of Education in Denmark at the time, who largely supported the ideas proposed by the schools, even suggested that children should start school at an earlier age than seven. His counterpart in the United Kingdom, who was of a similar political bent, was invited to Denmark and after twelve minutes in a Danish child care centre announced to the press that children did not learn enough at child care centres.

The political, educational and ideological fat was now well and truly in the fire, and the public was kept informed of the progress of the confrontation. The new school proposals seemed bound to win the day. Child care workers were up against the ropes. But gradually social care and child care workers joined forces to take up the struggle against seemingly overwhelming odds. The ideological battle was joined. After all, 'totality' can mean many things, depending on who defines it. The concept itself is all well and good, but it has no content.

To cut a long story short, the first battle ended with a small reduction of the age at which children should start school and a small increase in daily teaching hours for the youngest children. At the same time, the option of establishing school-age child care services in schools and subject to school legislation under the Ministry of Education (child care on school premises) was allowed. As a result, the entire field of school-age child care has been reorganized.

Child care centres, schools and Folk High Schools

This is not the end of the struggle, however. The same conflicting views may well lead to further confrontation. There is a clear difference between time spent at school and spare time. One of the main aims of schools is to prepare pupils for a life as adults, and grades are given for achievement (although in Denmark grades are not given until the last year). This has always been the role of schools, and preparing pupils for adulthood will probably continue to be the dominant task.

By contrast, child care centres focus on the here and now, on fellowship, enthusiasm and self-determination. No grades are given for achievement. So far, Danish child care centres have developed and maintained an independent philosophy of caring which can survive without the support of its big sister, educational theory. But with efficiency one of the most important values by which today's society measures success, it may be difficult to retain the daily routine of Danish child care centres, where the most valuable activities cannot be measured, controlled or planned in terms of rational or efficient norms. How can anyone measure friendship? Or good, close contact between children and adults?

This may be an over-simplification. Schools are not devoid of fellowship, and of course the experiences learnt at child care centres are of use in later life. At best, the two worlds can complement each other – just as work and family life complement each other for adults. There may be conflicts between the two, but discontinuing either would be far too radical a step to take!

This distinction between school and other institutions that are broader in concept and also without grades is not only part of the discussion about child care and school. Denmark has become an industrialized and urban society fairly recently: before, the vast majority of the citizens lived in rural areas and worked in agriculture and related activities. In this society the idea was raised of establishing a school for young women and men from the countryside, a school where discussion and fellowship were the first priorities. No grades were to be given, no examination was to be taken at the end of the schooling period which lasted from six months to one year.

The result was the Danish Folk High School. This institution has survived the big changes in society and still plays a role as an important meeting place for people of different ages, occupations and backgrounds. Many changes have been made but the discussion and the fellowship continue to be the top priorities. Danes are very proud of this valuable system.

The Folk High School movement, with a lot of schools spread throughout the country, may have contributed to a widespread understanding and acceptance in Denmark that life in child care centres is something more than education given to the next generation. In both High Schools and centres, fellowship and the ability to make close friendships are regarded as the most important values.

QUALITY TODAY

The Danish system is characterized by great variety. The system encourages variety instead of homogeneity, with a view to meeting everyone's needs; in my view, this is a sign of the quality of the system. Related to this, the system also encourages experimentation and the evolution of new types of centre. The alternative types of centre mentioned above (outdoor child care centres, age-integrated centres and so on) provide invaluable inspiration for the whole child care system; their existence has made a positive contribution to discussions and changes in other types of centres.

The system is also characterized by a high level of autonomy for individual centres. Individual child care centres in Denmark are now allowed a good deal of self-determination. The state and communes only lay down a few general guidelines and targets, leaving the rest up to the child care centre concerned. And ever since the over-enthusiastic days of the late 1970s, no problems have arisen as a result. On the contrary: decentralization has led to great activity in and around individual child care centres, and children, staff and parents all feel that they can contribute to an active democratic process in which changes are allowed and even approved of. This means that children, parents and staff at child care centres can be given the chance to be the leading figures in their own centre, as opposed to being the pawns in someone else's game. They have great influence on daily routines, the way groups are made up, the activities and rules in the centre and so on. This has led to a more flexible and open understanding of what is required and an ability to put good ideas quickly into practice.

Of course, the state or communes could easily lay down more detailed guidelines or plans for the activities that should take place at child care centres all year round. Indeed, this was attempted several years ago (without much success) by a number of Danish communes. The plans quickly became obsolete, and seemed restrictive when applied as the framework for child care centre activities. Instead of this 'top down' approach, quality in child care services in Denmark is very much discussed, implemented and reviewed at the level of the individual centre and includes children, parents and staff. The system permits and encourages diversity and change. What are the conditions that make this decentralized approach to quality possible?

As already discussed in Chapter 3, a children's culture is emerging which values listening to and involving children, including them in the life of centres. Parents have also become increasingly involved in the daily routines of child care centres. The days when parents had to hand their children over at the gate to reduce the risk of infection now seem like light-years ago. Parents today are an important presence in child care centres, and often have a cup of coffee there before taking their children home in the afternoons. The openness and lack of prejudice of workers in relation to the children is also extended to the parents.

The position of parents has been recently further strengthened. Danish legislation now states formally that parent committees should be established for all child care centres, to ensure that parents are not forced to accept the goodwill (or lack of goodwill) of child care workers looking after their children. This legislation is only a few years old and is supported from all parts of the child care system on the basis that it is impossible to run a centre with energy and enthusiasm if there is no support or understanding from the parents.

The trained staff has an important role, planning discussions and sharing insights arising from their professional background and daily experiences. Of course the discussions can sometimes be seen as conflicts. But it is seldom that you hear about a centre where there is an ongoing conflict between the staff and the parents. There is a strong willingness to negotiate and to find solutions, and staff do not see it as threatening if there are different demands from among the parents.

Autonomy, flexibility, working closely with others – all place demands on the staff and their training. I believe that the primary reason for the success of child care services in Denmark is the level of staff training. The basic training now takes three and a half years, and consists of a mixture of theoretical and creative subjects. The emphasis on creative work is very important: training and more training is needed if child care workers are to be able to deal with the whole gamut of cultural experience which is needed for fellowship with children (painting, singing, drawing, dancing, telling them stories until their eyes pop out of their heads, etc.) and it is not sufficient to know about theories of creativity, you have to be creative yourself.

As well as the great emphasis placed on the personal development of students during their training and the encouragement of a wide range of cultural skills, the training also includes lengthy placement periods during which students play an active role at child care centres. The basic training is a foundation which encourages child care staff to consider all sides of the problems with which they are faced as professionals.

Danish colleges which train both child care workers and other social care workers sometimes say that they train their students to care for people from the cradle to the grave. A wide and general training indeed! However, most graduates work with children and young people at different types of child care centre. But since child care centres vary considerably, a broad and general training has a number of undoubted advantages (e.g. graduates have the chance to work with various age groups during their careers, providing a variety of challenges during a working life).

A wide training and scope of activity like this sometimes leads to superficiality. This is a very real disadvantage, but on the other hand individual specialization after completing the college course (as well as supplementary training courses) very often enables staff to compensate for the problems that might arise. Thanks to post-college specialization, I regard the all-round, general nature of the Danish college training as a strength. It helps to ensure the development of a more coherent theory and practice throughout Danish child care and other social care services, instead of favouring the kind of specialization and age group division propounded by developmental psychology.

As already noted, students training to be workers are relatively mature and the system retains trained workers, who create a mature workforce. One recent survey shows that 79 per cent of child care workers in their forties are still active in the field. This is probably a high figure compared with other countries, and there may be many explanations for the phenomenon: the quality of the basic training, opportunities for development via further and supplementary training, and a wide scope of potential employment.

Two other conditions may contribute to the success of this decentralized system. Apart from an emphasis on basic and continuous training, there is support for experimental and development work. There is also, despite the decentralization and variety of provision, a strong underlying coherence in the system due to generally shared cultural values which manifest themselves in widespread support for certain priority objectives: fellowship, the importance of children's own play, self-determination.

CONCLUSIONS

In this chapter I have outlined how ideas about quality in child care centres have changed over the last twenty years or so. I have also suggested features in the system that I regard as signs of quality: variety to meet people's needs; autonomy for children; fellowship and other aspects of social relationships; self-determination; creativity. Finally, I have also tried to show how the high quality that I believe is apparent in much of the Danish system has developed not from regulation and direction from government or other authorities, but from individual centres and their main stakeholders taking responsibility for the issue of quality within a context of conditions that favour this autonomous and flexible approach.

In the past, 'quality' was generally used to provide a brief reference point in describing an experience and as a way of expressing in shorthand a complexity which was hard to define otherwise without using thousands of words – and even if thousands of words were used, the feeling remaining would often be that the description had only scratched the surface of what had actually been experienced. The concept of quality is used differently today, especially in Danish business life where the subject has been addressed for some time. The results achieved do not look promising, at least for child care services. The key words seem to be 'quality management' and 'quality control', and there is no mention of the kind of quality which might lead to indefinable change. These days, quality has to be defined and measured precisely. Perhaps true quality is no longer really required. Perhaps the main aim is simply to achieve tighter management and tighter control.

Quality charts, certificates, points and grades are being produced at a furious rate by business, a sort of 'quality-inflation'. And after all, many things can be weighed and measured or recorded in a table, formula or graph. But will this really improve the quality of what goes on in child care centres? My fear is that if this approach to quality, with its emphasis on weighing and measurement, comes to dominate the discussion in services for children then it will spoil more than it improves. A society with clearly defined ideas of how to measure art will be regarded as authoritarian and narrow-minded: true quality, like true art, cannot be reduced to simple statements.

REFERENCES

GOMBRICH, E. H. (1973) *Kunstens Historie* (The Story of Art) Gyldendal, Copenhagen.
POULSGAARD, K. (1975) *Børnehaven – Kritiske Arbejdspapirer* (Kindergarten – Critical Papers) Pædagogstuderendes Landsrads Forlag, Copenhagen.

CHAPTER 11

Evaluation and Regulation: a Question of Empowerment

GUNILLA DAHLBERG AND GUNNAR ÅSÉN

Sweden has long attracted international attention for its high quality early childhood services. In the context of recent changes in government and governmental policies, Gunilla Dahlberg and Gunnar Åsén consider the relationship between goal setting (what quality care goals will be), goal governing (by whom quality care goals are established) and the evaluation of goals (questioning the 'neutrality' of evaluation). In the closing pages they argue for an interactive, associative model of goal setting, goal governing and evaluation predicated on a reflexive discourse including the broader citizenry of the country utilizing a process structure of locally based forums or 'plazas'.

INTRODUCTION

In the context of the economic and fiscal crisis in Sweden, where serious efforts are under way to restructure the public welfare system, decentralization, goal-setting and evaluation have become new 'prestige' words. Questions about the value of the system of early childhood services for children, parents and society have been conspicuous by their absence, in debates as well as research. As a result, institutions bearing[1] cultural and social values have, in some respects, come to be treated as business enterprises, with children and parents viewed as consumers. One problem that will be addressed in the chapter is the fact that evaluation and goal-setting are still overly simplistic and instrumental concepts; evaluation is often regarded as a purely technical question, closely related to the construction of methods and tests to study effects. The chapter will discuss the dangers inherent in this very simplistic notion and explore different ways of negotiating the relationship between values and goals, generating different approaches – economic, political, professional and associative – to evaluating and determining quality. The 'associative approach' will be discussed more extensively as a valuable means of dealing with the meaning of quality and evaluation.

CHILD CARE AND EVALUATION – THE CASE OF SWEDEN

Political and economic changes over the course of the past ten years have brought about a change in public discourse about the Swedish welfare state and its responsibilities. Criticism has been aimed at the public sector and has focused on the financing of the public sector and the extensive involvement of the state. In discussions dealing with child care and education, two main demands have been voiced repeatedly: (1) the demand for greater choice, that is increased possibilities for parents and children to choose among different forms of child care and education; and (2) the demand for increased effectiveness and productivity in services. In the Swedish context, somewhat simplified, two solutions have been identified: on the one hand to let market forces play a greater role and, on the other, to decentralize and deregulate (Dahlberg, Lundgren and Åsén, 1991). In practice these two solutions appear simultaneously.

Underlying these demands and solutions are different values and different ways of looking at the responsibilities of the welfare state and its capacity to contribute to a more just distribution of resources. These profound changes will affect not only the responsibilities of the state and the local authorities in the future, but also citizens' responsibilities and their possibilities for exerting greater influence and enjoying more active participation in shaping the direction of policies and programmes.

A distinguishing feature of Swedish child care has been the relatively strong and centralized role of political governing as the main way to direct and control services. Historically a certain uniformity of quality has been guaranteed by way of central policy-making and the establishment of rules and regulations. The Swedish child care system has been controlled by three basic sets of instruments or national level governing systems: (1) the legal steering system; (2) the economic steering system; and (3) the ideological steering system (goals and content). By virtue of these steering systems, Swedish child welfare has been assigned a societal mandate, which is formulated in the Social Services Act. This Act establishes certain values, values that are inalienable in the Swedish society, such as democracy, equality, freedom of expression, children's rights and civil rights.

Through the different steering systems a national policy of early childhood education and care, closely related to social and family policy, has been developed. The expansion and development of child care services has been spurred by the desire to satisfy and unite various aspects: pedagogical, that is the importance of these services for the development and upbringing of children; socio-political, that is their importance for parents and children, family life and social equality; economic, that is their importance for the public economy, economic distribution and the private economy of parents.

On this basis, a national system of early childhood services has been developed since the mid-1960s. Today, when more than 80 per cent of all Swedish children between birth and six years of age have a working mother, 55 per cent of all children in this age group attend early childhood services. Although attendance is not compulsory, in 1991 the Swedish Parliament passed a resolution that all children from one and a half years of age shall have the right to participate in educational activities in early childhood services, whether full-time or part-time.

EVALUATION

A new steering system

In the context of the economic and fiscal crisis and efforts to change the public welfare system in Sweden (and in many other western countries) decentralization, goal-setting and evaluation have become new 'prestige' words. Goal governing has become the new way to direct and control services. The main idea of goal governing is that rules and relatively detailed plans are replaced by clear goals – 'management by objectives' – and strategies for evaluation of goal attainment.

With increased decentralization and deregulation, evaluation of the quality of early childhood education and care programmes will grow in importance as an instrument for governing, as it identifies, directly or indirectly, what is seen as important to govern and hence defines what is important in different programmes. As a consequence of this evolution, the evaluation system can be seen as a new fourth steering system (Lundgren, 1990).

This view of evaluation as a steering system is in keeping with the argument that 'evaluation in the modern state has a policing quality, whether we see it as part of the noble intent and desire of those who seek to improve school or as part of the darker side of social regulation' (Popkewitz, 1990, p. 105). Evaluation and its policing quality has also been discussed as a paradox of decentralization:

> Both decentralization and evaluation have to do with the exercise of power, and there is always the possibility that the power that decentralization gives away with one hand, evaluation may take back with the other.
>
> (Weiler, 1990, p. 61)

Evaluation and values

The concept of evaluation is difficult to define and has become more diffuse with its increased use for different applications. Basically, it is defined as the evaluation of the correspondence between goals and outcomes. The classic problem is then how goals and outcomes are made comparable (Lundgren, 1990; Dahlberg, Lundgren and Åsén, 1991).

Historically, the concept of evaluation has become a part of a rational paradigm. The legitimation of evaluation in an educational system has been strongly linked to objective measures. This demand for objectivity has in turn linked educational evaluation to the development of techniques for measurement and statistics within psychology and education. Lundgren (1990) describes evaluation, somewhat simplified, as 'a development of quantitative methods for measuring educational outcomes' (p. 38).

Until the mid-1960s evaluation and testing were almost synonymous (Thorndike and Hagen, 1955). Since then, new models and methods of evaluation have been developed hand in hand with the broadening functions of education. Even if the methods and models for evaluation in use today present a rather rich picture, expectations of what educational evaluation should be are primarily based on the use of tests. With growing demands for accountability, the pressure of having 'objective' evaluations reinforces a rather simplistic notion of evaluation (Kogan, 1986).

As we see it, there is a great risk of evaluation of quality being looked upon as a value-free activity and as a strictly technical question, whose main objective is to find methods to study effects. Another approach to evaluation is to consider it as part of a mental structure by which problems are defined, or, in the words of Popkewitz (1990):

> Evaluative strategies 'carry' cultural and social interests not evident in their formal rationales and publicly defined purposes. The concern for achievement, participation, community, collegiality and professionalization contain particular assumptions that may, in fact, reintroduce bureaucratic practices to schooling.
>
> (p. 107)

The notion of what is important in a programme or a process and what is viewed as a pedagogical practice of high quality will always be influenced – and perhaps even changed – by the evaluation strategies and tools. When evaluations are transformed into concrete techniques and methods and enter a concrete pedagogical process, they will always have an impact on the direction, structure and content of this process. Hence, evaluation will have great impact on how ideas and definitions of knowledge, as well as how social relations are manifested in pedagogical practice (Bernstein, 1990; Popkewitz, 1990).

There is always a risk that the instruments used for evaluation will replace the goals that have been established for a specific practice. Consequently, how evaluation is handled and how quality is defined in early childhood education and care must not be seen as isolated from the goals and the social and cultural values the institutions are bearing. What is defined as good quality or high efficiency must be viewed in relation to these values.

Goal governing and evaluation

When discussing evaluation it is imperative to begin by analyzing the question of goal governing, since evaluation, and hence indirectly how quality in early childhood education and care is defined, will assume different meanings depending on the nature of the goal governing involved. Below we will isolate and discuss in brief different models of goal governing that are relevant to continuing discussions about efficiency and quality improvement within early childhood education and care services. Each generates a different approach to evaluation and a different methodology for determining quality.

Four different approaches to goal formulation can be discerned: political, economic, professional and associative. It should be pointed out that while these types can be separated analytically, in practice they operate jointly. Even if this classification is an oversimplification it can provide a structure for analysis and discussion of how early childhood education and care can be governed, evaluated and developed. The models provide a structure in that they clarify the different meanings which goal governing and evaluation can have. We will start by discussing the first three models and then later in the chapter outline a fourth and alternative model, which we have called 'an associative model'.

As shown earlier, in Sweden a system for early childhood education and care has been developed, where the system has been governed by different national regulations and rules covering, for example, staff:child ratios and educational qualifications required of staff. Through this formulation of regulations, the state has, from a political position, tried to guarantee a certain quality and a degree of national uniformity in this respect. In Sweden one can say that *a political model* has dominated. In such a model the responsibility for setting goals falls to the politicians. According to this model, evaluation serves above all to evaluate the extent to which the political goals have been met in the pedagogical practice.

The move towards decentralization in Sweden has resulted in a shift from rule and regulation governing to goal governing. Parallel to this has been a shift towards a more market-oriented social welfare system (Marklund, 1992), which has resulted in a weaker role for political governance and influence. One can argue that recent discussion concerning deregulation of the public sector has had its foundation in *a market-oriented goal-governing model*, anchored in the world of private enterprise. This form of goal governing is based on the idea that institutions for education should be governed by market demands. This position has led to a focus on consumer freedom of choice and on the service different institutions provide to consumers. In this model consumers and users are given full responsibility for choosing between different centres and schools.

Today, the work being carried out in child care centres is often compared with the work carried out in private business. This is to suggest that the work in question is being performed under similar conditions. Some heads of centres, especially larger ones, do have a task which largely resembles that of a manager having to supervise 30–40 employees, serve more than 200 meals a day to more than 100 children and administer an annual budget equivalent to several million Swedish crowns (Dahlberg and Åsén, 1987).

Certainly there are similarities, if we look, for example, at the number of employees involved and some of the management-related tasks. But if we consider the type of organization concerned, some fundamental differences are apparent. The decision-making process of a manager of a private business is largely governed by the market. The value of the product the company produces is determined by the demand for the product in different markets, and the product is assigned an economic value which is a direct function of this demand. But child care centres are not producing products whose value can be determined by a given market. Here the 'production process' is concerned with basic human and societal processes whose aim is to integrate children into society and build some basic skills and competence among the coming generation. In other words, child care centres are culture-bearing institutions, whose value can neither be assessed in terms of what they produce nor determined in a simple and unambiguous fashion. Even if early childhood education is increasingly being discussed in market terms, the market will never be able to fully determine the value of the work carried out. Its value is more difficult to measure and is, above all, a function of its importance both for the individual and for society as a whole, and the degree of legitimacy it enjoys and confidence it inspires in different groups in the society (see Dahlberg and Åsén, 1992).

Evaluation in the market-oriented model has become a question of measuring efficiency and productivity in economic terms and the extent to which child care centres and schools have been able to establish a functioning relationship with the market. Evaluation and results from evaluation are used here to stimulate competition between different centres or schools, partly as a means of marketing the profiles and quality of specific centres and schools. As a consequence, children and parents are viewed as consumers and users, and it follows that an important function of evaluation is to determine whether the users are pleased with the service.

In evaluations of productivity and efficiency, as well as in media discussions concerning child care services, the market-oriented model has become dominant and almost taken for granted. To a certain degree, early childhood education and care has been assigned goals different from the existing, politically developed goals. This shift to a market-oriented perspective has taken place very rapidly in Sweden. Experiences in the United States and United Kingdom demonstrate the consequences of a market-oriented model. These kinds of changes do not necessarily lead to a higher degree of choice for children and parents. In the long run one can see the reverse take place, with schools choosing children (Ball, 1990).

With decentralization and increased local responsibility a discussion of the role of the professional teacher becomes increasingly salient. Historically, *a professional goal-governing model* was interactive with the politically determined goals. Professionals' inclusion had the effect of transforming political goals into pedagogical goals, with a subsequent evaluation of the pedagogical practice. Evaluation with this model becomes a question of determining how well the practice is carried out in relation to different goals. This can be accomplished by relating practice to specific criteria or standards of what is high pedagogical quality. These forms of evaluation are mostly internal, for example evaluations by colleagues and self-evaluations. An important starting point for this kind of goal governing is that evaluation will be able to contribute to the development of pedagogical practice and in this connection to lay the groundwork for common ethics and a common base of knowledge (Dahlberg, Lundgren and Åsén, 1991).

In the United States and the United Kingdom, where this form of evaluation is increasing in use, it is particularly the teachers' interest organizations or the local authorities who exert pressure to bring about the development of different scales or different forms of inspection systems to evaluate quality. These accreditation programmes have many purposes – from improving the quality of a specific service to functioning as a marketing instrument for daycare centres of high quality (Audit Commission, 1989; NAEYC, 1991).

However, questions concerning how educational evaluation should be handled must not be seen in isolation from basic values-based questions such as children's rights and social position, and the kind of competences children should develop (Dahlberg, 1992).

THE ACADEMIZATION OF EARLY CHILDHOOD EDUCATION

A phenomenon which has become evident throughout the industrialized world is the fact that the institutionalization of upbringing is encompassing younger and younger age groups. This is, among other things, a function of the ever-increasing number of women in the labour market and the concomitant need for some form of institutional care and upbringing. With the growth of the information society, new demands for knowledge and competence are emerging. It could even be said that institutionalization, in one form or another, has become the integrating factor in the new information society, comparable, perhaps, to the importance of work as an integrating factor in the industrial society (Dahlberg, 1982).

In a world of fierce economic competition, the focus of attention is turned towards the youngest children and the possibilities of educating ever younger age groups of children. This focus must be understood in terms of the renewed interest in how education can contribute to the economic growth of society, thereby laying the groundwork for a nation's capacity to compete successfully in international markets. As Olsen and Zigler (1989) have noted, the nationalistic interest in competitiveness, together with the 'excellence' movement in education, has fostered a turn towards instruction of basic skills from an early age. In many countries there has been increased emphasis on school readiness and acquisition of specific academic skills among young children (Spodek, 1982; Walsh, 1989). There is a risk of being guided by too narrow a view of knowledge, which emphasizes making the reproduction of knowledge more effective rather than making the child's learning and production of knowledge more effective. However, as shown by several studies, such a simplistic notion of knowledge as a foundation for working with young children does not produce the desired long-term effects: programmes relying on a more holistic and dynamic notion of child development seem to be more successful (Osborn and Milbank, 1987; Katz, 1987; Kärrby, 1990).

As the school system reaches younger age groups and places new demands on young children, new institutional definitions, as to what is good and what is bad, are created. At the same time, children, at earlier ages, are weeded out of the system on the grounds that they cannot meet the demands made on them. The problem is thus shifted to the child – with reference to his or her lack of capability and competence – ignoring the question of whether the demands in and of themselves are wrong or unreasonable. For some children this can be a very painful lesson. They come to believe from a very early age that they cannot succeed in kindergarten or nursery school and they enter a process of 'meta-learning'. In other words, what they learn is that they cannot learn. These changes in the demands on young children can also be related to the fact that modern society is increasingly measuring a person's worth by his or her achievements, which can easily result in attaching too much weight to what is rational and useful, and viewing the child, her nature and development, as a product (Dahlberg, 1982).

Parallel to this pressure to make the school system more effective, with the system catering to younger and younger children, there is a sign of increasing emphasis on evaluation, not only in child care services but in the compulsory school system as well. These evaluations may, through their aims and directions, influence what is seen as important and valuable in a pedagogical programme for young children. The strategies of evaluating the higher grades will also influence what is seen as excellent pedagogical practice in the lower grades.

In a discussion on the national evaluation of the Swedish compulsory school system, it has been pointed out that 'with a product evaluation of this type follows the risk that more basic problems will disappear from the school debate and be replaced by discussions which revolve around superficial product statements, that is children's test scores' (Franke-Wikberg, 1989, p. 13). Simple types of evaluations (scales and tests for example) are used more frequently today, despite the fact that there are many indications that they are of limited value and hardly contribute to developing educational practice and its quality (Shepard and Smith, 1986). Teachers often note that tests seldom provide any new information beyond what they already know. What is striking is the power that test scores have on parents, on politicians and on the public. How well children manage these tests can be totally decisive for the confidence and legitimacy of a specific school or child care centre.

UNDERSTANDING MODERN CHILDHOOD

How early childhood educational policy and practice are developed is always related to the eternal philosophical question of what a society hopes for and expects of its children – a question that must be raised by each generation. However, the 'solutions' that are adopted reflect not only our conception of children's potential, their civil rights and position in society, but also our own understanding of the past, the present and the future and how we should meet the requirements and challenges of the modernization process with its struggles between ideas and social forces.

If we hope to renew pedagogical practice and restore the legitimacy of early childhood education, it is of paramount importance to understand what kind of society children live in and what kind of future they will encounter. The societal process of modernization and the high rate of change in modern society results in new competency requirements and hence calls for new ways of thinking concerning early childhood education.

Evaluation of quality in education and upbringing cannot be seen in isolation from the question of the functions education and upbringing serve in a society. These processes are fundamentally concerned with the integration of the next generation into society. If we did not integrate our children into our civilization and tradition, our society would cease to function. Just a few decades ago, we lived in a society that was less complicated and more visible for children and adults alike: children could see adults at work in daily life, and their upbringing, to a great extent, was directly connected to the production process. In such a stable society, where the future is more or less marked out, the integrating elements of upbringing can be predominant. But integration is not sufficient in a society marked by rapid change. In such a changing society, where we can only hint at the contours of the future, children must be prepared to take an active and constructive part in developing and changing society.

Pedagogy in today's complex and invisible society must take into account the idea of *making the invisible visible* to children and youth. In a modern society, where information and knowledge are tied not only to the production of goods, but also to communication, symbols and relationships, it will become increasingly important to develop not only traditional basic skills, but *creativity, communicative competence and problem-solving capacity*.

Today's children and youth live and reside in many different contexts, each with somewhat different rules. The capacity to understand and interpret these rules, coupled with the ability to perform in different social arenas, becomes an important aspect of *social competence*. Modernity also places a greater demand on the ability of handling complexity – being able to integrate different experiences into a whole, to search for new knowledge and, together with others, to shape one's own identity.

Our society is also characterized by *increased choices*, which can mean not only uncertainty but also possibilities for cultural change. Thomas Ziehe, the German social-psychologist, notes the concept of 'ability-to-do' as becoming increasingly dominant in contemporary society (Ziehe, 1986). To understand what different situations offer, to be able to take a stand, and, above all, to make the 'right' choices consequently becomes an important skill to develop.

As we see it, the great pedagogical challenge today is to create a pedagogical practice that can match the demands of our changing world for new competences – not only traditional, basic skills – and, at the same, develop the rights and potential of *all* children.

HOW CAN LEGITIMACY BE RESTORED?

Economic recession, not only in Sweden but also in other countries, means that today we must argue for early childhood education in a completely different fashion than in the past. As shown earlier, the discussion on early childhood education and care is tied, more and more, to questions of economy, productivity and effectiveness. Hand in hand with the crisis in the welfare system, a new rhetoric has evolved in the field of educational policy, a rhetoric which is based on economic and management theory rather than educational philosophy (Telhaug, 1990). In this context, the discussion of its value for society, for parents and for children is no longer at the top of the agenda.

It is not by chance that many researchers are presently discussing questions concerning social justice and political democracy in a decentralized and deregulated system. Johan P. Olsen, for example, argues that the renewal of the public sector is based on apolitical rhetoric. The goals of economy and efficiency are presented as value-free, to be shared by everyone, while political and values-based questions, such as whose welfare the reforms improve, are avoided (Olsen, 1991).

However, the crisis in the welfare system is not only an economic crisis, but an ideological and moral one, where the values represented by the welfare state are seen as no longer valid.

We are convinced that the question of how to restore legitimacy under existing conditions can only be tackled if the economic aspects are more closely connected with the pedagogical and values-based aspects of early childhood education. A prerequisite for this is that pedagogical practice and its functions must be made visible outside the world of schools and child care centres and become a part of public discourse.

However, it is difficult to restore cultural legitimacy exclusively through economic, administrative and bureaucratic means (Habermas, 1985). One condition for the renewal of early childhood education is that the discussion of society's policies for children and youth must take a more central position in public discussion and action. As we see it, this requires the participation of a variety of concerned groups and a pedagogical practice based on empowerment, participation and reflective discourse between parents, staff, administrators and politicians. Another closely related question is how evaluation could function to support development of pedagogical practice and, at the same time, help to restore the legitimacy of early childhood education and care.

The associative model

It is here that an interactive or 'associative' model for governing could be an alternative. This model is based on an idea, a vision, of combining the professional and the political model with an idea of civic participation and democracy. Fundamental to the associative model is that institutions for early childhood education and care are viewed as institutions bearing cultural and social values, in which teachers take part in wider societal processes of acculturation. Accordingly, how quality in early childhood education and care is defined and evaluated will be a concern not only for politicians, experts, administrators and professionals, but will also be a matter for the broader citizenry.

In line with such a model it becomes important to create forums or arenas for discussion and reflection where people can engage as citizens with devotion and visions – not only as stakeholders positioned in an administrative perspective. Within these arenas a lively dialogue could take place, in which early childhood education and care are placed within a larger societal context and where questions concerning children's position are made vivid. One could say that it is the complex practice of early childhood services with which citizens have actively to engage. This is in line with the idea of Giroux that the school should ideally be understood as a polity, as a locus of citizenship:

Within this locus, students and teachers can engage in a process of deliberation and discussion aimed at advancing the public welfare in accordance with fundamental moral judgements and principles. To bring schools closer to the concept of polity, it is necessary to define them as public spaces that seek to recapture the idea of critical democracy and community.

(Giroux, 1989, p. 201)

By public space he means a concrete set of learning conditions where people come together to speak, to engage in dialogue, to share their stories and to struggle together within social relations that strengthen rather than weaken possibilities for active citizenship.

The idea of creating arenas for discussion and reflection also connects to Habermas' theory of communicative action. He criticizes modern political life and proposes a possibility for emancipation through communication between equals. Habermas' idea of communicative rationality presupposes a setting where one can explore different actions and reach a common agreement and understanding of future progress (Habermas, 1981).

The creation of forums for a locally-based public discussion, with the participation of different groups, is vital to this process. Examples of the development of reflexive discourse in early childhood and other human services are the growth in recent years in Sweden of numerous arenas or 'plazas'. In these plazas politicians, administrators, teachers and other representatives come together to discuss different aspects of early childhood education. Some plazas focus on the pedagogical work being done at the level of local services, while others focus on questions and problems related to the responsibilities of the community, regional or national level. The purpose is to establish a dialogue, characterized by debate, confrontation and exchange of experiences (Göthson, 1991).

The plaza should not be seen primarily as the place for traders, but as the place for a dialogue between independent citizens. It is the symbol of a vibrant democracy. 'Bring forward your experience into the plaza' has been the motto for one of these plazas, which says a lot about the underlying concept. This motto refers to

the idea that exchange of experience creates respect for different approaches and conditions and counters superficial acceptance of models and general organizational solutions . . . It also refers to the idea that everyday and practical work must be the starting point for all leadership and development work.

(Göthson, 1991, p. 11)

Documentation as a base for reflection

A reflective dialogue and a reflective practice presupposes material to reflect on, material that is visible for all whom it concerns. Another presupposition is that the pedagogue and the child are given a voice in this process, a voice that can be communicated to others. Seen against this background a conscious and well accomplished documentation of the pedagogical practice is exceedingly important. To document a pedagogical practice can imply many different things. We will here give some illustrations. The ideas behind our view of documenting have received much inspiration from the work carried out in the early childhood services in the town of Reggio Emilia in Northern Italy.

This view of documentation has to be understood in the context of the pedagogical philosophy underlying the work in these services: a deep respect for children's rights, for their potential and for their ability to create a learning organization. Reggio has succeeded in forging a unique way of working with children. What is most unique about Reggio Emilia is that a whole community, not just isolated centres, has been able to marry a common values system and an elaborate pedagogical philosophy, on the basis of a scientific approach. What is more, it has managed to put this philosophy into practice: 'nowhere else in the world is there such a seamless and symbiotic relationship between a school's progressive philosophy and its practices' (Gardner, 1993, p. x). This applied pedagogical philosophy for children has received widespread support from teachers, administrators, public officials, parents and citizens in the community.

The motto 'A child has a hundred languages but is deprived of ninety-nine' is closely associated with Reggio Emilia, a motto that signifies their endeavour to carry out pedagogical work characterized by a holistic view of language and communication. Their work is also characterized by an exploring attitude. The expressions 'the exploring child' and 'the exploring teacher' reflect the belief that adults, as well as children, must be guided by an exploring attitude towards work and towards life. When exploring reality, imagination and humour play a large role.

Project and theme work is used as a way of working from a holistic perspective and as a way of organizing and structuring the daily work. By testing hypotheses, thoughts and 'theories' on conditions and different phenomena in the outside world, the child's self-confidence, as well as his ability to create, understand, learn and exert influence, is enhanced.

As in Reggio Emilia, we are convinced that a pedagogic practice demands continuous adaptation and reflection if it is to evolve. *A reflective attitude* towards the practice makes large demands on the professionalism of teachers, but it is also a challenge that can spark curiosity, enthusiasm and involvement. This requires that the teachers take advantage of and build on acquired and well-tested experiences.

In Reggio Emilia much time and effort is spent *documenting the work* – to make the practice visible for staff, children, parents and others. To make the practice visible, the documentation is always a part of the daily work, and not something external. It is important, therefore, that it originates from everyday work and experiences. Through documentation by video-cameras, photos, tape-recorders and other means of the processes whereby children create and develop their understanding and knowledge of the world around them, a deeper awareness of the consequences of these processes is born, which provides a basis for changing and developing everyday work. In this way the act of documentation can become a learning process, which can lay an important foundation for further work. It can also furnish parents with concrete information about children's daily life at the child care centres, thus enhancing their insight and capacity for participation and promoting parental co-operation.

Through discussions in relation to what has been documented, documentation can additionally be a valuable base for connecting theory with practice. By starting out from documented examples of pedagogical processes, one can move from the specific to the more general. Accordingly, documented pedagogical processes can function as 'exemplary examples'. By documenting pedagogical processes, the practitioners can – on the base of documented examples – contribute new experiences and theoretical aspects concerning children's socialization, learning and ways of creating knowledge.

This process of documentation deals, in fact, with how we adults can provide the child with a voice, a visible identity, in contemporary society. Documentation can also be used as a way of visualizing and revealing pedagogical practice to the world outside the centre. Hence each child care centre can create a public voice and a visible identity with its own history. By making the practice visible, documentation can function as a base for the public dialogue about early childhood education and care.

It has to be emphasized that documentation per se is less important than the reflection and discussion to which it can give rise. The reflective discourse enables pedagogues to contribute to the production, not only the reproduction, of knowledge.

CONCLUSION

Decentralization implies a tug-of-war of power and influence, in which there are advocates of different models of goal governing. The professional, the political and the associative models provide the greatest potential for ensuring that national values, principles and goals are embodied in institutions for early childhood education and care. The market model is the least relevant when it comes to considering the societal and cultural functions of these institutions.

Seen in the light of a pedagogical perspective and in the light of the functions that pedagogical institutions serve, the associative model displays great similarities with the professional model in that it builds on the idea of the reflective practitioner (Schön, 1983), a teacher who analyses and reflects on the pedagogical practice in pursuit of a more elaborated understanding of the existing practice. However, a reflecting process requires a visible practice and it is here that our stress on documentation becomes critical. This requires in turn that pedagogical work is viewed as an intellectual activity and that teachers' work is given conditions that are compatible with such a view. Giroux (1989) underscores this concern when he writes:

Here I extend the traditional view of the intellectual as someone who is able to analyze various interests and contradictions within society to someone capable of articulating emancipatory possibilities and working towards their realization. Teachers who assume the role of transformative intellectuals treat students as critical agents, utilize dialogue, and make knowledge meaningful, critical, and ultimately emancipatory.

(p. 175)

The ideal would be a power-free discourse between equal partners who share an interest. In this discourse ideas and arguments can be diverged. The purpose is to test – in a free exchange of ideas – the power and capacity of arguments. Better arguments receive greater weight.

This ideal is in line with the emancipatory perspective of the Enlightenment, in which people assume responsibility for the governance of their own lives. However, power and power relationships must not be ignored:

> The task of the Enlightenment is bound with a recognition that there are multiple claims, that these claims are historically bound and emerge from the social struggles and tensions of a world in which we live, and that the production of human possibilities always contains contradiction
>
> (Popkewitz, 1990, p. 114)

In this chapter we have not presented a completed model, but some preliminary sketches marking out in which direction evaluation should go if one wants to guarantee questions of values and quality in early childhood education and care and if one wants to use evaluation to improve pedagogical practice. First and last, our associative model approach is concerned with how we value the society's institutions for early childhood education and care, with children's rights and position and, above all, with the forms and practices of democracy. The associative model could be a way of restoring cultural legitimation for early childhood education and care. This model opens up and forms the basis for a new type of evaluative thinking – a thinking in which evaluation can be seen as a learning process building on documentation and reflection.

REFERENCES

AUDIT COMMISSION (1989) *Assuring Quality in Education. A Report on Local Education Authority Inspectors and Advisers*, Her Majesty's Stationery Office, London.

BALL, S. (1990) *Markets, Morality and Equality in Education (Hillcole Group Paper 5)* Tufnell Press, London.

BERNSTEIN, B. (1990) *The Structuring of Pedagogic Discourse. Class, Codes and Control; Volume 4*, Routledge, London.

DAHLBERG, G. (1982) *Kulturöverföringens Rationalisering* (The Rationalization of Cultural Reproduction) Högskolan för Lärarutbildning i Stockholm, Stockholm.

DAHLBERG, G. (1992) *Child-Parent Relationship and Socialization in the Context of Modern Childhood*, Paper given at the Vth European Conference on Developmental Psychology, Seville, 6–9 September.

DAHLBERG, G. and ÅSÉN, g. (1987) *Föreståndarna och Förskolans Ledning* (Supervisors and Preschool Leadership) HLS Förlag, Stockholm.

DAHLBERG, G., LUNDGREN, U. P. and ÅSÉN, g. (1991) *Att Utvärdera Barnomsorg* (Evaluating Early Childhood Education) HLS Förlag, Stockholm.

DAHLBERG, G. and ÅSÉN, g. (1992) Mot vad leds barnomsorgen? (Towards what is early childhood education headed?) *Locus*, no. 2, pp. 7–17.

FRANKE-WIKBERG, S. (1989) Utvärdering i olika skepnader (Evaluation with different shapes) *Läroplansdebatt*, no. 42, pp. 11–13.

GARDNER, H (1993) Complementary perspectives on Reggio Emilia, in C. Edwards, L. Gandini and G. Forman (eds.) *The Hundred Languages of Children: The Reggio Emilia Approach to Early Childhood Education*, Ablex Publishing Corporation, Norwood: NJ.

GIROUX, H. A. (1989) *Schooling for Democracy: Critical Pedagogy in the Modern Age*, Routledge, London.

GÖTHSON, H. (1991) *Torget. Från Kommunala Riktlinjer till Utvärdering* (From Community Policies to Evaluation) Utbildningsförlaget, Stockholm.

HABERMAS, J. (1981) *Theorie des Kommunikativen Handelns*, Suhrkamp, Frankfurt.

HABERMAS, J. (1985) Den nya oöverskådligheten – om välfärdsstatens konsekvenser (The new unlucidity – on the consequences of the welfare state) *Ord & Bild*, no. 3, pp. 60–74.

KÄRRBY, G. (1990) *De Äldre Förskolebarnen – Inlärning och Utveckling* (The older Preschoolers – Learning and Development) Utbildningsförlaget, Stockholm.

KATZ, L. (1987) *What Should Young Children be Learning?* ERIC Digest.

KOGAN, M. (1986) *Education Accountability: An Analytic Overview*, Hutchinson, London.

LUNDGREN, U. P. (1990) Educational policymaking, decentralisation and evaluation, in M. Granheim, M. Kogan and U. P. Lundgren (eds.) *Evaluation as Policymaking: Introducing Evaluation into a National Decentralised Educational System*, Jessica Kingsley Publishers, London.

MARKLUND, S. (1992) The decomposition of social policy in Sweden, *Scandinavian Journal of Social Welfare*, Vol. 1, pp. 2–11.

NAEYC (1991) *Guide to Accreditation by the National Academy of Early Childhood Programs: Revised Edition*, National Association for the Education of Young Children, Washington: DC.

OLSEN, D. and ZIGLER, E. (1989) An assessment of the all-day kindergarten movement, *Early Childhood Research Quarterly*, Vol. 4, pp. 167–87.

OLSEN, J. P. (1991) Modernization programs in perspective, *Governance*, Vol. 4, no. 2, pp. 133–57.

OSBORN, A. F. and MILBANK, J. E. (1987) *The Effects of Early Education: A Report from the Child Health and Education Study*, Clarendon Press, Oxford.

POPKEWITZ, T. S. (1990) Some problems and problematics in the production of evaluation, in M. Granheim, M. Kogan and U. P. Lundgren (eds.) *Evaluation as Policymaking: Introducing Evaluation into a National Decentralised Educational System*, Jessica Kingsley Publishers, London.

SCHÖN, D. A. (1983) *The Reflective Practitioner: How Professionals Think in Action*, Basic Books, New York.

SHEPARD, L. A. and SMITH, M. L. (1986) Synthesis of research on school readiness and kindergarten retention, *Educational Leadership* Vol. 44, pp. 78–86.

SPODEK, B. (1982). The kindergarten: a retrospective and contemporary view, in L. Katz (ed.) *Current Topics in Early Childhood, Vol. IV*, Ablex, Norwood: NJ.

TELHAUG, A. O. (1990) *Den Nye Utbildningspolitiske Retoriken* (The New Rhetoric Within Educational Policy), Universitetsförlaget, Oslo.

THORNDIKE, R. L. and HAGEN, E. (1955) *Measurement and Evaluation in Psychology and Education*, John Wiley, New York.

WALSH, D. J. (1989) Changes in kindergarten? Why here? Why now? *Early Childhood Research Quarterly* Vol. 4, pp. 377–91.

WEILER, H. (1990) Decentralisation in educational governance: an exercise in contradiction, in M. Granheim, M. Kogan and U. P. Lundgren (eds.) *Evaluation as Policymaking: Introducing Evaluation into a National Decentralised Educational System*, Jessica Kingsley Publishers, London.

ZIEHE, T. (1986) Inför avmystifceringen av världen. Ungdom och kulturell modernisering (Toward demystification of the world. Youngsters and cultural modernization) in M. Löfgren and A. Molander (eds.) *Postmoderna Tider* (Postmodern Times), Norstedts Förlag, Stockholm.

NOTE

1. The English word *bearing* has been used throughout this chapter to translate the Swedish word *bärande*; however, it is a literal translation and does not convey the full sense of the Swedish original. *Bärande* refers to the way that institutions are permeated with cultural and social values, both growing out of these values and sustaining these values through their work.

CHAPTER 12

Towards an Inclusionary Approach in Defining Quality

ALAN PENCE AND PETER MOSS

A DIFFERENT PARADIGM FOR QUALITY

This volume commenced with the statement that 'quality in early childhood services is a relative concept'. As such, quality in early childhood services is a constructed concept, subjective in nature and based on values, beliefs and interest, rather than an objective and universal reality. Quality child care is, to a large extent, in the eye of the beholder – and that beholder can be anyone or any group from among a range of stakeholders, each with an interest in early childhood services.

Historically, defining quality child care and the application of definitions through research studies, assessment instruments, regulations and so on have been the prerogative of a limited set of powerful stakeholders. Discussion, description and evaluation of quality child care has been dominated by experts from government, certain professions and academic research. The approach, therefore, has been *exclusionary* in nature, and as such has involved the exercise of power and control – even though the stakeholders exercising this power and control may be motivated by benign concerns and are often unaware of exercising control, excluding others or operating on the basis of values, beliefs and interests.

Models of quality based on private market approaches to early childhood services which treat services as businesses and which emphasize the criterion of consumer satisfaction have been equally exclusionary, albeit in rather different ways. The consumer-producer relationship at the heart of this approach is private in essence. There is little place for the involvement or interests of others.

This volume poses a challenge to this exclusionary paradigm for defining quality – not to the experts, providers and users of services (all of whom are important stakeholders with a continuing role to play in defining quality) but to the exclusionary approach itself. The challenge is to develop a new paradigm for defining quality based on participation by a broad range of stakeholders, and recognition of values, beliefs and interests underpinning definitions. Within this alternative paradigm, the roles, processes and principles typically found within the exclusionary paradigm are transformed: limited participation is replaced by broad access to the process of definition; power concentration gives way to power distribution; few voices make way for many; an assumption of rational objectivity is challenged by recognition of the essential subjectivity of the process and the role of values, beliefs and interests; the search for quality universals becomes the exchange of quality perspectives leading to definitions specific to a particular spatial and temporal context and capable of evolving through a dynamic and continuous process.

Much remains to be understood about this new approach – what we call the 'inclusionary paradigm'. At this stage, however, we can discern some of the main parameters. Most important of all is *who* participates in the process of defining quality. What is the range of stakeholders involved? There is a continuum here. The New Zealand chartering procedure described by Anne Smith and Sarah-Eve Farquhar was intended to include management, staff and parents. Denmark, as described by both Ole Langsted and Claus Jensen, is moving towards the inclusion of children. Perhaps most inclusive of all is the 'associative model' for goal governing, proposed by Gunilla Dahlberg and Gunnar Åsén, in which definition is the concern not only of politicians, experts, administrators and professionals but also of all citizens. They also instance the Italian town of Reggio Emilia, and the involvement of the whole community there in the development of a system of early childhood services based on a common value system and pedagogical philosophy.

Another important dimension to be considered within the inclusionary paradigm is the *nature of participation* by different stakeholders. Helen Penn's chapter about Strathclyde presents a range of stakeholders involved in the process of developing quality; but they often related to each other in an adversarial manner with a high level of conflict. By contrast, Alan Pence and Marie McCallum, working in a very different context, describe an approach which prioritized the development of a partnership based on respect, trust and caring. Gunilla Dahlberg and Gunnar Åsén recognize the virtues of partnership, positing power-free discourse between equal partners as an ideal, but also recognize that in reality power and power relationships will intrude and need therefore to be recognized and accommodated.

Participation can also be defined in terms of the *extent of involvement* and actual influence of those stakeholders who participate in the process of defining quality. Do all play a full and active part? Or are some (like parents in some of the centres described by Anne Smith and Sarah-Eve Farquhar in their chapter about the New Zealand chartering exercise) included but mainly in a marginal or tokenistic way?

Finally, defining quality should involve *many levels*. Definitions of quality are needed for different levels: as Julia Brophy and June Statham conclude, we need to be able to describe and evaluate quality at the level of service systems (national, regional, local) as well as within individual services. The process of definition, whether of systems or of individual services, needs to operate at different levels, from national and regional government though to individual organizations and services. The extent and nature of inclusion can vary between levels, as can the scope for decision – or what is open for different levels to define. The New Zealand chartering process sought, not altogether successfully in practice, to combine certain centrally defined and non-negotiable aspects of child care quality with other aspects which were delegated for determination by individual centres.

Defining quality on a multi-level basis raises the important issue of whether boundaries should be imposed on the extent of relativism. In a pluralistic society, where definitions of quality are recognized as values-based, are certain values and certain parts of the quality definition to be deemed non-negotiable and hence to be imposed, thereby limiting the scope for an inclusionary process? If so, what values? And how and by whom should they be determined? Pat Petrie suggests that in democracies this is a task for legislatures, expressing certain core values which reflect common interests and social cohesion. Carol Joseph, Jane Lane and Sudesh Sharma put the case that one such core value must be equality and suggest a second basis for determining such non-negotiable values – internationally agreed value statements such as the UN Convention on the Rights of the Child.

WORKING WITH THE NEW PARADIGM

The inclusionary paradigm is complex and difficult. Developing principles, processes and structures will require a great deal of exploration. The editors' personal values, however, lead us to identify with the paradigm: we are committed to the process of exploration as a way forward in contemporary, international discussions of quality in early childhood services. This approach, we believe, is not only right, it is also necessary. For, as Gunilla Dahlberg and Gunnar Åsén argue, a more inclusionary approach is an essential condition for the social legitimacy of early childhood services and hence securing public support for them.

So far, however, there is a limited base of experience and knowledge on which to build. Neither paradigm, exclusionary or inclusionary, has been the subject of much research (there is of course a huge literature on 'quality' but, apart from the work of Anne Smith and Sarah-Eve Farquhar on the New Zealand experience of charter development, pitifully little specifically on the process of defining quality within either paradigm). The chapters in this book, however, enable us to increase the base a little more by incorporating a range of experiences from different countries. They suggest a number of areas that are important for the further development of work on quality within the new paradigm.

1. CULTURE: Progress in applying the inclusionary paradigm does not start with building structures or processes. As Ole Langsted stresses, the starting point is the cultural climate, at both societal and political levels, for this determines whether inclusion is valued and wanted. Without this level of commitment, structures and processes are unlikely to be developed; or, if they are initiated, they will have only limited success.

At the most general level, an inclusionary approach assumes a strong and pervasive democratic culture, with a robust and valued tradition of debate and participation; civic participation and democracy are basic to the associative model proposed by Gunilla Dahlberg and Gunnar Åsén.

More specifically, the book suggests the need for a culture, reflected in public policy values, that accepts a broad societal interest in and responsibility for children, parents and early childhood services. In this respect, the dominant values in the United States described by Mary Larner and Deborah Phillips, namely family privacy and exclusive maternal care, seem much at odds with the values, such as shared responsibility, which have underpinned the development of extensive publicly supported early childhood services in Denmark. Gunilla Dahlberg and Gunnar Åsén also presume a strong public responsibility for children and early childhood services which requires the involvement of all citizens, through discussion and reflection, in defining quality. Services are not private concerns, cannot be treated like businesses; they are a public responsibility, not least because they bear cultural and social values. Their contribution also emphasizes that consideration of early childhood services needs to be placed in a wider context of childhood, the place of children in society and the purposes of upbringing and education; quality in early childhood services, therefore, should not be considered in isolation from these wider concerns.

In his chapter, Ole Langsted emphasizes the importance of a child-oriented culture. In such a culture, children are recognized as citizens and are treated as experts about childhood. In such a culture, adults want to listen to children. He provides evidence of how this type of culture is currently evolving in Denmark, while similar developments may also be occurring in parts of Northern Italy where the development of services in towns such as Reggio Emilia is based on a deep respect for children's rights.

Finally, in societies which are, in most cases, increasingly diverse, an inclusionary approach requires a culture which recognizes, respects and values diversity and plurality. Carol Joseph, Jane Lane and Sudesh Sharma argue for equality as a core value in society and that equality must be addressed with children from the earliest age. The chartering process in New Zealand and the reform process leading up to it, described by Anne Smith and Sarah-Eve Farquhar, reflected a strong ideological and political commitment to recognition and support for cultural diversity and the survival and transmission of Maori and other minority cultures.

2. PRACTICE: The social and political culture of a society will determine whether or not an inclusionary approach to quality can take deep root and flourish. Once the concept has taken root, work is needed to put it into practice. Once people want to work on an inclusionary basis, then processes, structures and other requirements for implementation can be addressed.

The chapters in the book point to a number of qualities and skills that will be required of stakeholders in the process of defining quality based upon an inclusionary approach. Both Helen Penn in the approach she consciously adopts to her chapter and Gunilla Dahlberg and Gunnar Åsén in their exploration of the associative model recognize the importance of reflection. Dahlberg and Åsén further argue that reflective dialogue and reflective practice require a strong and widely visible documentary base.

Respect for other groups is advocated by Alan Pence and Marie McCallum, while Helen Penn provides examples of the consequences of failure to establish respect. Respect must be based on recognition of equality with others. It also involves valuing what others bring to the process of defining and developing quality and an awareness of personal limitations of experience and knowledge, an important factor in the success of the partnership between university workers and First Nations people described by Alan Pence and Marie McCallum.

The chapters by Helen Penn, Julia Brophy and June Statham and Pat Petrie raise the relationship between subjectivity and objectivity. All point to the need for stakeholder groups, especially experts, to be aware of themselves as stakeholding insiders, bringing their own values, beliefs and interests to the process of defining quality, rather than acting as dispassionate outsiders.

Other qualities are more implied than explicit within the book. While some inclusionary processes may be based on genuine respectful partnerships, others may be more adversarial and conflictual. In such cases, some participants will need to have skills to be able to manage disagreement and conflict and turn them into a constructive part of the process. And working in an inclusionary way, based on mutual respect and equal valuation of different stakeholder groups, implies both a commitment to the approach and considerable self-confidence. Groups who feel devalued or threatened are more likely to be resistant (just as Mary Larner and Deborah Phillips draw attention to how a system of early childhood services, where funding of services relies heavily on parental fees, may inhibit different stakeholders working together to define and improve quality since this may have threatening economic consequences for one or more of the stakeholders).

An inclusionary approach makes many demands of workers in early childhood services. Apart from working on an equal basis with a range of other stakeholders in a process which has profound consequences for their working lives, Gunilla Dahlberg and Gunnar Åsén argue that work in early childhood services should be viewed as an intellectual activity requiring a reflective attitude. To meet these and other demands, workers will require support from training and other sources. Claus Jensen points to the critical importance of a high level of basic and continuous training for workers in child care services; Denmark is unusual in having achieved this for workers with children both under and over three.

As well as developing an ability to work with children, training may provide workers with skills and confidence to participate in an inclusionary approach to defining and developing quality. However, it also carries with it the risk of creating a workforce that, on the contrary, seeks more exclusionary ways of working to vest more control in its members. This poses a critical issue. Must professionalization of workers in early childhood services inevitably create an obstacle to an inclusionary approach? Or can it facilitate wider inclusion and, if so, under what conditions? Even with training that successfully prepares child care workers to relate to parents as equals, Mary Larner and Deborah Phillips still envisage tensions between workers and parents and the need for workers, as professionals, to recognize that a respectful and inclusive relationship with parents is an essential part of good practice.

The chapters in the book also point to a number of examples of structures, processes and methods which have been developed within the inclusionary paradigm. The development of charters in New Zealand, described by Anne Smith and Sarah-Eve Farquhar, required centres to institute a participatory process for developing statements on philosophies and policies and specified which stakeholders should be involved in that process. Claus Jensen describes how staff, parents and, to some extent, children are jointly involved in determining the direction for their centres to take, an informal and decentralized process but reinforced by government requirements for centres to listen to children and to have parent committees and give parents influence. Gunilla Dahlberg and Gunnar Åsén describe plazas or arenas in Sweden, where stakeholders can come together to debate practice and policy, and also the potential contribution of documentation to this process of reflection and give workers and children a voice in that process. The Generative Curriculum Model evolved in the Meadow Lake project provides an example of an interactive and participatory process which might be applied beyond the area of curriculum development to provide a way of integrating different stakeholder perspectives.

3. EVALUATION AND RESEARCH: Although we treat research and evaluation separately, these related activities should also be treated as a necessary part of the process of operationalizing an inclusionary approach. The chapters in this volume suggest that the new inclusionary paradigm requires and encourages new roles for research and evaluation in relation to quality, as well as new ways of undertaking these roles. As with other activities, this means moving from exclusionary approaches, in which experts define and impose their own concepts of quality – although, of course, there will always be a place for researchers to pursue their own interests and those of their disciplines, but on the basis that it is made clear what perspective and what values they are adopting. Alan Pence and Marie McCallum call for research to move away from a singular focus on measurement of 'environmental variables' towards seeking greater understanding of the perspectives on quality of a wide range of stakeholders, many of whom are under-represented or totally invisible in current research literature – a shift from a search for 'quality universals' to a search for 'quality perspectives' based on a recognition and understanding of cultural, environmental and social diversity.

Mary Larner and Deborah Phillips, in a similar but more specific conclusion, urge researchers to expand their efforts to understand parents' perspectives, adding this to the perspectives of workers in early childhood services to create a more comprehensive conception of quality.

A number of approaches to research and evaluation are offered in this volume which would be supportive of a more inclusionary approach to quality. Helen Penn describes how research was initiated by a local authority within its programme to improve quality and as a tool to help the implementation of that programme. A survey of mothers provided one way of including the perspective on services of this group of stakeholders. The chapter by Mary Larner and Deborah Phillips shows an increasing body of research on parent perspectives in the USA, which is also increasingly exploring differences between groups of parents. The participatory research tradition influenced

Pat Petrie's study of school-age child care services, which she approached with a desire to understand the values underpinning different services and to look at their work in relation to these values, rather than impose her own set of values and her own concept of quality; her aim was to clarify, rather than judge, what staff in different services were seeking to achieve. The *BASUN* research project in Scandinavia, in which Ole Langsted participated, sought to understand young children's own everyday experience and views about quality through the children's own accounts; he emphasizes the need for more work to elicit children's views.

Julia Brophy and June Statham suggest the need for a greater diversity of evaluative measures with some developed for specific services, and that in developing such measures, underlying values should be addressed and made explicit. Similarly, Gunilla Dahlberg and Gunnar Åsén emphasize the importance of evaluation not being isolated from how quality is defined in early childhood services and the social and cultural values of those services; they highlight the danger that evaluation measures can become service goals, the tail wagging the dog so that quality becomes defined in terms of the ability of services to pass muster on evaluation measures. This is a point of prime importance. A crucial role of research and evaluation in an inclusionary paradigm is to develop within and from the process of defining and improving quality. Research and evaluation should be at the service of the stakeholders in defining, implementing, evaluating and reviewing quality; they should contribute to a learning process.

They should also provide a means of understanding services, in this way addressing the analytic concept of quality, defined in Chapter 1 as the essence of a service. Evaluating performance in relation to goals needs to be complemented by understanding how and why a service operates in the way it does. Such understanding will not only provide context for interpreting the results of evaluation, but also guidance to support and help a service respond constructively to evaluation.

We see each of these three areas – culture, practice and research and evaluation – as providing pointers to how to pursue the inclusionary paradigm and what may constrain or promote this pursuit. They do not, and cannot, provide a blueprint about how to proceed. Not only do we lack sufficient knowledge and understanding to attempt a blueprint, but to do so seems actually inappropriate given the extent of national differences. These differences require different approaches, grounded in analysis of each country, and imply different potentials for progress.

POSTSCRIPT

This book is neither prescriptive nor definitive but exploratory. The evolution of an inclusionary approach will proceed differently in different settings. The paradigm supports a range of possibilities. Settings will learn from settings and over time there will be inclusionary progress and evolution.

Similarly, our own thoughts have evolved considerably from the time when this volume was first conceived. The setting then was the 1992 Summer

Institute on Child Care Research and Policy Development held biennially at the University of Victoria in British Columbia. In informal discussions during the course of the Institute, we discovered that we shared many ideas about quality in early childhood services, starting with the idea that it was values based and a relative concept. While we each knew other colleagues who shared a similar perspective, it seemed to us that these ideas had not been adequately presented and discussed in the child care literature. Initial planning of this volume emerged from these early discussions.

Some of the evolution in our own thinking since then was evident as we reviewed Chapter 1 in preparation for writing this chapter of conclusions. Chapter 1, written in the autumn of 1993, focuses primarily on quality as a values-based and relative concept and also on the dual meaning of 'quality' and the issue of multiple stakeholders – these last two themes emerging since our original discussions in 1992. By the time we have come to write this final chapter, in late spring 1994, these issues in Chapter 1 still seem pertinent and relevant but our thinking has now moved on to exploring exclusionary versus inclusionary paradigms. We view it as natural and important that such a progression of ideas and emphasis take place. The inclusionary paradigm is dynamic and interactive: it is not a search for One Best Way but an exploration of Many Good Ways.

Already we have begun to explore a number of trails, leads and ideas which do not appear, at least in any substantive form, in this volume. They represent ideas that we may return to at some point in the future. For example, an earlier draft of this final chapter focused primarily on the elusive nature of caring itself: that the essence of caring cannot be achieved by imposition, regulation and enforcement; that the essence is transcendent and a shared communion between individuals; and that such an experience cannot be created, but can at best be supported within an environment of caring. That 'conclusion' proved elusive to develop, but the ideas and philosophy behind it remain as a potentially interesting avenue for future exploration.

The good news about work in a newly identified paradigm is that there is much that is innovative and creative to be done. The bad news is that it may be difficult to take forward, but also that it may be difficult to search for relevant examples that already exist and which could add to the knowledge base. We invite you, the reader, to join us in the search. The journey we are on is not exclusionary. We welcome your reactions, ideas and examples. We believe that this volume represents early steps in the evolution of a different way of looking at and understanding quality child care, quality early childhood services. We invite you to join with us in identifying the next steps in the journey.

VICTORIA, BRITISH COLUMBIA
May 1994

* * *

BELFAST PUBLIC LIBRARIES

If you have any comments, ideas or examples please write to:

Peter Moss,
Thomas Coram Research Unit,
27/28 Woburn Square,
London WC1H 0AA
or
Alan Pence,
School of Child and Youth Care,
University of Victoria,
P.O.Box 1700,
Victoria,
British Columbia V8W 2Y2

Index